MOTIVATION IN SPORT AND EXERCISE

Glyn C. Roberts, PhD

University of Illinois at Urbana-Champaign

Editor

Human Kinetics Books

Champaign, Illinois

Library of Congress Cataloging-in-Publication Data

Motivation in sport and exercise / editor, Glyn C. Roberts.
   p. cm.
   Papers previously presented at a symposium held at the University
of Illinois in November of 1989.
   Includes bibliographical references and index.
   ISBN 0-87322-345-4
   1. Sports--Psychological aspects. 2. Exercise--Psychological
aspects. 3. Motivation (Psychology) I. Roberts, Glyn C.
GV706.4.M68   1992
796'.01--dc20   91-22864
                                           CIP

ISBN: 0-87322-345-4

Papers presented at the Human Kinetics Symposium on Motivation and Sport were sponsored by the University of Illinois Department of Kinesiology and Human Kinetics Publishers, November 1989, at the University of Illinois at Urbana-Champaign.

Developmental Editors: Sue Mauck and Mary Fowler
Assistant Editors: Laura Bofinger and Kari Nelson
Copyeditor: Vickie West
Proofreader: Karin Leszczynski
Indexer: Theresa Schaeffer
Production Director: Ernie Noa
Typesetter: Kathy Boudreau-Fuoss
Text Design: Keith Blomberg
Text Layout: Denise Peters
Cover Design: Jack Davis
Illustrations: Tom Janowski
Printer: Braun-Brumfield

Photos on pages 3, 129, and 161 courtesy of the Champaign (IL) Park District; photo on page 31 by The Daily Illini, University of Illinois at Urbana-Champaign; photos on pages 57, 93, 177, and 199 courtesy of University of Illinois Sports Information.

Printed in the United States of America

10 9 8 7 6 5 4 3 2 1

Human Kinetics Books
A Division of Human Kinetics Publishers, Inc.
Box 5076, Champaign, IL 61825-5076
1-800-747-4457

Canada Office:
Human Kinetics Publishers, Inc.
P.O. Box 2503, Windsor, ON N8Y 4S2
1-800-465-7301 (in Canada only)

Europe Office:
Human Kinetics Publishers (Europe) Ltd.
P.O. Box IW14
Leeds, LS16 6TR
England
0532-781708

Contents

Preface

Achievement behavior and motivation in sport have been the subject of much debate in both coaching and academic circles. Given this long history of concern, one would expect that motivation in sport has been thoroughly studied. But the systematic study of motivational processes in sport and, more recently, in exercise has only in the last 20 years received significant and sustained attention by those scholars specializing in sport and exercise settings. However, our knowledge is increasing each day, and this volume reflects the excellent efforts of some of the major contributors to motivation studies. The distinctly cognitive flavor of this book reflects the most influential contemporary approaches to motivation.

This volume reviews and integrates important modern contributions to the study of motivation in sport and exercise. It provides insight into state-of-the-art research on motivation. The group of authors are distinguished contributors to the theoretical and applied literature, and each author represents a major avenue of research. The themes of this volume are twofold: understanding motivation and enhancing motivation. In the understanding motivation section, each contributor attempts to shed some light onto the dynamics of the motivational process and upon the variables and constructs that affect our understanding of motivation. Each contributor examines the cognitions that impact achievement behavior in exercise and sport. In the enhancing motivation section, each contributor discusses enhancing motivation and enjoyment in the sport and exercise experience. These approaches, too, are cognitive in that each contributor discusses the individual's perceptions within the achievement context.

The impetus for this volume came from a symposium sponsored jointly by the Department of Kinesiology and Human Kinetics Publishers, held at the University of Illinois in November 1989. Nine speakers were invited to present their research and interpretations of the motivation process. This resultant collection contains each of the invitees' presentations. To my fellow contributors, I acknowledge a debt of gratitude; they all responded professionally to my editorial requests. Their individual and collective contributions make this volume unique—the first of its kind dedicated to clarifying the process of motivation in sport and exercise, and to understanding the enhancement of motivation.

Having acknowledged my fellow contributors, I must also acknowledge the secretaries and staff of the Department of Kinesiology who contributed to the running of the symposium. Deep appreciation is also extended to Rainer Martens and Human Kinetics, who gave financial support in organizing the symposium. Thanks are also due to all of the University of Illinois graduate students in sport psychology who faultlessly ran the symposium and contributed in many other ways to its success, which directly led to this volume. To Jay, Olga, Vance, Joy, Phyllis, Kim, Billy, Fiona, Susan, and Anita, I give my heartfelt thanks. In particular, to my colleague Eddie McAuley, who became an Illini "overnight," your unstinting efforts for the symposium, and your advice and counsel for this volume were appreciated. To all, my thanks.

Glyn C. Roberts

Introduction

This book is firmly placed within the present zeitgeist of social cognitive perspectives on motivation. Motivation and achievement behavior are manifestations of cognitions and thought processes within dynamic social contexts; and it is these thoughts and thought processes that govern motivated action. Cognitive theory has, in the last 10 years, increasingly dominated the study of human motivation. All of the perspectives within this book may be termed cognitive, although they examine a variety of thought processes as determinants of action.

Cognitive theory has given motivation research a new life, and a very lively area of interest has developed that utilizes cognitive perspectives. In 1971, Bernard Weiner signaled the beginnings of this new era in motivation research when he argued that individuals who were high or low in motivation were likely to *think* differently about success and failure. The notion that thoughts, or more particularly, attributions were the critical variables in the motivation process led to an interest in such thoughts and how these thoughts and meanings change as the social context changes. Weiner's attempt to introduce cognitions into the motivation equation transformed the study of motivation.

Cognitive views now prevail on motivational questions. The study of motivation and achievement behavior is dominated by the effects of mediating cognitions relating to control and competence, perceptions of purpose, and value and meaning. In this book, all of the constructs and models to explain motivated behavior are derivatives of attribution theory; however, all of the chapters go beyond the view that attributions are the most significant cognitive events in understanding achievement behavior.

The chapters are grouped into two parts: The first presents theory and empirical research on understanding the processes of motivation and achievement behavior in sport and exercise; the second presents applications to enhance motivation and enjoyment in sport and exercise. All these chapters represent the culmination of a decade of systematic efforts to unravel the process of motivation, and to understand and enhance motivation in sport and exercise.

Each chapter deals with thoughts and how these thoughts are related to action. Each contributor has studied the processes over some time, and each has reached individual conclusions about the motivation process. Thus, each contributor has a perspective that differs from that of the others. To some extent, these perspectives differ on what the spring of action is in motivated behavior (e.g., goal perspective, desire for information, valued goals, enjoyment); on how attributions contribute to the thought-action sequence; on how the social context affects the determinants of action; and on how we change the motivational state. These contrasting views are clearly seen among the chapters, but complementary and convergent lines of thought are also evident. Whether or not we are moving toward a more comprehensive theory of motivation is still under debate, but the power of using social cognitive processes to understand motivated behavior is clear. This common social cognitive theme permeates all of the chapters.

The common perspective is evident in the assumption that thoughts, or a constellation of cognitions, are the major antecedents of the energization, direction, intensity, and duration of achievement behavior. But at a more specific level, there is an emerging convergence on the importance to the motivation process of two kinds of thought processes: (1) thoughts about self (such as competence, control, and confidence), and (2) thoughts of purposes, goals, values, and meaning.

How This Book Is Organized

As stated earlier, the book has been organized into two major parts. The first one is on understanding motivation, and the second is on enhancing motivation. The first section has six chapters and attempts to extend our views of the determinants and energization of achievement behavior in sport and exercise.

Understanding Motivation

The first chapter is by myself. In this chapter, I try to set the stage for the later chapters in the book. I briefly review past approaches to understanding motivation, but primarily focus on the importance of the cognitive revolution to our understanding of motivation and achievement behavior in sport and exercise. I argue that, should we wish to understand motivation, the critical variables to study are social cognitive variables. Then, I proffer a model which specifically identifies motivational climate, goals of action, and perceived ability as the prime determinants of adaptive and maladaptive achievement striving in both sport and exercise. I utilize this model to criticize other models of motivation and to suggest that a critical element has been ignored by some conceptualizations of motivation: the conception of ability assumed by various theories. Some theories assume a task-involved concept of ability, whereas others adopt a more ego-involved, or social comparison, concept of ability. I argue that the fundamentally different conceptions of ability inherent in these theories affect the interpretation of some of the findings utilizing these theories. I conclude my chapter by calling for a convergence of some of the conceptual models of motivation.

The second chapter by John Nicholls is important in that not only does he reflect upon his sterling efforts to understand motivation over the past 15 years, but he also underscores the fact that sport is a unique achievement context; we need to attend to the particulars of the context if we wish to understand achievement behavior within that context. Nicholls focuses on the development of the perception of ability and the meanings of ability for individuals, whether they be in academic or sport contexts. In the second half of the chapter, Nicholls deals with lay theories of achievement and addresses the importance of individual perceptions of meaning of task involvement. It is these individual perspectives of meaning that give substance to achievement striving. But these meanings change from individual to individual and from sport context to sport context. Thus, to understand motivation in sport, Nicholls argues that we must come to terms with the changing meanings of the sport experience.

The third paper is by Joan Duda who presents very dramatic evidence of the efficacy of the goal perspective approach to understanding achievement behavior in sport. Continuing the theme of my own prior chapter, Duda underscores the converging aspects of the various goal perspectives of the major theorists. But the strength of the Duda chapter is her welter of evidence demonstrating the pertinence of the goal perspective approach to sport motivation. She presents evidence that task involvement relates to intensity and high persistence, and that ego involvement leads to low persistence. In addition, Duda argues that goal perspectives shape one's views of sport, and that acceptable behavior in one's perception of fairness is determined by goal perspectives. Duda concludes by asking pertinent questions that should shape future research efforts in this realm.

The next two chapters by Feltz and McAuley, respectively, are a change of pace as they both deal with the self-efficacy perspective to achievement behavior. Feltz reviews the corpus of work in sport and discusses how self-efficacy cognitions are more predictive of motivated behavior in sport than are outcome expectations. Feltz states that the failure to demonstrate the utility of self-efficacy in sport is due more to inappropriate measurement than to any weakness in the conceptual basis of self-efficacy theory. Feltz reports that research within sport is limited and highlights some directions for future research, including the need to investigate team efficacy. Feltz concludes by noting that researchers need to establish better the relations among self-efficacy and other social cognitive variables such as causal attributions.

McAuley discusses the growing body of evidence dealing with self-efficacy in exercise and health contexts. After reviewing the benefits of exercise,

McAuley details the importance of procedures for the microanalytic measurement of self-efficacy. McAuley reviews the research on adoption and adherence in exercise behavior and details the methodological flaws of some of the studies. McAuley also addresses the effects of efficacy on exercise performance, noting the consistent, if modest, ability of self-efficacy percepts to predict exercise behavior. Although McAuley admits that self-efficacy is but one among a host of explanations for analyzing exercise behavior, his chapter builds a strong case for the merit of pursuing the relationship of self-referenced percepts of personal agency to motivated, health-related behavior.

The final chapter in the section on understanding motivation is the one by Rejeski. Rejeski notes that much research in sport and exercise motivation has been atheoretical. Rejeski explains the need for theory and provides criteria by which theory may be assessed. He argues for a return to the conceptual approaches dealing with Expectancy × Value. Rejeski argues that theories need to be used for their intended purpose, and underscores my own point that we should not go beyond the constraints of theory. Rejeski concludes by critiquing a number of existing theories, particularly in the exercise behavior area, and very appropriately points to some of their weaknesses. As an example, Rejeski points to the need to consider incentive in self-efficacy work, and the need to consider value within the goal perspective approach. Rejeski clearly demonstrates the need for a theoretical basis for research in intervention, and he challenges us to expand our horizons about the utility of theory. Rejeski's chapter provides a useful bridge between this section and the next section of the book on enhancing motivation.

Enhancing Motivation

The three chapters in this section reflect three important research programs that are likely to influence future research on enhancing motivation. It will be surprising if these approaches do not also considerably influence educational practice over the next few years. A rich variety of methods are employed, yet a careful reading shows some degree of convergence. But the important point to note in each one of these chapters is that the enhancement procedures employed are driven by conceptual percepts.

The first chapter is by Ames. Ames argues that we, as adults, teachers, or coaches, need to pay particular attention to the motivational climate we create for children within the classroom or on the playing field. Clearly, this care would be appropriate for exercise settings too. Ames points out that adults (parents, coaches, or teachers) convey values to children by the use of cues, rewards, and expectations that lead to the development of particular goal orientations. Ames maintains strongly that the way achievement situations are structured by coaches and exercise leaders affects the goal orientation that is developed by the individual. The psychological climate and the children's interpretation of the environment influence the degree of mastery attempts and the extent to which achievement behaviors will be adaptive. In describing her research in progress on motivational climate issues, Ames states that her initial findings encourage the assumption that altering the psychological climate of the classroom can help prevent the decline in motivation often witnessed by teachers and coaches. Ames concludes with a suggestion that recognition for effort, improvement, and personal bests will foster a mastery orientation within sport contexts and will lead to motivationally effective strategies on the part of the children.

The second chapter in this section is by Weinberg, who reviews the general literature and research on goal-setting within physical activity. He notes that there is but little research in sport and physical activity, and much of that research is equivocal in some of its findings. Weinberg then discusses methodological design considerations of goal-setting research in sport, and notes that one of the methodological limitations in goal setting is spontaneous goal-setting. He emphasizes that examination of goal-setting within sport is a very useful activity. Weinberg concludes by looking at the future directions of goal-setting research. He argues that we need to consider goal orientations and the value of longer term studies, and we should investigate some of the conceptual underpinnings of goal-setting effects.

In the last chapter in the book, Scanlan and Simons bring affect into the study of motivation in sport and exercise. Scanlan and Simons argue that sport enjoyment per se is worthy of study, and that enjoyment is the cornerstone of motivation in sport. They attempt to identify the sources of enjoyment, and, therefore, the sources of motivation. They explain how enjoyment is different from intrinsic motivation and how perceptions of competence and challenge are among a wide range of sources of enjoyment. Scanlan and Simons discuss their research with elite figure skaters; they demonstrate a great array of sources of enjoyment, some of which reflect the cognitive themes in the earlier chapters of this book. Finally, Scanlan and Simons suggest how their findings might be applied, and they assert the centrality of positive affect in sport enjoyment and sport motivation.

Conclusion

I have attempted to provide the reader with an appropriate cognitive map of the concepts, theory, and research foci of the contributors to this book. The schematic structure introduced here of goals, cognitions, and moment-to-moment thoughts should highlight the theoretical relationships across the chapters. The chapters in this volume discuss many of the major elements of a cognitive theory of motivation, and, in particular, they illustrate how sport and exercise participant's goals and cognitive operations operate on motivational content that affects moment-to-moment cognitions. These chapters should underscore the importance of considering the social context of sport and exercise, of considering the constellation of cognitions, and of attending to the pertinent structures of each context. Collectively, the chapters in this volume expand our thinking about the roles, self-referent percepts, goals, and cognitions in motivated behavior in exercise and sport contexts. Each of us may now begin to utilize the lessons learned from the research efforts of these contributors to sensitize our own future research. By so doing, we will elaborate a cognitive theory of motivation that is pertinent to sport and exercise settings.

Part I
Understanding
Motivation

Motivation
in Sport and Exercise:
Conceptual Constraints
and Convergence

Glyn C. Roberts

Motivation is one of the central issues in human affairs. Whether it is politicians discussing the will of societies, business leaders concerned with the effectiveness of the work force, parents discussing the efforts of their children, teachers bemoaning the study habits of pupils, coaches complaining about the commitment of players, or exercise leaders lamenting the persistence of exercise participants, all are dealing with levels of motivation.

In achievement contexts, whether at the national or individual level, motivation is implicated. For example, at the present time the role of motivation in society is a popular point of discussion, particularly when the United States compares itself to Japan and West Germany. What has happened to the initiative and drive of the American work force to reduce its worldwide competitiveness? A proposed solution is offered in an article in the *New York Times* ("Motivation Factor," 1983, p. 1) where Lester Thurow (an economist from the Massachusetts Institute of Technology) argues that the United States needs to upgrade the motivation of the work force. He points to Argentina, a country with excellent natural resources, and to Japan, a country of few natural resources, and states that the difference in the economies of the two countries is directly attributable to a motivated work force.

A motivational solution to the nation's economic ailments is neither new (e.g., Inkeles, 1980) nor trivial. But motivation research has primarily addressed itself to the role of motivation in individual lives. Whether it is the issue of managing the motivation of others, as does a coach or a teacher, or the issue of managing self-motivation, it is this level of motivation that has primarily consumed the efforts of researchers. This chapter, and this book, are no different.

The role of motivation in individual lives is very important. However, despite being an important topic, it is a regrettable fact that motivation is a poorly understood phenomenon in the trenches—the classroom, the auditorium, the workbench, the playing field, and so forth. For some reason, conveying information to coaches, teachers, and other individuals about motivation has not been totally successful. But nowhere is the concept of motivation more misunderstood than in sport. Coaching is a very conservative occupation, and coaches often coach as they were themselves coached and are resistant to change. Thus, coaching folklore perpetuates past misunderstandings.

One common misunderstanding is the assumption that motivation is synonymous with arousal. Coaches assume that pregame locker room inspirational talks and other procedures "motivate" the players to better performance. This is why coaches often employ bizarre tactics (such as biting the heads off day-old chickens!) in order to arouse players prior to a game. Clearly, despite coaching folklore (and business perceptions regarding inspirational talks to sales staff, etc.), arousal and motivation are separate and independent constructs.

A second misunderstanding revolves around what coaches call "positive thinking." The parable of "the little engine that could" is legend in coaching circles, and coaches often exhort players on that assumption. Although there is evidence that holding certain expectations can affect achievement behaviors, if the expectations are not realistic, they have little long-range benefit.

Lastly, many coaches believe that motivation is "hard wired" into the human organism—that the inner state of motivation is a given. If a player is judged to be low in motivation, these coaches do not believe that this will or can change, and, consequently, they often give up on that particular individual. But these inferences are all made from observing achievement behavior patterns and assigning stable attributes to sport participants. All of these misperceptions are grounded in certain half-truths, yet they do not come close to understanding the complex phenomenon of motivation in sport and exercise.

This volume attempts to shed some light upon this complex phenomenon. Herein, some of the major researchers in sport and exercise motivation report on their efforts to understand both the process of motivation and interventions to enhance motivation. The focus is firmly on contemporary cognitive theories and models of motivation. This book unashamedly assumes that the most important efforts to understand motivation are predicated upon contemporary social cognitive approaches.

The purpose of my own chapter is to set the stage for the subsequent chapters in the book. I begin by defining motivation in contemporary motivation research, and then I briefly trace the development of our understanding of motivation, describing various approaches that have been used. This segment concludes with current work in the social cognitive tradition. The next segment presents a social cognitive framework that assumes that there are common elements that run through many of the contemporary approaches to motivation. The existence of these common elements is typically ignored by contemporary research. I present a model to help clarify the complex interaction of the variables that impact motivation. Then, the chapter continues with an attempt to illustrate the conceptual convergence that exists in these approaches to motivation. The chapter concludes with an argument that the concepts utilized in motivation research should be looked at for that convergence.

Before I begin, however, let me confess to the bias and limitations of my analysis. This chapter is not a careful review of the literature which inexorably gives way to firm propositions. Rather, I am presenting a very personal essay on motivation and motivation issues in sport and exercise. I present an *a priori* understanding of motivation, but it is a position that is forged from years of working in the area. The issues I shall present are critical to debate if we are to advance our collective understanding of motivation and come to grips with appropriate procedures to enhance motivation in the future.

What Is Motivation?

Typically, in the research literature motivation refers to those personality factors, social variables, and/or cognitions that come into play when a person undertakes a task at which he or she is evaluated, enters into competition with others, or attempts to attain some standard of excellence. At such times, it is assumed that the individual is responsible for the outcome of the task and that some level of challenge is inherent in the task. Moreover, such circumstances are assumed to facilitate various motivational dispositions and/or cognitive assessments that influence human behavior in achievement situations. Specifically, it has been hypothesized that the determinants of achievement behavior are approach and/or avoidance motives, expectancies, incentive values of success and failure, and/or cognitive assessments of success and failure.

In the extant literature, achievement behavior, which motivation theories purport to explain, has typically been defined as behavioral intensity (trying hard), persistence (continuing to try hard), choice of action possibilities, and performance (outcomes). In sport, achievement behaviors are those behaviors witnessed when participants try harder, concentrate more, persist longer, pay more attention, perform better, choose to practice longer, and join or drop out of sporting activities. These behavioral patterns are probably not all-inclusive. Further, they represent assessments of behavior from which we infer motivation. But they suffice to define what we refer to when we state that an individual is or is not motivated (Maehr & Braskamp, 1986).

Theoretical Approaches to Understanding Motivation and Achievement Behavior

The history of motivation theory has been the search for the ''right'' theory, and, as such, it was assumed that when that theory evolved, a whole range of achievement behaviors would not only be better understood, but intervention opportunities would also present themselves (see also Rejeski, this volume). Despite the efforts of many, this Holy Grail remains elusive and certainly not within our grasp as yet. But the search continues. The chapters in this book reflect the excellent efforts that are ongoing in search of theoretical concepts to understand and enhance achievement behaviors within sport and exercise.

The study of motivation is the investigation of the energization and direction of behavior. Theories are not motivational unless they address both aspects of behavior. Thus, some avenues of research which describe the direction of behavior without specifying *why* the behavior was energized are not motivational, even though they may describe achievement behavior. Goal-setting is such a case in sport. Goal-setting specifies the direction of achievement behavior, but to date it has no sufficient psychological explanation. Motivation theories are predicated upon a set of assumptions about individuals and about the factors that give impetus to achievement behavior. Motivation theories ask *why*. (Robert 1992)

When motivation matters, various theoretical models have been proposed as governing motivation and achievement behavior. Motivation theories may be viewed as being on a continuum ranging from mechanistic to cognitive, or organismic. Mechanistic theories view humans as being passive and driven by psychological drives, while cognitive theories view humans as being active and initiating action through subjective interpretation of the achievement context. In the early part of this century, mechanistic psychoanalytic drive theories dominated the field and terms such as equilibrium and hedonism were utilized. But motivation is more than striving for equilibrium or maximizing hedonism. Theorists gave credence for a while to behaviorism during the 40s and 50s, but the attraction of attempting to understand humans as input/output connectors waned as the cognitive revolution had its effect on psychology.

However, among the many alternative approaches advocated, four major research traditions may be identified: need achievement theory, test anxiety theory, expectancy of reinforcement theory, and the cognitive approach. A brief overview of each approach now follows.

Need Achievement Theory

The most influential research tradition, especially in sport contexts, began with Murray (1938) and was further developed by McClelland and Atkinson and their colleagues (Atkinson, 1957, 1958; McClelland, 1961; McClelland, Atkinson, Clark, & Lowell, 1953). This approach believes that motive states are the mainsprings of action. These motive states—the *motive to achieve success* and the *motive to avoid failure*—formed the central constructs of the theory. McClelland believed that the motives interact with cues in the environment to arouse affective states (pride and shame, for example) which elicit instrumental approach or avoidance behavior. The approach incorporates a hedonic quality of behavior into an essentially affective arousal model (for more detailed reviews see Dweck & Elliott, 1983; Roberts, 1982).

The McClelland and Atkinson research tradition is an exemplary model of psychological theorizing with empirical research conducted to verify the constructs. However, the research in sport generally has been inconclusive. Research has supported the prediction that individuals driven by the *motive to achieve success* select challenging tasks and demonstrate heightened performance, but research has not always supported the prediction that individuals driven by the *motive to avoid failure* avoid intermediate risk and demonstrate low performance. The theory also has been criticized for its ethnocentric bias, the weight it places upon personality as the crucial variable, and its failure to account for heightened performance of low-achievement-motivation individuals in some situations (Maehr, 1974; Roberts, 1982). But the approach has been very important to understanding motivation, and many of the insights into motivation are intact in contemporary approaches.

The Test Anxiety Approach

Based upon the extensive research relating test anxiety to achievement in task performance, Sarason and colleagues (Mandler & Sarason, 1952; Sarason, Davidson, Lighthall, Waite, & Ruebrush, 1960) formulated a theory emphasizing the parent-child interaction during the preschool and elementary school years and the evaluative aspects of the school situation. The major motivational variable here was anxiety with evaluation. The search has focused on anxiety-evoking situations such as test taking and performing before peers. The line of research has produced a convincing body of evidence indicating that performance on achievement tasks and before peers is strongly influenced by motivational factors. However, this approach has not been popular in sport psychology despite a deep interest in anxiety per se. This is surprising given the increased awareness of the debilitating effects of anxiety in competitive environments. But the approach has given us insight into the affect-cognition linkages and how these linkages affect the ongoing stream of behavior in achievement contexts.

Expectation of Reinforcement

The third major school of thought in motivation and achievement behavior is based upon social learning theory. Crandall and her colleagues (Crandall, 1963, 1969) were interested in academic and intellectual achievement, particularly in situations where personal skill is important. The major motivational variable is the individual's expectancy of reinforcement. These researchers emphasize overt behavior rather than motives; in Crandall's view, achievement behavior is behavior directed towards the attainment of self-approval and the approval of others, and it is specifically contingent upon criteria for performance competence (Roberts, 1982). The expectancies and values of this Expectancy × Value theory were precisely measured and the findings pertaining to specific individual differences (e.g., sex differences in expectancy of success) remain among our most robust and important. Even though Crandall was interested in sport achievement, little work has been completed on the topic, and its value in sport psychology circles remains undetermined despite interest in social reinforcement phenomena and in coaching effectiveness programs (e.g., Smith, Smoll, & Curtis, 1979).

The Cognitive Approach

The most evident way in which the study of motivation has changed in the past 20 years is in the resurgence of the cognitive paradigm. There are, of course, many who do not accept this view, but in the main, the cognitive paradigm is now dominant in the study of motivation.

The essential task for a cognitive perspective on motivation is to study the way in which knowledge is acquired, represented, and used by humans. The emphasis is on the creation of models to understand how cognitions or thoughts govern behavior. Cognitive theorists believe that behavioral variance in sport and exercise is better captured by models that incorporate the cognitions and beliefs of individuals; in other words, the cognitions and beliefs of individuals mediate their behavior. To a cognitive theorist, thought governs action. As one wit put it recently: Having lost it during the radical behaviorism era of Skinner and others, psychology has finally regained its mind! It is up to us as scientists to describe and explain what constellation of cognitions affects the ongoing stream of achievement behaviors in sport and exercise.

It can be argued that Tolman (1932) was the first motivation theorist to utilize the cognitive approach. Tolman argued that achievement behavior required a more flexible explanatory mechanism than that provided by the behavioristic approach. Tolman stated that an organism may have a belief that a particular event will be followed by another event, and that a particular course of action will have consequences. Thus, Tolman introduced expectancy into the psychological literature, and choice and decision making began to replace stimulus-response associations to explain achievement behavior.

The major resurgence in motivation research can be dated to the late 1950s. It began with unexpected findings in the laboratory of Harlow, and these led to deCharms (1968) coining the terms *origin* and *pawn* to describe the perception of control that individuals have over their behavior. But the works of Heider (1958), White (1959), and McVicker-Hunt (1965) are also important, and the terms *extrinsic* and *intrinsic motivation* were utilized to distinguish respectively, the older behavioristic tradition from the newer cognitive research forms. Indeed, Csikszentmihalyi and Nakamura (1989) go as far as to state that the cognitive revolution that overtook psychology in the 1970s resurrected the study of motivation. Whether this is true or not, it certainly gave the study of motivation new life, and new concepts and variables to study. It is fair to state that the cognitive revolution has made the area of motivation a lively and interesting topic of discussion.

In 1971, Bernard Weiner and his colleagues (Weiner et al.) signaled the beginning of a different era in the study of motivation with the argument that individuals who were high or low in need achievement were likely to *think* differently about success and failure. Weiner argued that thoughts and, particularly, causal attributions were the important variables to consider in understanding motivation. As Maehr (1989) stated, Weiner's modest attempt to insert causal attributions into the achievement motivation equation transformed the focus of motivation research. The situation and its meaning became more important; individual differences and personality aspects became less important. A brief review of the approach of Weiner now follows.

Attribution Theory

The attribution approach to motivation is reflected in the body of research generated from *attribution theory* (Weiner, 1979, 1986; Weiner et al., 1971). Attribution theory deals with the rules that the average individual uses in attempting to account for the causes of behavior. It involves a naive psychology, and the scientist must assume the phenomenological outlook of the man in the street who attempts to determine the causes of everyday events (Heider, 1958). Attribution theory is concerned with the methods people use and the naive attributional schema or theories that individuals adopt in order to make sense of their lives. This approach regards the human organism as an active information processing organism with the inclusion of higher mental processes as determinants of human action.

The overwhelming emphasis of the attributional approach has been on expectancy within an Expectancy × Value framework, with particular weight placed upon the changes in expectancy as a function of success and failure outcomes. The manner in which one attributes the causes of outcomes affects expectancies of future success and failure, and is assumed to affect achievement striving. Different attributions reflect different expectations of future outcomes. It is this pattern of attributions that has interested researchers the most.

The most heavily studied aspect of sport and physical activity settings has been winning and losing. Studies have been conducted to investigate how individuals determine the cause of their own and other people's success or failure in these settings. Winning and losing have been studied in experimentally manipulated settings, in natural settings, or in imagined settings, in which individuals have been asked to imagine themselves or someone else winning or losing a sporting event (Roberts, 1982). The studies assume that information about the outcome affects the expectancy for future wins and losses and also the feelings of affect; these in turn affect achievement behaviors. The research has established that both children and adults utilize information in systematic ways in order to arrive at causal attributions for wins and losses. Individuals analyze sport outcomes in terms of the information provided concerning the influence of a given causal factor, and causal attributions are made based upon the perceived covariation of cause and effect.

During the 70s and 80s, attribution work in sport and exercise grew in both interest and volume. This corpus or work has been reported elsewhere by recent reviews (Brawley & Roberts, 1984; McAuley & Duncan, 1990; Rejeski & Brawley, 1983; Roberts, 1982, 1984), and it is not my desire to repeat that information here. Suffice it to say that while the work has demonstrated that motivation is very much a product of cognitive processes, the work has not been without criticism. Many of the concerns with attribution work in sport and exercise revolve around these elements:

1. The specified causes or attribution elements in studies. These elements are richer than have traditionally been recognized within the sport literature.
2. The dimensional relevance of particular attributional elements. The relevance of these elements is often assumed, and researchers simply ignore whether the meaning of the attributional element is pertinent to the sport participant.
3. The meaning of outcome to the individual. In sport, we often assume that winning and losing are synonymous with success and failure.
4. The process of measurement of attributions (Roberts, 1982).

Many of these issues have been addressed, and satisfactory resolutions to the criticisms have been advocated (e.g., Brawley & Roberts, 1984; McAuley

& Duncan, 1990), but attribution theory has never been able to overcome the criticism that it is less a psychology of motivation than a social psychology of perception (Roberts, 1982). Indeed, when we consider interventions to enhance motivation, attribution theory is weak. Although it may be useful for telling us why things go wrong, it does not tell us how to put them right (Roberts, 1982). Some attributional models were useful in interventions in the classroom (e.g., attribution retraining, see Dweck, 1975), but these never translated to sport.

weak *ness*

In sum, the attributional approach has opened up significant avenues of investigation and must constitute an important ingredient of any comprehensive theory of motivation from a cognitive perspective, but it does not constitute a comprehensive theory in itself. The theory has not addressed value in any systematic manner. The theory has focused upon why people expect to succeed, but not on why they want to succeed (Dweck & Elliott, 1983).

Any comprehensive theory of motivation must integrate affect and cognitions and explain how they interact in order to affect the energy and direction of achievement behaviors. A number of investigators have begun to propose achievement motivation approaches that incorporate affect, expectations, and values in order to explain motivated behaviors. It is to these more recent approaches we now turn.[1]

Social Cognitive Approaches

The social cognitive approach draws upon past theories to portray a dynamic process incorporating sets of cognitive, affective, and value-related variables that are assumed to mediate the choice and attainment of achievement goals. In this brief review, I shall focus on the specific formulations and suggest the flow of the process. The social cognitive approach is built around expectancies and values that individuals attach to different goals and achievement activities. But the social cognitive approach has, imbedded within it, several mini-theories that purport to describe and/or explain motivated behavior. Even though I shall argue for some conceptual convergence later in the chapter, it is better to review each mini-theory separately.

The major mini-theories utilized in sport and exercise are self-efficacy (Bandura, 1977a, 1986), perceived competence (Harter, 1975, 1980), and the various achievement goal perspectives (Dweck, 1986; Dweck & Elliott, 1983; Maehr & Braskamp, 1986; Maehr & Nicholls, 1980; Nicholls, 1981, 1984a, 1984b, 1989). Work in sport and exercise using these theories has exploded in the last few years. Let me briefly discuss how each approach has been used in sport and exercise.

Self-Efficacy

The *theory of self-efficacy* has been the most extensively used theory for investigating motivational issues in sport and exercise. For detailed reviews of this work, see Feltz (1988b, this volume) for sport research and McAuley (this volume) for exercise research. Let us review the sport research first.

Originally proposed as an explanation of the various intervention procedures used in the treatment of anxiety, self-efficacy has been used in sport to explain achievement behavior. Bandura (1977a) used the term *self-efficacy* to describe the conviction one needs to successfully execute the behavior necessary to produce a certain outcome. Self-efficacy is not concerned with one's ability per se, but with one's assessment of what one can do with one's abilities (Feltz, this volume; McAuley, this volume). This is why some sport psychologists have utilized the term *self-confidence* synonymously with self-efficacy (e.g., Vealey, 1986). The motivational mechanism of self-efficacy theory is the assessment of one's capability to perform at a given level in an achievement context of value to the participant. In short, mastery expectations influence performance (Bandura, 1977a, p. 194).

Research in sport and motor performance has focused on one of two issues: (1) the methods used to create self-efficacy; and (2) the relationship of self-efficacy to performance. Both areas of research have typically used performance measures as dependent measures. The research that has looked at methods of enhancing self-efficacy has established that participant modeling, vicarious experiences, and other antecedents have affected self-efficacy in the predicted directions. However, not all studies show an enhancement of performance (Feltz, 1988b). In those studies that have looked at the relationship of self-efficacy to sport performance, the results show that a positive relationship exists, but the relationship is more modest than most reviewers admit. Indeed, in some cases the relationship is, at best, weak (Feltz, 1982; McAuley, 1985a). The general findings suggest that while self-efficacy has shown itself to be a reliable, albeit modest, predictor of sport performance, other mechanisms can and do contribute to behavioral change (Bandura, 1986; Feltz, 1988b).

In the exercise area, self-efficacy fares better. Several researchers have identified that self-efficacy affects exercise compliance, reliably predicts adherents from dropouts, and predicts cardiac recovery of patients (see McAuley, this volume).

The reason that self-efficacy fares better in predicting exercise achievement behavior will be discussed in more detail later when I argue for conceptual convergence. However, briefly, self-efficacy is a better predictor of performance when performance is defined in terms of persistence, as in exercise settings (e.g., adherence to an exercise regimen). Sport studies that use persistence as the performance measure (e.g., an endurance task) also show a reliable relationship to self-efficacy (Feltz, 1988b). It is the studies that use sport performance criteria that appear to have a weaker relationship (e.g., McAuley, 1985a). Later in this chapter, I shall argue that the psychological climate of the context affects the participant's perception of the task demands, and it is this that has a powerful effect on motivational variables such as self-efficacy.

In other words, there are some constraints to the efficacy of self-efficacy in sport.

Perceived Competence

Another series of motivation theories revolves around the perception of competence on the part of the participant. The work of Harter (1978, 1981b) has been used in sport in particular. Based on the seminal work of White (1959), Harter attempts to explain why individuals feel impelled to engage in mastery attempts in achievement contexts. To Harter, perceived competence is a multi-dimensional motive which directs individuals in cognitive, social, and physical domains. Success and failure in these domains are evaluated by significant others, and the perceived competence and intrinsic pleasure gained from success are seen to increase achievement striving, while perceived incompetence and displeasure are assumed to lead to anxiety and a decrease in achievement striving. The popularity of Harter's model in sport was specifically due to a talk she gave in 1980 to our national organization in sport psychology, and to the intuitive appeal of the model. The appeal of the model is obvious, especially for those of us who work with children. Further, the fact that she had a measurement technology that included the physical domain helped. Typically, studies have looked at the relationship of perceived competence to actual competence, at the antecedents of perceived competence, and at the relationship of perceived competence to participation in competitive sports.

A prediction of Harter's model is that children who perceive themselves competent in sport should be likely to participate in sports. With some colleagues (Roberts, Kleiber, & Duda, 1981), I found that sport participants were higher in perceived competence, as measured by the physical competence scale of Harter, than nonparticipants in sport. The relationship was not strong, and while other research has supported this initial finding, the relationships continued to be weak (Feltz & Petlichkoff, 1983; Ulrich, 1987). Even when Harter's scale was modified to be more sport specific, the relationships have remained weak (Feltz & Brown, 1984).

It has been suggested that children may participate for many reasons other than the demonstration of competence. Klint and Weiss (1987) found that children with high scores of physical competence did engage in sport, but that some engaged for affiliation or social reasons. For children, the reasons to engage in the competitive sport experience may be many (Feltz, 1988b), but continued engagement in a context where physical competence is at a premium may favor those who wish to demonstrate competence.

Researchers, looking at years of playing experience, predicted that those who were higher in perceived competence would remain in the competitive sport experience longer; however, the relationship remains weak (Feltz & Brown, 1984; Feltz & Petlichkoff, 1983; Roberts et al., 1981). Indeed, my colleagues and I have suggested that sport participation may have little effect on children's perceptions of competence; rather, the domain of sport is attractive to children who already perceive themselves to be high in perceived competence. But this contention is difficult to substantiate. Harter's model assumes a mastery perspective to achievement striving (Ames, this volume; Duda, this volume), but the Harter scale assumes an ego or competitive perspective in that children are asked to compare themselves to their peers. Children are notoriously inaccurate in estimating their comparative ability (Nicholls, 1978), thus, the scale may not be sensitive to the children's actual perceptions of competence.

Achievement Goal Approaches

Based upon the joint and independent theoretical and empirical work of Maehr, Nicholls, and Dweck (Dweck, 1986; Dweck & Elliott, 1983; Maehr & Nicholls, 1980; Nicholls, 1981, 1984a, 1984b, 1989), it is argued that to understand motivation and achievement behaviors in all their forms, the function and meaning of behavior must be taken into account so that the goals of action may be identified. By so doing, multiple goals for action are identified, not one. Variation in behavior may not be the result of high or low motivation, but rather may be the manifestation of different perceptions of appropriate goals. An individual's investment of personal resources such as effort, talent, and time in an activity is dependent upon the achievement goal of that individual for that activity.

The first step toward understanding achievement behavior is to recognize that success and failure are psychological states based upon the interpretation of the effectiveness of that person's achievement striving (Maehr & Nicholls, 1980). If the outcome of achievement striving is seen to reflect desirable attributes of the self, such as high effort, then the outcome is interpreted as a success. Conversely, if the outcome is seen to reflect undesirable qualities of the self, such as laziness, then the outcome is a failure. Success, failure, and achievement can only be recognized in terms of the goal of behavior. What is success for one, may be failure for another.

Many forms of achievement goals have been identified, but the ones which emerge consistently across studies in sport generally conform to the original hypotheses of Maehr and Nicholls (1980). Even though Nicholls, Maehr, and Dweck advocate somewhat different approaches today, the original goal orientations are the ones most studied and, one can argue, the ones most relevant to sport and exercise.

Specifically, the achievement goal approach assumes that the major focus of individuals in achievement contexts, such as sport and exercise, is to demonstrate competence or ability (Dweck, 1986; Maehr & Braskamp, 1986; Nicholls, 1984a). But ability has two conceptions in achievement contexts, and these lead to the development of two major goal perspectives that are assumed to be pursued by individuals in achievement contexts (Nicholls, 1984a, 1984b). The first goal is the goal of maximizing the probability of attributing high ability to oneself and minimizing the probability of attributing low ability to oneself (Ames, 1984a; Dweck, 1986; Maehr & Braskamp, 1986; Nicholls, 1984a). This goal drives achievement behaviors in circumstances where social comparison is extant, such as competition. Perceptions of ability are normative and referenced to the ability of others. Success or failure is dependent upon the subjective assessment of comparing one's ability with that of relevant others (see also Duda, this volume). This goal is termed *ego involvement* by Nicholls (1984a), but others call it *performance goal* (Dweck, 1986) and *ability-focused goal* (Ames, 1984a). For the purpose of this chapter, the term *competitive goal* will be used to make it more pertinent to the contexts important to sport and exercise psychologists. There are considerable data to support the existence and relevance of this goal in sport and exercise (Duda, 1989a, this volume).

The second achievement goal is the goal of demonstrating mastery or learning of a task (Ames, 1984a; Dweck, 1986; Maehr & Braskamp, 1986; Nicholls, 1984a). This goal drives achievement behavior in circumstances where learning or mastery is deemed important. Perceptions of ability are self-referenced and dependent upon improvement and/or learning. Success or failure is dependent upon the subjective assessment of whether one achieved mastery, learned, or improved on a task (see also Duda, this volume). This goal is termed *task involvement* by Nicholls (1984a), but others call it *learning goal* (Dweck & Elliott, 1983) and *mastery goal* (Ames, 1984a). For the purpose of this chapter, the term *mastery goal* will be used to make it pertinent to exercise and sport psychologists. There are considerable data to support the existence and relevance of this goal in sport and exercise (Duda, 1989a, this volume).

There are two literature surveys that have critically reviewed the achievement goal approaches in sport (Duda, 1989a; Roberts, 1984), but I would refer you to the chapter by Duda in this volume for an excellent review of the research pertinent to the goal perspective approach in sport and exercise. In brief, the evidence clearly demonstrates that multiple achievement goals exist in sport and exercise, and the approach has given much insight into the determinants of achievement behavior, as well as into enhancing achievement striving. But the approach is not without criticism. The approach has difficulty in operationally defining and measuring goal perspectives; the number of goal perspectives is under debate, and the relative contribution of each goal to achievement behavior is not well understood.

Conclusion

We have discussed the major theories and empirical approaches most common in sport and exercise. The approaches briefly reviewed have opened up clearly important avenues of exploration for understanding motivated behavior, and we have many individuals from many perspectives gathering data on motivational issues in sport and exercise. These people are producing powerful insights about the process of motivation, and many of them have chapters in this book. These researchers have illuminated crucial mechanisms of achievement behavior but have not identified all the elements that energize, direct, and sustain achievement behavior. As is clear, no one theory has emerged as "the theory." Each has its band of supporters, each its band of detractors.

I am not suggesting that motivation theory in sport and exercise is in disarray. We have a great deal of data on the process of motivation, and we do have many theories that give meaning to the data. What we need now is to move toward integration and a synthesis of theory and data, so that we might better understand what we already have. There is a danger in seeking universal applicability, as it may blind us to the very real cultural and social dynamics that modulate the ongoing stream of achievement strivings. In our quest for understanding, we may have to tolerate apparent inconsistencies, but we must attempt to move forward to a more general set of concepts to synthesize our respective efforts. In the next section, I shall try to draw on the range of social cognitive theories and their research findings to suggest an integrative framework within which the elements discussed thus far might work to affect motivation and achievement.

The Dynamic Process
of Motivation in Sport and Exercise

The integrative framework I shall propose draws upon past theories to portray a dynamic set of variables that may guide an individual's choice and pursuit of achievement goals (see Figure 1). The concepts are not new, or original. I advocated the basis of this approach in 1984 (Roberts, 1984). Further, the

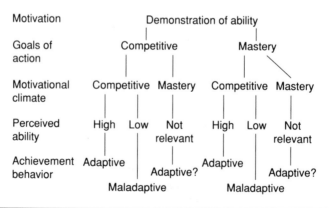

Figure 1. The dynamic process of motivation.

approach draws heavily on the joint and independent efforts of Ames (1984a), Dweck (1986), Maehr (Maehr & Braskamp, 1986), and, especially, Nicholls (1981, 1984a, 1989). However, some attempt is made to integrate concepts and findings from the different social cognitive traditions. The framework is cast in expectancy-value terms, as are most achievement motivation theories.

The framework is intended only as an idealized representation of the dynamic process of motivation (Dweck & Elliott, 1983). Whether or not the variables are considered in the explicit way I suggest is not the issue here. Rather, the information is processed in a selective and subjective manner so that the resultant achievement goal is represented as it would be in the mind of the sport or exercise participant, and the subsequent behavior is in response to this assessment. Thus, my position is that the variables and subjective assessments occur as the framework suggests, but not necessarily in the order presented. However, I will argue that the variables presented are important in the understanding of the ongoing stream of achievement behaviors of sport and/or exercise participants. To ignore any of these variables means that we, as students of motivation, ignore important elements of the dynamic process.

The concept adopted in this chapter as being particularly relevant to sport and exercise are ones articulated by Ames (1984a; this volume), Dweck (1986; Dweck & Elliott, 1983), Maehr (Maehr & Braskamp, 1986; Maehr & Nicholls, 1980), and Nicholls (1984a, 1984b, 1989). The framework specifies achievement incentives and the most economical behaviors required to attain those incentives. The individual is assumed to be an intentional, goal-directed organism who operates in a rational manner (Nicholls, 1984a). The energizing construct in this framework is assumed to be the goal of demonstrating competence or ability in achievement contexts. This goal becomes the motivational construct undergirding the dynamic process of motivation. In nonachievement contexts, other goals are assumed to operate. But when achievement is desired, when a standard of excellence is implicated, and when the activity is one of value to the participant, then the assumption of this framework is that the energizing construct is the demonstration of ability. (For a more detailed explanation, see Nicholls, 1984a.)

Conceptions of Ability

One of the real insights of the work of Nicholls (1984a, 1989), is the argument that two conceptions of ability exist, not one. Most of the theories we have discussed previously have assumed a uniform definition of ability. Nicholls argues for two. The first conception is present when an individual's actions are aimed at achieving mastery, improving, or perfecting a skill or task. The individual is merely attempting to produce a higher level of perceived mastery. This is termed a task-involved criterion of ability by Nicholls (1984a). The second conception of ability is based upon social comparison processes, where the individual judges his or her capacity relative to that of others. The focus of attention here is more on the self when compared to others, and this is termed an ego-involved criterion of ability by Nicholls.

The important point of Nicholls's argument is that both the subjective experience of the individual and the social constraints within the environment are likely to engage one conception of ability versus the other; the individual develops goals of action that are based upon ego- or task-involved ability assessments. In other words, these conceptions of ability lead to a competitive goal of action and/or a mastery goal of action. Nicholls specifies those elements that may engage ego- versus task-involved ability conceptions as being tests of valued skills, competition, or factors that increase self-awareness, such as an audience in sport and exercise.

It is at this point that the research efforts of Ames (1987, this volume) become important. Ames argues that parents, teachers, and coaches create psychological climates that affect participants in achievement contexts. Ames has looked at how the structure of achievement situations influences the adoption of ego or mastery conceptions of ability. Children are exposed to goal structures created by adults who govern the achievement context. It is these goal structures that create different processes of self-evaluation and attribution assessments in terms of performance assessment. Coaches, for example, when they talk to participants about their performances, whether in practice or competition, have choices to make about how to present the information. It is these *choice points*, as Ames calls them (Ames, this volume), that become critical in determining the motivational climate. By giving certain cues, rewards, and explicit expectations, the coach structures the motivational climate so that task-involved or ego-involved conceptions of ability are the criteria by which performance is evaluated. The coaches' goal preferences become manifest and children perceive the goal structure and act accordingly. In this way, the goal structure creates a motivational climate that makes one conception of ability or the other manifest. The child is exposed to the explicit criteria that impinge upon his or her own performance assessment within that context.

The work of Ames (1987, this volume) underscores the work of Nicholls (1989) in that the goal structures created by the significant others lead to the adoption of goals of action that are based upon the conception of ability manifest in the context. A sport participant recognizes that ability is assessed in a task- or ego-involved manner, thus he or she *develops* goals of action consistent with the conception of ability. It is in this way that individuals become socialized to the goals of action that are either mastery or competitive in orientation (see Ames, this volume). Thus, the motivational climate created by parents, coaches, or any other persons with influence in the achievement context may lead to the development of competitive or mastery goal perspectives.

Goals of Action

As Nicholls (1989) states, situations can make us more competitive or mastery involved, but this is not to deny that individual differences in the susceptibility to those types of involvement exist. This susceptibility becomes translated into achievement goals, so that individuals develop goals for action that are competitive involved when they wish to demonstrate ability to others, or mastery involved when they wish to demonstrate mastery or learning.

The goal perspectives have been discussed earlier (see also Duda, this volume). As previously stated, there is much evidence to demonstrate that these goals exist and are important to study if we wish to understand motivated behavior either in academic settings (Ames, 1984a, this volume; Dweck & Elliott, 1983; Maehr & Braskamp, 1986; Nicholls, 1989), or sport and exercise settings (Duda, 1989a, this volume; Roberts, 1984; Roberts & Balague, 1989). Even though other goals of action may exist and be important for understanding motivation in academic, industrial, and/or sport and exercise settings (e.g., Ewing, 1981; Maehr & Braskamp, 1986), I would agree with Duda (1989a) that the two most important goal perspectives in sport contexts are mastery and competitive goals of action. Thus, to better understand achievement behaviors, investigators must recognize multiple goals of action. Assuming one universal goal, as many theories of motivation do, is to ignore important dynamics of the process of motivation.

Motivational Climate

We have discussed how the psychological climate created by parents and coaches has the effect of socializing individuals to one goal perspective or the other. But the process of motivation is affected at yet another level—the motivational climate created by coaches in practice and competition. Again, this is where the work of Ames (this volume) is insightful.

Within sport and exercise settings, competitive and mastery climates exist. Clearly, competitive climates exist in competitive sport when winning is the criterion of success for the coaching staff. But competitive sport can also have a mastery climate when getting better, or improvement from game to game, is the coaching staff's criterion of success. Similarly, practice sessions can be mastery or competitive in orientation depending upon the cues and evaluative feedback given by the coaches (and parents!). But the important issue to be addressed here is the consistency of the motivational climate created by the coaches with the achievement goal perspective held by the individual participant.

We may have individuals predisposed toward a mastery goal perspective who find themselves in a mastery climate (see Figure 1). Thus, we would expect these individuals to be comfortable within this context and be motivated to achieve. However, we may have individuals predisposed toward a competitive goal perspective who find themselves in a mastery climate. We would expect these people to perceive some conflict and not be as motivated to achieve. Indeed, as a means to motivate themselves, these individuals may seek to introduce competition into the mastery climate. But this is a much understudied area in motivation research, and we can only speculate at the present time.

The same scenarios may exist with individuals predisposed toward a competitive goal perspective who find themselves within a climate consistent or inconsistent with their predisposition. The climate may not always override the goal of action when the climate is inconsistent with the goal; thus, the achievement behaviors of these individuals might be in conflict with the expectations of the coach.

As stated earlier, it is difficult to know how this situation would affect the achievement behavior of individuals when the goal of action is inconsistent with the motivational goal structure created by the coaches. It is an understudied area, and an area of research that has the potential to be most productive. For example, parents who do their best to create a mastery goal perspective for a child and then place the child in a sports program that clearly is competitive in climate have a dilemma: Do they keep the child in the program, recognizing that the child may have to adopt a competitive goal perspective?

The adoption of one goal perspective or another may not be important in and of itself. However, the evidence we have from both academic (e.g., Ames, 1984a; Dweck, 1986) and sport research (e.g., Duda, this volume) shows that the adoption of a competitive goal perspective often leads to maladaptive patterns of achievement behaviors by some individuals. A reason for this lies in the next variable of importance in the dynamic model—the perception of ability.

The Perception of Ability

A persistent aspect of the research in academic and in exercise and sport settings is the emergence of perception of ability as an important construct in the understanding of achievement behavior (Roberts, 1984). A growing body of evidence suggests that the perception of ability, in a variety of guises, is the central mediating construct of achievement behavior (Bukowski & Moore, 1980; Covington & Omelich, 1979; Diener & Dweck, 1978; Dweck, 1986; Dweck & Elliott, 1983; Duda, 1989a, this volume; Nicholls, 1976, 1978, 1984b, 1989; Roberts, 1975, 1984; Roberts, Kleiber, & Duda, 1981; Spink & Roberts, 1980). Ability attributions and the self-concept of ability play an important role in understanding the ongoing stream of achievement behavior. Various terms have been used to describe the construct, but it is argued here that there is a great deal of similarity in the function of this construct as it is described in the various theories under the social cognitive rubric. Whether it is termed self-efficacy (Bandura, 1977a, 1986), perceived ability (Dweck, 1986; Nicholls, 1984a, 1989), perceived competence (Harter, 1978, 1981a), sense of competence (Maehr & Braskamp, 1986), or perceived capacity to meet environmental demands (Csikszentmihalyi & Nakamura, 1989), the self-concept of ability in its various forms is considered to be an important mediator of the ongoing stream of achievement striving. The individual is expected to assess his or her competency to achieve the task, or have confidence in his or her capacity to meet the environmental demands; and this assessment affects maladaptive or adaptive achievement striving.

Adaptive achievement behaviors are those that promote the likelihood of achievement. Adaptive achievement patterns are characterized by challenge seeking and effective persistence in the face of failure (Dweck, 1986). In brief, adaptive behaviors are those where the individual exerts effort, values the task, enjoys exerting effort, and exhibits sustained persistence. Maladaptive patterns of behavior are those that do not promote effective strategies for achievement. Maladaptive behaviors are those where the individual avoids challenges and reduces persistence in the face of difficulty. In brief, maladaptive behaviors are avoiding challenge, not exerting effort, failing to persist in the face of difficulty, and, in sport, dropping out if achievement of desired goals appears difficult (Roberts, 1984).

The perception of one's own ability is predicted to mediate the adoption of maladaptive or adaptive achievement behaviors depending upon the perception of the motivational climate and one's goal for action (see Figure 1). Thus, if the goal perspective is competitive and the individual perceives him or herself to be in a competitive climate, the perception of ability is expected to mediate behavior depending upon whether ability is seen as high or low. If high ability is salient, then adaptive behaviors are predicted. If ability is low, then maladaptive behavior is predicted. There is evidence to support those predictions (Duda, this volume; Roberts, Hall, Jackson, Kimiecik, & Tonymon, 1990).

If one is competitive in goal orientation and is placed in a mastery climate, then the perception of ability becomes irrelevant. The goal structure of the context de-emphasizes social comparison and assessments of ability relative to others. Therefore, it is difficult to predict what behaviors will be manifest if the climate does not override the goal perspective. Thus, adaptive behaviors are assumed to predominate. But only research with both climate and goal perspective considered will resolve this question.

Ability assessments for competitive-goal-perspective individuals in sport are complex. The focus of attention is on the self, and at least three evaluations must be made: an assessment of the opponent in relation to all other opponents; how one's own ability compares to the opponent's ability; and how much effort is being applied by the self and by the opponent (Roberts, 1984). While we have briefly touched upon the implications of holding a competitive goal perspective in a sport and exercise context, I would refer readers who wish to pursue the arguments more fully to the research of Dweck (1986) and Nicholls (1984a, 1984b) for academic contexts, and the efforts of Duda (1989a, this volume) and Roberts (1984), for sport and exercise contexts.

When individuals are mastery involved, then similar predictions emerge. A mastery person in a competitive climate may find him or herself utilizing adaptive or maladaptive achievement behaviors, depending upon his or her perception of ability. Assuming that the competitive climate is not so salient that it overrides the mastery orientation (see Roberts, 1984), then the perception of ability is irrelevant, as the person engages in adaptive behavior anyway. But for the person who finds him or herself becoming competitive in orientation, then perception of ability is crucial. For high-perception-of-ability individuals, adaptive behaviors are used. But if perception of ability is low, then the person may engage in the activity for a while, but may adopt maladaptive behaviors over time. Again, research will have to be undertaken to assess these predictions. However, some evidence to support these predications is available (Duda, this volume; Roberts et al., 1990).

Ability assessments for mastery goal-directed individuals are self-referenced and are thereby less complex than competitive ability assessments (Roberts, 1984). Sport or exercise participants do not have access to the competencies of others in order to reach judgments of demonstrating ability. Rather, the individual focuses upon information provided by the task to establish simply whether he or she is performing optimally or improving. Effort is important, but only in that it leads to greater learning. For mastery individuals, they cannot display low ability. Social comparison ability assessments are irrelevant (see Figure 1).

It is this type of involvement that elite athletes sometimes reflect upon when describing peak experiences. Indeed, we have some data to show that people who experience peak experiences can be described as being mastery involved (Jackson & Roberts, 1989). Further, the work of Feltz and Mungo (1983) with subjects who had problems with backward diving, and McAuley (1985a) in a physical activity setting has shown that motivational climates that may be termed mastery oriented can lead to enhanced achievement striving and enhanced performance. For readers who wish to pursue these arguments in greater detail, I would refer them to the research of Dweck (1986) and Nicholls (1984a, 1989) for academic contexts, and the work of Duda (1989a, this volume) and Roberts (1984) for sport and exercise contexts.

Conclusion

I have stated that the framework proffered is an idealized one, but there is evidence to support that the dynamic process of motivation does integrate the constructs discussed in a systematic manner. Whether it is exactly as outlined is not the issue. Rather, I have argued that the achievement goals of individuals, the perception of the motivational climate, and the perception of the appropriate conception of ability manifest in the context are crucial to consider in order to understand motivation in all its forms. Taking any one variable in isolation makes us vulnerable to a myopic and static view of the motivation process. It is these variables acting in concert that need to be understood.

The question to ask here is whether this framework allows us to integrate the various approaches in some way. To begin to discuss this issue, we need to know what behavior in sport and exercise we are attempting to understand.

I believe we need to ask a very simple question: What is motivated behavior in sport and exercise? It is the resolution of this question that will help us understand our own approaches and whether the research each one of us conducts contributes to the insight of another approach.

Motivated Behavior

The answer to the question of what is motivated behavior in sport and exercise has been very varied. One researcher is interested in youth sport dropouts, another with participation motivation or the choice of activity. Some researchers are interested in exercise adherence, others in performance variables and accomplishment—and the list goes on. Certainly, the fact that these people chose these behaviors while testing motivation theories implies that these researchers consider these behaviors to be motivated. The choice of dependent measures by which we explore the efficacy of our theories is crucial, but the decisions we have made in the past are sometimes debatable.

Once a measure is selected, researchers tend to concentrate upon that one dependent measure to the exclusion of others. Sometimes, a convenient measurement technology exists that influences the decision. Consequently, if we have the measurement technology and believe in the approach we are adopting, why entertain other approaches? Thus, at meetings we declare our approach and present our data. Under the assumption that our approaches are appropriate, we spend most of our time debating the efficacy of our operational definitions, their power, and the behavioral variances for which they account. We worry more about the psychometric properties of our variables than about their conceptual relevance. We may be accused of studying data, not people (Roberts, 1989).

One of the biggest errors, in my opinion, has been the uncritical use of ''performance'' as a dependent measure when studying motivation in sport and exercise. This is where I take exception to Maehr and Braskamp (1986) when they advocate performance as an appropriate dependent measure in motivational research. In some achievement contexts performance may be appropriate, but in sport and exercise the validity of performance may be questioned.

First, when we look at performance as a dependent measure, we infer that achievement change is the result of motivational ebb or flow. While this may be true, performance is affected by an array of other constructs that may also be ebbing and flowing at the same time. As Feltz (1988b) pointed out in the self-efficacy area, when performance findings do not conform to predictions, other constructs not measured are assumed to have affected performance. On the other hand, we cannot assume every instance of performance enhancement is the result of motivation. It is sobering to realize that the relationship between motivation and performance is a great deal more modest than we assume.

Second, as Nicholls (1989) is at pains to remind us, we often assume that if we enhance achievement, we have enhanced motivation. In other words, we associate achievement with motivation. This is because we assume that success is what other people strive for, and success is often defined in terms of achievement or accomplishment. But as I stated earlier, success is subjective. Other variables affect perception of success in addition to accomplishment (Roberts, 1984).

Third, another concern with performance as a dependent measure is that it focuses the participant on the ego-involved conception of ability (Ames, 1984a). The constraints of the social context of sport have been discussed elsewhere (e.g., Martens, 1975; Roberts, 1984), but, in sport, the only means by which we can assess performance is in comparison with others. The social context of sport elicits social comparison processes and, by definition, the ego-involved concept of ability. This in itself is not a problem if the theory being tested also assumes that the concept of ability being used is ego involved. But this is not always the case. Some theories assume a task-involved concept of ability, others utilize an ego-involved concept of ability. We are in danger of violating the constraints of the theory being tested if we utilize dependent measures that are predicated upon a different conception of ability than that assumed by the theory.

We have all been guilty of this error in the past. However, in the future we must all be sensitive to the conceptual constraints of the theory we are using and make certain that the dependent measures used are consistent with the assumptions underlying the theory. To aid us in this approach, let us look at the theories that we have used in sport and exercise and attempt to decipher the appropriate means to adequately remain within the constraints imposed by the theory.

Task- and Ego-Involved Conceptions of Ability

It is sometimes difficult to determine with confidence exactly which conception of ability is assumed in some theories. The work of Harter (1980), however, primarily deals with the task-involved conception of ability. Harter deals with mastery behaviors even though she discusses challenge-seeking and curiosity. Therefore, when we introduce performance within a competitive sport context, we typically (but not always) force the participants to assume an ego-involved conception of ability. This is outside the constraints of the theory as proposed by Harter (1980), and I argue that Harter's theory must be interpreted cautiously within the competitive sport context when sport performance is the criteria of achievement behavior. Sport performance is often based upon competitive conceptions of ability, yet Harter's theory only addresses task-involved conceptions. I believe this is why the findings of the research using Harter's concepts are equivocal. There is an added difficulty with the Harter model. Her scale of physical competence assumes an ego-involved concept of ability. Therefore, even her scale is not consistent with her theory when used in sport. Even though the insights gained from the work using Harter's theory are important, we must ensure that in the future we are sensitive to the limits of the theory.

The same argument may be made for the use of goal-setting procedures as advocated by Locke and associates (Locke, Shaw, Saari, & Latham, 1981). Locke's empirical approach to enhancing performance is atheoretical, but it is predicated upon a task-involved conception of ability. The use of goal-setting in work and school settings has been remarkably successful in enhancing performance. But this is performance from a mastery perspective. As Weinberg (this volume) and Hall (1990) have pointed out, the findings in the sport literature are equivocal and difficult to interpret. I am arguing here that two different conceptions of ability are involved and that we need to rethink our work involving goal-setting in sport when conceptual issues are under debate. I am arguing that past goal-setting research is only relevant for mastery-oriented motivational climates. I would refer readers to the works of Hall and Byrne (1988), and Hall (1990) who are conducting valuable work in attempting to understand the conceptual undergirding of goal-setting.

The same may be said for self-efficacy research. However, the issue here is not as clear-cut. Bandura's (1977a) arguments are consistent with a task-involved concept of ability, but in other places they suggest a more ego-involved concept (Nicholls, 1989). One of the problems of self-efficacy theory is that, although Bandura (1977a, 1986) has specified the directive influence of self-efficacy, he has not clearly specified the energizing concepts. Bandura argues that self-efficacy is a mediator of achievement striving. Thus, it can be argued that self-efficacy is not a true motivational theory, in that it does not clearly specify the energizing as well as the directing aspect of self-efficacy. Generally, however, the theory does lend itself to a task-involved conception as Bandura discusses mastery, mastery attempts, and one's efficacy in executing these attempts. Therefore, when sport researchers have used self-efficacy in sport contexts where a competitive climate is extant, we may argue that they may be violating the constraints of the theory. That is a strong statement, but it may explain why a weak relationship has been found with self-efficacy research in sport contexts. Competitive environments force the participant to be more concerned with social comparison processes than with mastery or learning. This is not to deny that competitive sport can have a mastery motivational climate, especially for elite participants and young children, but to the extent that a competitive motivational climate is perceived to exist, participants will not focus upon adaptive achievement striving when perception of ability is also low.

The work done by Feltz (1982) and her colleagues using backward diving, and the work by McAuley and colleagues (McAuley & Jacobson, 1990; McAuley & Rowney, 1990) in exercise behavior is, in contrast, more consistent with a mastery goal perspective and a task-involved conception of ability.

With Feltz, backward diving was a skill the subjects learned to master; therefore, mastery was pertinent. Similarly, exercise behavior most often deals with adherence and with personalized goals that elicit the task-involved concept of ability. This is why this line of research is easier to interpret. This is what I mean when I advocate that we should be more aware of the constraints of the theories we use in sport and exercise, and that we should ensure that our dependent measures are within the conceptual constraints of the theory.

There are many theories involving ego-involved conceptions of ability, but the ones most used in sport are *need achievement theory* (Atkinson, 1957; McClelland, 1958) and *attribution theory* (Weiner, 1979, 1986). Both theories have been utilized in sport for a number of years, even though conceptual problems exist in both areas (Brawley & Roberts, 1984; McAuley & Duncan, 1990; Roberts, 1982). However, my position here is that when these theories were used in sport, an ego-involved assumption of ability was made, and, most often, ego-involved concepts of ability were investigated. The dependent variables were consistent with the constraints of the theory (see Nicholls, 1989).

This illustrates the need to be more concerned with our use of dependent measures. Our assumption that the dependent measures always meet the conceptual constraints of the theory has already confused the motivational literature in sport and exercise. If the dependent measure does not fall within the conceptual constraints of theory, then we run the risk of generating random noise in the literature—against which the true signal of advancement will be difficult to discern. We must be more critical of our approaches and be more careful that our measures are consistent with what we wish to study. A failure to do this will limit our understanding of motivation and achievement striving.

Toward Conceptual Convergence?

Does the previously presented framework help us toward a synthesis of theory and data? Are there generalities to the conceptual undergirding of the various theories that move us toward theoretical convergence? Are we moving toward a more general and comprehensive theory of motivation in sport and exercise? As is evident from my prior discussion, I think we are making some progress toward convergence and integration. But this progress will only continue if we begin to be more sensitive to the issues addressed in this chapter and begin to critically examine our own approaches as well as the approaches of others. Then we may be able to move toward a convergence of theories, and we can all better understand the dynamic process of motivation in sport and exercise.

What, then, are the tasks to be undertaken that will allow us to move closer to this comprehensive understanding of motivation and achievement behaviors? Clearly, much more research is needed into both the elements and the association between the elements that will allow us to understand the total dynamic process. I have used the concepts and the research findings of many investigators that I might suggest some of the critical variables I believe we need to address. But this framework is not meant to be exhaustive. Other variables and other processes may emerge as our ongoing research efforts unfold. While this framework is not meant to be definitive, I do believe the variables discussed in the framework are the critical ones to study at the present time. I do not assume, however, that the process unfolds as described. Only further research will reveal the dynamics of the process. Much more research is needed into the dynamic subprocesses identified in this framework. Let us discuss some of the most critical.

1. We must learn how individuals become socialized to adopt goal perspectives that are mastery and/or competitive in orientation. The work of Ames (this volume) and Nicholls (this volume) is crucial and gives us insight into the dynamics of this process. What Ames also addresses is the role of parents, as well as sport or exercise leaders, in this socialization process. We clearly need much more effort in this area if we are to understand this process more fully.

2. We must decide how important the goal perspectives are to understanding motivation. The proposed framework differs from most other approaches in that multiple goals are assumed. Separate goals and separate predictions are made in achievement contexts (see Figure 1). The importance of this distinction is sustained by the evidence (e.g., Duda, this volume; Nicholls, this volume). But as I have elsewhere (Roberts, 1984) argued, other goals may play a central role in any comprehensive theory that ultimately emerges (see also Maehr & Braskamp, 1986). I believe it is clear that researchers ignore the existence of multiple goals at the peril of ignoring important subprocesses of the process of motivation.

3. We cannot underestimate the importance of the motivational climate. Motivational climate can override predispositions toward goal perspectives. The importance of the goal structure created to affect the motivational climate must be studied to understand the conflicts and the attributional processes undertaken by the participants within sport and exercise. When, and under what circumstances, do motivational climates override the predisposition to one goal or another?

4. We need to recognize that different conceptions of ability exist, and that these put a premium on the measurement of ability perceptions. It is not sufficient to measure perception of competence without concern for the concept of ability held by the participant. In some contexts, for some people, ability perception has become irrelevant. But for others, it is paramount to understanding achievement behavior. We must be sensitive to the different conceptions of ability that are manifest in the contexts of importance to our individual research efforts.

5. We should ask, as Duda (this volume) and others have asked (e.g., Gould, 1982; Roberts, 1984), how developmental issues impact on the process

when the motivation of children is under the microscope. We need much more informed research on this topic than has been the case hitherto.

6. We must be sensitive to the measurement of the variables under scrutiny. For example, Duda (1989a, this volume) and Roberts and Balague (1989) have developed scales to measure the achievement goal perspectives of individuals in sport and physical skill contexts. More research and more concern with carefully operationalizing the dependent and independent variables is needed in our quest to understand motivation.

7. Last, and certainly not least, we can no longer set aside the one issue that has been ignored by most theorists in the cognitive realm—the issue of value in the Expectancy × Value framework (see also Rejeski, this volume). Value is assumed in all the models, and each theorist actually states that the value of the activity for the participants is assumed. But can value always be assumed? When we observe maladaptive behaviors by participants, we often assume that the process has impinged upon the expectancy constellation of cognitions. In fact, it may well be that the value of the activity for the participant may be low. Even though evidence exists that shows that sport is valued by participants (Duda, 1981), not all participants value the activity to the same level. Therefore, in our research efforts in the future, value must be investigated and understood for a complete understanding of achievement behavior. Among others, I have deplored the high dropout rate from sports programs and have advocated intervention to prevent dropouts in the future (Roberts, 1984). But it could well be that some of these people value the achievement context so little that employing adaptive patterns of behavior just does not make rational sense. Therefore, dropping out becomes a rational and desirable act. We should be concerned with value so that when we do intervene, we intervene with those participants who value the activity.

Conclusion

This chapter has pleaded for all of us to expand our conceptual lenses, to incorporate the concepts and findings of each of our approaches, and to begin to synthesize our theories and data. I believe that if we do this, then we will better understand the process of motivation in sport and exercise. We must consider the multivariate complexity of information processing, bidirectional causality, cognitions, and feedback, because such concern is more likely to capture the individual and social reality of individuals in exercise and sport. In the real world, effects are the result of multiple causes in complex interaction. Thus, we must spend more time creating appropriate hypotheses that emanate from an understanding of both the cognitive complexity of the individual and the situational constraints of the contexts. We need to describe, document, and conceptually represent the cognitive functioning of exercise and sport participants. Only then can we begin to consider which intervention strategies may be appropriate for particular cognitive deficits underpinning deviant, inappropriate, or ineffectual behavior.

In the social and cognitive systems we investigate, we need to be aware of the effects of the outcome of multiple causes in complex interaction. Therefore, our measurement procedures must be sensitive to the multiple causes acting in a bidirectional manner. We need to recognize the obsolescence of some of our current methodologies (Roberts, 1989). We must change our research practice so that we will better cope with the conceptual constraints of the theories that we utilize, and with the dirty data of the real world. But I am optimistic. I am certain that when we begin to do our own research and our microanalyses with the appropriate populations and informed dependent measures, and that when we recognize the congruence in our approaches and operate accordingly, then we cannot help but advance our collective understanding. This book is but a modest attempt to begin to address the multiple issues in our understanding of motivation, and to begin our interventions to enhance motivation in sport and exercise.

Note

[1]In my review of attribution research in 1982, I concluded my review by reporting a "new" direction in motivation research. I discussed the exciting work that centered upon the various ways that the self-concept of ability and one's perception of competence to complete the task had taken motivation research in new directions (e.g., Bandura, 1977a; Harter, 1978, 1981b; Maehr & Nicholls, 1980). I stated at the time that these new directions held the most potential for understanding motivation. Little did I realize how prophetic this statement would be: This is now the mainstream approach to motivation.

The General and the Specific in the Development and Expression of Achievement Motivation

John G. Nicholls

Psychologists commonly exalt abstract and general theories over descriptions of the unique features of life in particular times and places. One commonly finds attempts to apply, without modification, theories of motivation such as that of Atkinson to activities as diverse as mathematics and shuffleboard. It is less common to find researchers interested in what is unique about motivation in different domains of accomplishment. After having long looked the other way, I am now trying to attend to the unique features of motivation in different activities.

A cursory glance reveals that different achievement activities offer different sources of satisfaction. Marathon runners, for example, must enjoy solitary exertion. This seems an alien form of pleasure for American football players, who swarm together on the sidelines of fields and huddle together talking and holding hands after each play.

Research on motivation that ignores such differences is incomplete. But while examining particulars, we need not ignore features that are common to many achievement activities. Accordingly, I suggest the beginnings of a framework for the study of the nature and development of achievement motivation that encompasses features that are common to academic and sporting activities as well as features that are unique to specific activities within each domain.

There are two main parts to this story. The first concerns developmental change in concepts of ability, intelligence and physical skill, knowledge, and fairness. In this part, my concern is with people's cognitive competencies, not their use of these competencies—with how people can construe ability or fairness in contests, for example, when they are stimulated to think as effectively as they can about these topics.

The second part of the story concerns which concepts people use and how they use them. It concerns people's theories about achievement. People who have similar concepts of the nature of fairness in contests, for example, might differ in their use of these concepts when they interpret academic and sporting events. Fairness might have a central role in one person's interpretations of school or games, but might be inconsequential in the interpretations of another person. In the same way, people with similar conceptions of the nature of physical ability will not necessarily have similar analyses of the role of high ability in physical accomplishment.

The first part of this chapter, then, deals with concepts while the second deals with theories about achievement activities. For both concepts and theories, I will consider possible similarities and differences for sport and academic-intellectual activities. (Possible similarities and differences for concepts are outlined in Table 1.) As for scientific theories, it is useful to think of concepts as components of theories—a theory is "bigger" than a concept. It is also useful to recognize that theories involve people's goals or values. In post-modern conceptions of science, differences among scientific analyses of any phenomenon are often seen as reflecting the different goals or concerns of different scientists. This turns out to be a useful perspective for studying lay interpretations of achievement.[1]

Achievement-Related Concepts and Their Development

Students of achievement motivation have had a rather constricted vision of the field of achievement-related concepts. Self-concept of ability, for example,

Table 1   Achievement Related Concepts and the Likely Similarity of Their Meanings in Intellectual and Sporting Activities

Concept	Likely similarity of meanings
Ability and performance	
Luck and skill	Equivalent
Difficulty and ability	Equivalent
Effort and ability	Equivalent
Nature and growth of skills	
Intelligence	Specific but parallels possible
Athletic skills	Specific but parallels possible
Knowledge	
Regulative conventions	Specific but parallels likely
Constitutive conventions	Specific but parallels likely
Fairness	
In tests	Equivalent
In contests	Specific but parallels likely
In learning situations	Specific but parallels possible
In "fun" situations	Specific but parallels possible

Note. Specific implies that concepts are likely to be specific to sport or intellectual activities. *Parallels* implies the possibility that though concepts of intelligence and physical skill (for example) might be specific, similar though not equivalent characteristics are likely.

has commonly been seen as an important concept. It refers to individuals' conceptions of how much ability they have. Perhaps this concept is especially popular because it is often highly related to attainment. Correlations run as high as .80. But the fact that people, when given ample information, can figure out where they stand is not necessarily very enlightening (Nicholls, Cheung, Lauer, & Patashnick, 1989). Yet the question of what individuals think ability is has, until relatively recently, been accorded little attention. I start with this question, and distinguish conceptions of ability, as it limits immediate performance from the nature and long-term changeability of different intellectual and physical skills.

Freud's dictum that a full life demands love and work has achievement motivation comprising about half of a meaningful life. If that half is no more than the business of proving how able we are or increasing our abilities, we have small lives. The field of achievement concepts can be broadened to include conceptions of the culturally constructed rules that define what it is we are about when we write poetry or kick an inflated pig's bladder around a field. Conceptions of the fairness of the practices we adopt in these diverse settings also deserve a share of our attention. Let achievement motivation research live a fuller life.

Ability

If one takes Heider's (1958) perspective or Weiner's (1972) early position, the concepts of luck, difficulty, effort, and ability play leading roles in people's interpretations of their *immediate performance* outcomes. If you win a race, for example, you might attribute this to superior ability, good luck, an incompetent field of runners (an easy task), or to your high effort. These concepts have each been shown to undergo considerable change over the elementary and junior high school years. The development of the concept of ability can be seen as a process of differentiating the concepts of luck, difficulty, and effort from ability. Only when this differentiation is complete—at about 12 years—do children understand ability in the way that adults do. Accompanying changes in self-evaluation, behavior, performance, and expectations about others' evaluations indicate the importance of these conceptual changes.

Note that the question here is what children think ability is—the meaning of ability. The concern is not with causal attributions or the schemes children use to infer ability in themselves or others. For example, if I think that my success in academe is due to my ability but observers conclude that it can only have resulted from luck, it does not follow that we have different beliefs about the nature of ability or luck. These related, but not equivalent, matters are commonly confused (Nicholls, 1989).

Children's conceptions are often difficult for adults to understand—especially without the opportunity to actually interview children or to study interview transcripts (Nicholls, 1989). It is hard not to project our own conceptions on children when they lack understandings that are, for us, axiomatic. Axiomatic for us is the distinction between luck or pure gambling tasks and tasks involving skill. Young children (below about nine years), however, confound the concepts of *skill* and *luck*. The skill tasks used in the study on which these claims are based required subjects to select, from among a number of similar line drawings, the only drawing that matched a standard (Nicholls, 1989). The parallel luck tasks required students to guess which of several drawings that were turned face down matched a standard. Only in early adolescence was it clearly seen that effort and skill could have no role in the luck task. Adolescents were correspondingly more selective than young children in the effort they applied to luck (chance) versus skill tasks: Adolescents spent less time than did young children concentrating or working on luck tasks and more time on skill tasks.

There is every reason to suppose that use of physical tasks would show comparable trends in conceptions and in effort deployment. Indeed, Weisz (1984) reports similar age-related trends for children's interpretations of skill carnival games (such as those that involve throwing balls at a target) and chance games (such as those that involve devices like roulette wheels).

The concept of normative *difficulty* develops considerably earlier—at about eight years. It involves the understanding that task difficulty and a person's competence are best understood with reference to the performance of members of a reference group. That is, a task of high difficulty is one that few people can do and mastery of such a task is taken as evidence of high ability (Nicholls, 1989, 1990).

A number of changes in responsiveness to social influences that occur at about seven years of age appear to reflect the development of the normative conceptions of difficulty and ability (Nicholls & Miller, 1984). For example, Butler (1989) found that after about eight years children showed reduced subsequent interest in a task when it was said that the experimenter wanted to see which member of a group could draw the best picture. This effect was not observed in younger children.

It seems likely that these cognitive and motivational developments will be essentially the same for sporting activities. It would be ironic if the development of the normative conception means that children become better able to understand the meaning of competition in sport, but also that their intrinsic interest is more readily undermined by an emphasis on competition (Deci & Ryan, 1985; Nicholls, 1989; Ryan, 1982). This would occur, for example, when coaches emphasize winning over doing one's best (Chaumeton & Duda, 1988), or when they emphasize the hierarchy of competence on a team by selectively benching less able players or by making comments that focus attention on the relative standing of players rather than on strategies for improving each one's performance or for helping the team (Butler, 1987).

Finally, there is the differentiation of the concepts of *effort* and *ability*, which culminates in attainment of the conception of *ability-as-current-capacity* at about 12 years. This conception involves the assumption that effort can increase how well one *performs* relative to others but only up to the limits of one's *present* capacity on the task of interest. To test for the conception of ability-as-current-capacity, we presented children with the problem of how someone who applies little effort at a short-term task can perform as well as another who applies high effort. It is not until about 10 to 13 years that children recognize that the "lazier" person must be more able and could outperform the other if she tried as hard as the other. This means a sense of increased limits on immediate performance and on the effectiveness of effort. It is not surprising, therefore, that when students expect to look incompetent, greater impairment of performance occurs after this conception is attained (Miller, 1985). There are a variety of other accompaniments of this development that suggest its importance as a landmark of early adolescence (Nicholls, 1989; Nicholls & Miller, 1984).

There is no reason to expect any significant differences in the nature of the conception of ability-as-current-capacity or its development for the field of sport or games. Note that the interview questions used to assess this conception are devoid of reference to the nature of the task or ability involved. The task could be mathematics problems (as in one study), unspecified puzzles (as in another), or almost any skill task. Note also that the interview does not address the question of how one could become more able or what the limits are on how able one can become. It deals only with the effects of ability (however one comes to acquire it) and effort on *immediate performance*. The question of the changeability of intellectual abilities—as distinct from the changeability of performance—is the topic of the subsequent section, not this one.

It is reasonable to speculate that dropping out of voluntary sport activities, which increases in early adolescence (Roberts, 1984) might partially reflect the development of the conception of ability-as-current-capacity. Boys dropping out from wrestling at early adolescence report low perceived ability at wrestling, but not at other sports (Burton & Martens, 1986). This suggests the importance of perceived ability in dropping out. The role of the conception of ability-as-current-capacity is suggested by evidence that when it develops, expectations of incompetent performance become more incapacitating (Miller, 1985).

"Merely" doing one's best also comes to be valued less than doing well with little effort when the conception of ability-as-current-capacity develops (Nicholls, Patashnick, & Mettetal, 1986). In schoolwork, this means that when they expect to perform worse than others, students with this concept are more likely to feel on the horns of a dilemma: If they try their best, they might please the teacher and, possibly, perform well; but, if after doing their best they fail, they will establish their incompetence more decisively than if they had applied little effort. In sport, where performances are often very public and effort more obvious, this dilemma might be experienced especially acutely. This would make the prospect of performing worse than one's peers more threatening after the concept of ability-as-current-capacity develops.

Incidentally, although the concept of ability-as-current-capacity will lead to reduced effort, it does not follow, as is commonly claimed, that this will lead to reduced effort so as to protect one's sense of competence at the task. For some reason, people (including researchers) assume that other people might do this but do not see it as a viable option for themselves. We now believe that it is indeed not a viable self-protective mechanism. To reduce effort to avoid demonstrating incompetence is to acknowledge that one cannot perform competently. The mechanism would be self-defeating (Jagacinski & Nicholls, 1990). What happens is, more likely, that people facing this dilemma devalue the skill at issue and, therefore, withdraw from the task. They might protect their overall feelings of competence to some degree by doing this. But they could not, thereby, convincingly avoid the implication that they are low in the particular skill at issue.

In summary, the conception of ability-as-current-capacity, like those of difficulty and luck, seems general in the sense of being equally applicable to physical and intellectual activities. It also seems likely to play roles of similar importance for motivation in sport as it does in intellectual and educational activities (Duda, 1987). With age, children are more able to see the point of competition as do adults. At the same time they become more likely to have their interest undermined by competition and, when they see themselves as incompetent, to find the experience of competition unpleasant and to withdraw.

Intelligence

In studying the development of concepts of intelligence, we (Nicholls et al., 1986) started with evidence that adults make a distinction akin to that between fluid and crystallized intelligence (Sternberg, Conway, Ketron, & Bernstein, 1981). This is contrary to Dweck and Elliott's (1983) thesis that adults think of intelligence as a single global entity or as a collection of ever-increasing skills. Our interview was designed to see (a) when concepts akin to fluid and crystallized intelligence were attained, and (b) the nature of antecedent conceptions. Therefore, we interviewed students about how people might improve (through their own efforts to learn or with the help of teachers) in accumulated knowledge or information (relating to crystallized intelligence) and in abstract reasoning ability (relating to fluid intelligence).

Everyone we interviewed thought one could improve in both areas. That is, we had no subjects that Dweck and Elliott (1983) would call entity theorists. Yet there were clear age trends in conceptions of intelligence. The task of improving a person's standing (relative to others) on these intellectual tasks was interpreted by most elementary school children simply in terms of how hard the tasks looked to them. From early to late adolescence a "trivial pursuit" conception of intelligence predominated. For these intermediate-level students, gaining in intelligence meant gaining in facts or accumulating information by hard work or systematic teaching. Only toward the end of high school was reasoning ability (fluid intelligence) distinguished from accumulated information and seen as appreciably harder to change. At this point, students thought of reasoning ability as reflecting many experiences including unplanned, informal learning experiences—the whole nature of one's life. (See also Leahy & Hunt, 1983.) A lack of such background was seen as difficult to overcome. Formal teaching and trying hard to memorize were not seen as likely to be effective. Note that as well as being a qualitatively different developmental sequence, this occurs very much later than does the development of the conception of ability-as-current-capacity.[2]

Here, it seems that the study of achievement-related concepts must diverge for intellectual and sporting activities. Sport abilities are surely not equivalent to intellectual abilities. In informal interviews, Michael Patashnick and I gained the impression that senior high school students distinguish basic skills like running speed from ability at games, where many skills must be coordinated (as in most team games) and where strategy is important. They appear to see the former as harder to change. But these were very casual interviews of a few children.

The research we need to start on this topic is research modeled on that of Sternberg et al. (1981). We need a picture of adults' conceptions of sport abilities. The practice of measuring skills when selecting professional football players suggests that at least some people whose livelihood depends on their ability to choose winners think there are important and measurable sport abilities. How many dimensions do they, and less specialized adults, distinguish? Do they think there are important skills that cannot be assessed with discrete tests of agility, speed, endurance, and strength? Are some skills more "basic"? Is there a conception of the "natural athlete"? If so, what might natural mean? What intellectual and social skills are seen as important to sport and are these distinguishable from other more "purely" physical and intellectual skills? Are different skills developed in different ways and are some more readily improved? Research on these questions would provide the necessary framework for developmental studies.

In the intellectual domain, the veneration of abstract reasoning—as exhibited by our awe of "pure" mathematics—might depend on the differentiated conceptions of intelligence. Only those adolescents who have established conceptions akin to fluid and crystallized intelligence value reasoning ability over accumulated information. Younger students value amount of information—the sort of intelligence exhibited in most quiz shows. Also, the apparently greater fear of math than of other subjects might reflect the belief that it is harder to change fluid intelligence. If one lacked fluid intelligence, one's chances of catching up would look more hopeless than if one lacked specific information. There are likely to be age trends of valuing different types of sport abilities that are not completely parallel to those for intelligence. Such trends are likely to reflect, in part at least, changing conceptions of the nature of different skills.

Knowledge

Concepts of ability and intelligence both involve social comparison. Conceptions of knowledge, as that term is used here, do not. Conceptions of knowledge bear on questions such as where do our ideas about the world come from, how do you tell what are useful ideas, how do you recognize truth, and whether or not the concept of truth is a useful one. Who is faster at getting answers right is a question about ability. How one increases one's ability to get right answers is a question about the educability of intelligence. What is a right answer and how one tells this is a question about knowledge. There are many directions one could go to study conceptions of knowledge and the picture here is, I suspect, more complex than questions about ability and intelligence.

We have begun with a distinction between types of knowledge that cuts across intellectual disciplines. This work is inspired by that of Nucci (1982), Smetana (1981), Turiel (1983), and others on moral and conventional domains of social cognition. In the intellectual-academic sphere, students (from Grade 1 and up) make analogous distinctions between intellectual conventions (such as what symbols stand for, how a word is spelled, how a letter is formed, or how a geometry theorem is presented) and matters of substance (such as the logic of a geometry theorem). Intellectual conventions are seen as alterable by social consensus whereas matters of substance are not. And, among matters of substance, students distinguish matters involving logic and laws of nature (e.g., stones drop when you let them go) from facts about the world that do not directly reflect laws of nature (e.g., bikes are normally smaller than cars). Such matters of empirical fact are seen as more likely than matters of logic or natural law to be changeable (Nicholls & Thorkildsen, 1988).

In school, much time is spent mastering these different types of knowledge. All have a legitimate and important place in the curriculum. Spelling, a category of convention, is often taught as a separate subject in the elementary school. It is also the basis of school, state, and national contests. Spelling is also learned and, to varying degrees, emphasized by teachers in the context of other subjects like history and science.

Spelling can be seen as a set of regulative conventions. The term regulative implies that these conventions help us get on with the substance of what we are trying to do. Thus, standard spelling facilitates communication whether it be about science or sport. It does not, however, change the nature of what we say about these matters. Sport involves somewhat parallel regulative conventions that serve to help people get on with the games or sports they have decided on. The nature and use of uniforms, for example, is specified in what can be termed the regulative rules or conventions of sport. One could play baseball with different uniforms without altering the essential nature or constitution of the game. Such conventions can be distinguished from constitutive rules or conventions that define the very nature of a game (Gruneau, 1983). If one changed the number of bases or the method of pitching, one could quickly reach the point where the game was not what we construe as baseball.

Literary forms like the novel and the sonnet are constitutive conventions. As Naipaul (1987) notes, forms such as the novel

> are constantly changing to match the new tone and mood of the culture . . . literary forms are necessary; experience has to be transmitted in some agreed or readily comprehensible way. But certain forms, like fashions in dress, can at times become extreme. And then these forms, far from crystallizing or sharpening experience, can falsify or be felt as a burden . . . it takes great care and tact . . . for the nature of the experience not to be lost, not to be diluted by the wrong forms. (p. 7)

In a similar way, the constitutive rules of sports change over time in quite a dramatic fashion (Dunning & Sheard, 1979; Gruneau, 1983). And, at any time, a given set of constitutive game conventions will favor some skills more than others and might or might not satisfy the needs of players, administrators, and spectators. When a game becomes unsatisfying, it either dies or evolves so as to become more meaningful. For example, changes in rules governing the three-point shot and the shot clock in college basketball change the meaning of the game in appreciable, if not dramatic, ways for participants and spectators.

Constitutive conventions can involve more than the formal rules of sports. Indeed the sport of mountaineering, though governed by well-established practices, is (or used to be) almost devoid of formally agreed upon rules. The amount of bodily contact allowed in basketball could go up without formal rule changes. The game might then lose some appeal to those who value quickness but not intimidation or aggressiveness. Consider the impact of Suzanne Lenglen on women's tennis:

> [She was the] first woman tennis player who wore short skirts (short then meant simply "not full-length") and hit like a man. She hit very hard and angled her shots: she was fit. The Ladies' Tennis Clubs naturally associated her force, her Frenchness, and her victories with all sorts of allegations about her life. Well, that was the price of victory in 1921. (Inglis, 1977, pp. 6-7)

She did more than violate a regulative convention about dress. That convention was so compatible with the reigning conception of the game and so incompatible with the more physical game that Lenglen promoted that it had substantive, constitutive significance. She helped make the game hospitable to different skills and purposes.

One cannot always make a categorical distinction between regulative and constitutive conventions. Given the confusion about the apparently fundamental distinction between the determinants of immediate performance and the determinants of intelligence, we might expect even more confusion on this topic. In writing this, for example, it became clear that, until now, we (Nicholls & Thorkildsen, 1989) have blurred the distinction made here between constitutive and regulative conventions. Yet it seems likely that even young children would see the essential difference in sport and in intellectual activities. Furthermore, it is likely that Turiel's (1983) evidence of developmental changes in conceptions of regulative social conventions would (though he does not distinguish regulative and constitutive conventions) be replicated for academic disciplines as well as sport and games. How understanding of constitutive conventions might change remains to be seen, but (as evidence reviewed in the next section indicates) different patterns will surely be found for different activities.

Understanding the constitutive conventions governing one's activities means understanding the essence of what one is about. Examination of conceptions of these conventions seems important for understanding socialization in education and in sport—important for understanding developmental changes in the ways people construe the essence of what they are doing. If writing novels is construed as different from doing geometry, and baseball is seen as different from mountaineering, much of these differences might be captured in people's conceptions of the nature and point of the different conventions whereby we constitute these different activities. There is scope for much interesting work on the development of understanding of constitutive and regulative conventions in sport and academe.

Fairness

There has been some attempt to apply perspectives on moral development such as that of Kohlberg to the study of sport and education. These attempts are analogous to attempts to apply general theories of motivation. The unique moral issues involved in sport are not easily addressed within these general frameworks. Furthermore, the established approaches to moral development focus on the morality of the conduct of individuals rather than on people's conceptions of the fairness of social practices or of the rules of games or institutions.

Socialization in sport must involve the development of understanding the fairness of game rules. The very nature of any game or sport activity is defined by its constitutive rules. That is, games or sporting activities exist by virtue of implicit or explicit social contracts. Perceptions of fairness of sporting practices should, then, be seen to vary with the way activities and game situations are defined.

These ideas about fairness have been elaborated and tested by Thorkildsen (1989b) in the areas of education and sport. She found that in academic and sporting activities where learning or task mastery was defined as the goal, competition (attempting to surpass others) was seen by elementary school students as unfair, likely to harm individuals, and unlikely to be an effective strategy for learning. Cooperation, on the other hand, was judged to be fair, likely to be effective, and unlikely to harm in learning or task mastery situations. Competition was, however, generally seen as fair in contests, whether sporting contests (a race) or academic contests (a spelling bee). Some harm was expected to occur as a result of competition—even though it was seen as fair in these contexts. Tests were seen as different again. Here competition was seen as unfair, but individual striving was seen as fair and effective.

Thorkildsen's results support the view that even early elementary school students see the fairness of practices as dependent on the implicit social contract or on the way the social situation is defined—that is to say, on the constitutive conventions of the situation. Competitive practices, for example, are judged fair only when the situation is defined as a contest. Children's recognition of the contractual (or at least consensual) basis of fairness was confirmed by their belief that practices like competing in school learning (which would normally be unfair) could become fair if people all agreed to change things. The finding that they thought competing in learning might be fair for people in some other countries also supports this thesis.

Thorkildsen's work points to limits on the value of global approaches to the study of the socialization of fairness in sport or education. Developmental changes in conceptions of fairness will vary depending on the nature (constitutive conventions) of the specific game, sport, or intellectual activity.

Consider, for example, cooperation in testing and academic learning situations. Cooperation in academic tests is seen as clearly unfair by third and fifth graders, but not by first graders. Similar results were obtained for tests of physical skills (Thorkildsen, 1989b). Conceptions of ability (but not intelligence) are important for interpreting test performance. It makes sense that about the time that children develop the normative conceptions of ability and difficulty (Nicholls, 1989), they see cooperation—which would tend to make everyone appear equally able—as unfair. Presumably this is because the normative conceptions involve a clearer recognition of the fact that everyone is not equally able—a recognition that would make practices that promoted the appearance of equal ability seem unfair for the more able.

The picture is quite different for fairness in school learning. When the situation is defined as concerned with learning, cooperation that increases equality of learning is seen as fair through the elementary school and most of the high school years (Thorkildsen, 1989a). (There are no comparable data for sport.) How could there be such different reactions to the idea of equal test and learning outcomes? This appears to reflect the different conceptions that are relevant to testing and learning. For testing, conceptions and ability are, as just suggested, relevant. These conceptions concern the limits on performance in the short term—as in tests. For learning, where the issue is who learns faster in the long term, conceptions of intelligence are relevant. Conceptions of intelligence (not conceptions of ability) concern the limits on the growth of one's competence. It is only at about the age when the conception of fluid intelligence or reasoning ability is developed (about 17 years) that students argue that cooperation is unfair if it tends to hold back the more able students. Fluid intelligence, which is seen as relatively hard to change, becomes a more limiting factor than is found in earlier conceptions of intelligence. This is probably part of the basis for the late adolescent view that having everyone learn the same amount is unfair.

School was clearly construed as a place for learning by the children Thorkildsen interviewed. But it is also a place where contests and tests occur. Sport also has a similar range of types of situation, with contests being more predominant in sport. Regardless of this, one could examine conceptions of fairness in school contests, tests, or sports where promotion of physical health, strength, and agility are aims.

If a variety of types of physical skill are distinguished by people, we should expect a corresponding variety of conceptions of fairness when development of different types of skill is involved. My hunch is that there will be differences for "simple" skills like sprinting, weight lifting, and skills that involve complex strategy, collaboration with others, and coordination of many simple or basic skills. Team games raise many unique issues of fairness, both within and between teams. Exploration of such matters is likely to produce a picture that is, in some respects at least, unique to sport.

Retrospect and Prospect

The preceding categorization of achievement-related concepts is surely not exhaustive, and there must be other ways of slicing the pie. Nevertheless, I hope to have shown that there is more in the pie than cognitions about how able we are. The newer question, how is ability construed, also turns out to raise more complexities than has often been realized, and there is much more to achievement-related cognition than conceptions of the nature of ability. For example, I have not even touched on conceptions of character and motivation. Presumably skydiving, novel writing, marathon running, and basketball favor different types of character or motivation. Conceptions of such motivation must undergo developmental changes that have yet to be plotted.

Because there are many questions that can be asked about sport and intellectual achievement, in this complex and messy world where people ask their own questions we find different people asking different questions. This means that, though they might have the same collection of concepts, they often use different parts of their collections. These differences are the topic of the second half of this chapter.

Lay Theories of Achievement[3]

Attribution theory represents the individual as a lay scientist and makes a dichotomy between attributions that are logical, scientific, or based on a "pure" desire for knowledge and those that are guided by personal, biased motives (Kelley, 1973; Weiner, 1979). In keeping with this view, many researchers (including, in a former life, myself) have attempted to distinguish logical from motivationally biased aspects of causal attributions.

In a Kuhnian post-modern world, this particular view of the lay person as a naive scientist is unsatisfactory. As William James (1907) and many since have argued (e.g., Barnes, 1977; Rorty, 1983; Toulmin, 1983), any scientific interpretation can be seen as useful for some human purposes and not useful for others. Rather than speaking of mere accuracy or logic as the mark of good theory or reasoning, we might speak of the usefulness of particular scientific interpretations for specific purposes.

I would note here that the terms useful and pragmatic have gained the implication of base, materialistic, "bottom line" value. When I write that a theory can be seen as useful for a particular purpose, this purpose could be that of making life more exciting, a moment more aesthetically pleasing, or the book one is reading more comprehensible. The proclivity for assuming that useful means useful-for-bringing-in-bread or useful-for-taking-out-garbage seems to reflect the materialism that is often alleged to pervade our society.

Adaptiveness or usefulness cannot be judged from any abstract or absolute position. Rather, what is valuable or adaptive depends upon one's purposes. Lay people, like scientists, always approach their work with certain purposes. The concepts they employ, the data they collect, and the ways they interpret it can be understood in terms of these purposes. That is to say, people's theories reflect their concerns (Dennett, 1978; McArthur & Baron, 1983; Nicholls, 1989). Different theories about schoolwork and sport and how to do well at these activities involve different concerns or purposes. Different concerns mean that different concepts will be *employed*, but not that people (of any given developmental level) will *have* different concepts. The implication is that people will differ in which of their concepts they use and in how they use them. This argument is similar to that of Cole and Scribner (1974), that cultural differences are more often manifest in the ways concepts or processes are employed rather than in those concepts or processes themselves.

None of this implies that any lay or scientific theory is as good as any other. What is "good" depends on what one is trying to do. And, when one has a specific purpose, one theory will work better than others, and that theory can always be improved to serve one's purpose more effectively. Weiner's (1979) attributional approach to academic motivation, for example, is useful for explaining how inequality of academic motivation can come about. It is, however, of less value for guiding efforts to increase equality of optimum motivation in school (Nicholls, 1989) and sport (Roberts, 1982, this volume). We can shape up a theory for any purpose. But we cannot anticipate all the different purposes that, now or in the future, people might have for a theory of motivation.

The contention that the usefulness of a culture or theory depends on one's context and one's concerns highlights the possibility that the search for the one best theory or culture is likely to turn into an attempt to enshrine one's own context and concerns as of universal validity. Alternatively, the search for the one best theory might occasion attempts to deny one's own impulses or feelings about what makes sense because these have no place in one's view of decontextualized, impersonal, absolute truth. Cultural imperialism is an example of the former, while the attempt to fit the human sciences to the Galilean thesis that everything in the book of nature is written in the language of mathematics is an example of the latter.

The notion that theories always reflect one rather than another collection of human concerns means that the psychological study of lay people's theories about how to succeed must proceed differently to the study of their achievement-related concepts. When studying achievement-related concepts, we must try to ensure that everyone answers the same question. It quickly becomes apparent when interviewing children (let alone talking to our friends) that what appear to be simple and unambiguous questions are often subject to diverse and unexpected interpretations. In effect, when you ask them one question, different people answer different questions.

Consider the interview on the conception of ability-as-current-capacity. When shown two students gaining the same score on a test during which only one works hard, one girl said that the hard worker is smarter "because it's dumb to goof off" but the other is smarter "because she knows more about the subject." Few children are this conscious of different possible interpretations of what "smart" might refer to. We cannot rely on them to make such distinctions for us. If we simply ask children which one is smarter, we will have no way of telling whether they differ in what they think we are asking about or in what they think about what we take to be our question. Interviews must be designed to clarify such ambiguities.

Another trap occurs because some children will suggest that the student who didn't work hard gained her score by copying the other's work. This is a plausible and potentially legitimate interpretation. But if the researcher's purpose is to see if children understand that more able people don't need to try as hard as others to perform as well as them, this interpretation is nothing but a nuisance because it implies that ability and effort weren't relevant. Accordingly, the researcher must explain to the child that although some children do cheat, this one didn't. This is something that some children simply assume to be the case. But because many do not, one must attempt to standardize not just interview stimuli, but children's interpretations of them (Nicholls, 1989; Turiel, 1983).

When studying concepts, one must attempt to ensure that everyone answers the same question and that each answers to the best of his or her ability. For this reason, we cannot effectively study children's concepts of intelligence or sport competence by simply asking (in the fashion of Dweck and Bempechat, 1983) whether such skills are changeable or not. Intelligence can have many referents. As Vernon (1969) has pointed out, it commonly refers to genetic potential, realized potential, and displayed competence. And, each of these can be thought of with respect to different types of intellectual skill. Change also can have several meanings when applied to human skills (Nicholls, 1990). When studying concepts of intelligence, we need to be able either to discern or to control the many possible senses of change and intelligence the child is employing. We also need to make sure they answer these questions to the best of their current abilities.

But the "real" worlds of sport and education do not constrain people so that they all address the same questions. Nor does this real world constrain us to reveal our fullest understandings. Most of the time, the world is like a poorly controlled, sloppy interview. Thus, in school and sport some people are prone to be preoccupied with questions about their ability whereas others address entirely different questions. It is important to know what people are preoccupied with as well as how they construe these things.

To assess habitual achievement preoccupations or orientations, we ask people what makes them feel successful in, for example, sport? We also pose questions about reality—what do people have to do to succeed in basketball or in mathematics? The first type of question concerns personal goals or motivational orientations—that is, personal criteria of success. The second concerns beliefs about the way the world is. The second, not the first, is like a common sense request for someone's theory about success or achievement. Yet, as post-modern conceptions of science would have it, people's beliefs about the way the world works might be bound up with their personal concerns about the world. Data reviewed in the next section confirm that we can speak of lay theories of achievement as involving both personal goals and beliefs about the world.

Some General Dimensions of Lay Achievement Theories

Despite dramatic developmental changes in concepts like ability, students from at least second grade up show considerable similarity in dimensions of theories about how to do well in school. Two independent dimensions of student goals and beliefs emerge in most of our studies—ego orientation and task orientation (Nicholls, 1989). None of our studies offer any support for the practice of speaking of or measuring a dichotomy or continuum of task versus ego orientation. Only with second graders have we found the two dimensions negatively related and this association was slight, with task and ego orientation forming clearly separate factors. On the few occasions when task and ego orientation are not close to orthogonal, they are positively—not negatively—associated. See also Spence and Helmreich (1983), and Maehr and Braskamp (1986). (This highlights but one of the differences between our formulation and that of Dweck and Leggett, 1988, who propose and measure learning versus performance goals as a dichotomy.) These dimensions are not a recent discovery. A thoughtful earlier discussion is given by Solomon Asch (1952).[4]

Scoring high on the first dimension, ego orientation, are students whose purpose in school is the egotistical one of establishing their superiority over others and who also tend to believe that, to do well in school, one must have more ability than others and attempt to beat them. Such students do not emphasize helping one another learn, nor do they emphasize the necessity of attempting to make sense of academic tasks if one is to succeed. The second main dimension, task orientation, involves the purposes of gaining skill or knowledge and performing one's best, and the beliefs that success in school depends on interest, on effort, on attempts to understand rather than merely memorize, and on collaborating with one another. Students high on this task-oriented dimension, but low in ego orientation, do not emphasize superior ability as necessary for academic success. They habitually assess their accomplishments in a fashion similar to that of young children for whom a sense of competence derives from performing at a personal peak or from gaining knowledge (Nicholls et al., 1989).

The same dimensions of goals and beliefs are evident in sport (Duda, this volume; Roberts, this volume). Furthermore, separate sport and academic dimensions are not found (Duda, this volume). That is, if a person is ego-oriented, this tends to apply for both sport and academic work. Here is a case where the parallels between the two domains are clear.

From Grade 2 and up, it is possible to identify ego-oriented students who, more than those low in ego orientation, see high ability (as they construe it) as necessary for academic success. What distinguishes ego-oriented students is their use of conceptions of ability, not the nature of their conceptions of ability. In this respect we differ from Dweck and Elliott (1983) who argue that different achievement goals are associated with different conceptions of the nature of intelligence.[5] Practically everyone at the 8th grade has a differentiated conception of ability as (current) capacity to accomplish a task (Nicholls, 1989). There is virtually no individual variation in this concept after about 14 years. Yet, variation to the extent in which individuals are preoccupied with their current ability and see superior ability as essential for success is, at this and other ages, considerable (Nicholls, 1989; Nicholls, Cobb, Wood, Yackel, & Patashnick, 1990).

Among second graders, valuing of collaboration was not associated with ego orientation nor was the belief that collaboration leads to success. Helping one another learn was, however, valued by task-oriented students. Indeed, the purpose of helping one another in schoolwork was not distinguishable (in factor analyses) from the purpose of gaining understanding (Nicholls, Cobb, Yackel, Wood, & Wheatley, in press). Therefore, it seems that, because helping is seen as the fairest method of learning (Thorkildsen, 1989b), the concept of fairness in dealing with individual differences in ability will be relevant to the theories of task-oriented students but not of ego-oriented students. We have not examined this question directly. However, Duda (this volume) has obtained data consistent with this hypothesis in sport.

We also find that academic motivational orientations and beliefs about the causes of success are correlated meaningfully with what might be called wider academic values—views about what the ultimate purposes of school should be (Nicholls, 1989; Nicholls, Patashnick, & Nolen, 1985; Thorkildsen, 1988). One's view of the place of school in the world has some connection to one's theory about how to do well in school and is related to one's personal criteria of success in school. For example, task but not ego orientation is moderately associated with the view that school should help prepare one for work that will contribute to the well-being of others. Ego but not task orientation is moderately associated with the view that school should help prepare one for positions with high incomes and superior social status. Duda (1989c) has obtained parallel results for views about the larger purposes of sport. One's theories about success are related to what might be called one's philosophy of the place of school and sport in life.

Most of what has been said above with respect to individual students' theories of success in school applies—with only slight modification—to whole class environments (Nicholls, 1989). That is to say, the dimensions of task and ego orientation can be used to describe the subjective environments or (average) theories of whole classrooms. Presumably the same can be said for sport teams—whole teams might be described in terms of these dimensions.

There is, however, one qualification to be made about group theories of success. This comes from two studies of second grade mathematics classrooms. In these we compared classes where collaborative problem solving predominated with more traditional, more individualistic classrooms (Nicholls et al., in press). The two types of classroom differed more clearly in beliefs about success than in goal orientations. The problem-centered classes more strongly believed that the way to succeed was to try to make sense and to collaborate with others to this end. Perhaps beliefs about how success occurs are more easily changed than are personal criteria (goals) of success. They are, after all, beliefs about social reality. So if that reality changes, a change in beliefs about the causes of success is not surprising. Personal goals might follow more slowly.

Our studies of academic motivation suggest that task-oriented sports teams might, more than others, value helping one another and believe that success follows from a team spirit. Such teams would presumably be more socially cohesive than more purely ego-oriented teams. They would also be expected to find playing more inherently satisfying and to play without the pressure of a contest or demands from a coach. If a coach increased the emphasis on rivalry within the team, such a team would presumably increasingly see superior ability (but not effort and collaboration) as necessary for success. These changed beliefs might be followed by an increase in ego orientation and a decline in intrinsic satisfaction. But some players are likely to find the new reality too inconsistent with their goals and, therefore, drop out. Dropping out might be more marked in those who see themselves as less competent than others. However, given the generally low associations between the motivational orientations and perceived ability (Nicholls, 1989), even those who rightly see themselves as very able might pack up and leave (Dunning & Sheard, 1979).

There might appear to be a parallel between ego orientation and a "professional" orientation to sport and between task orientation and a "play" orientation to sport. In Webb's (1969) analysis, a play orientation means an emphasis on having fun and playing fair. At the conceptual level, this parallels task orientation. The professional orientation, however, involves the goals of winning and playing well. As Coakley (1986) observes, a concern for winning is part of the constitutive definition of most formally organized sports. From the present perspective, to say that someone desires to win or compete is to be ambiguous. It might mean no more than that they want to play. People who abhor competition would presumably not join in most sports. Among those who do join, however, there are various motives. The question is, why do they want to compete or win? Many fine players are known for their absence of egotistic tendencies. Respect for them, if nothing else, requires that we not confuse a desire to compete with ego orientation.

A win as such is not informative about a player's competence. We need to know who the opponent was to know how competent the player is. Similarly, to say that there is a desire to win is not very informative about a player's motives. To the extent that they seek to win to maximize their superiority or dominance over others, players are ego involved. This goal might lead to a tendency to run up the score when winning. Alternatively, hot dogging when ahead might also serve to make one's superiority more obvious. For such players, winning is neither everything nor the only thing. Rather, it is not enough. Winning can be but part of the business of establishing one's dominance.

On the other hand, one might take winning (or even, depending on the score, losing to a clearly superior opponent) as an indication that one is gaining in skill or fitness (Spink & Roberts, 1980). To the extent that they do so, players would be task-involved. Things might be yet more complex because people can focus their attention on task performance and avoid worrying about how well others are doing with the belief that not thinking about one's standing is the best way to win. Though it might be difficult to detect, there is a difference between running one's own race mainly to do one's best and running one's own race to show one is the best.

The two leading characters in the film *Chariots of Fire* wanted to win. But they wanted this for different purposes, and these purposes were associated with different beliefs about the way to succeed, and different views about the place of sport in the wider scheme of things. They had different theories about running: One was a classic case of ego orientation; the other was more task-oriented.

Theories About Specific Activities

Whether we speak of individuals or classes, the picture given so far of the theory of success of task-oriented individuals remains vague. To say that such people see success as involving performing one's best, working at understanding, or performing as an end in itself is not as enlightening as it might be. This is because the concepts of intrinsic motivation, task involvement, or doing one's best remain generic. Consider a statement of intrinsic involvement from a former film actress, Lina Basquette, in her old age. "I never married anyone or had an affair for an ulterior motive. I never did it for money or career . . . I'm a reformed nymphomaniac" (Paris, 1989, p. 73). The intrinsic satisfactions Basquette refers to are presumably not those of most sports or the academic disciplines. And, the nature of intrinsic satisfaction must vary across sports and intellectual activities as well as within any activity. This means that if we are to describe adequately the theories of success of task-oriented individuals in sports and different academic subjects, we will have to go beyond abstract and general formulations about task involvement or intrinsic motivation. We will have to examine people's valuing of the various conventions that define their activities as well as their associated motivational orientations and beliefs about how these are best performed.

The purpose in this section is, then, to unpack the sources of feelings of success or accomplishment and associated beliefs about how one can develop or perform successfully that might fall within the rubric of task orientation or intrinsic motivation. The concern is no longer with aspects of ego orientation or other obviously extrinsic goals. The strategy adopted was to break down the different aspects of different types of task.

The broad distinction between matters of substance (including constitutive conventions) and regulative conventions provided one starting point. Students think they should learn standard positions on matters of logic, laws of nature, empirical fact, and convention (Nicholls & Thorkildsen, 1988). The weight students accord to regulative conventions relative to matters of substance when both are involved in an intellectual activity is, however, another question. Spelling and punctuation, for example, must be considered along with one's message when communicating in writing. The average tendency is to see conventions as less important than matters of substance (Nicholls & Thorkildsen, 1989). There also appear to be reliable individual differences in readiness to accept variation in intellectual conventions and in the importance attributed to them relative to matters of substance (Nicholls & Thorkildsen, 1988, 1989). Observation in classrooms reveals some young students who enjoy writing without regard to spelling and, in the same class, others who want to spell each word correctly before they proceed to the next one. In effect some of them define success in terms of mastery of regulative conventions. For others, regulative conventions are largely a nuisance.

Similar phenomena probably also occur in sport. In mountaineering, for example, I and my friends were occasionally frustrated by certain authorities and instructors who came close to turning the established conventions of safety in climbing into the very definition of mountaineering. They almost ignored what we viewed as the constitutive conventions of climbing. They overlooked the very features of the sport that made it worthwhile. For us, the point was to explore, to seek excitement, to scare ourselves, to have adventures, to make wondrous journeys, to climb new routes that were as challenging as we could manage, as dramatic and as beautiful as we could find. In this context, safety is critical because unsafe practices lead to death and an end to all climbing. As Geoffrey Winthrop-Young said, above all other sports, mountaineering must be taken seriously. But seriously need not mean solemnly. The safety conventions advocated by the experts we knew were only means to our ends, and in that sense of secondary importance. We studied safety procedures, but avoided mountain safety enthusiasts who made the safety conventions the very substance of climbing. If they had been in control of the sport, we might have been truants or troublemakers. As it was, they had little effect on our activities.

In sport, as in education, there are probably considerable differences among individuals in the emphasis they place on constitutive, relative to regulative, conventions. And, in this respect, teachers and coaches might be in tune or out of tune with the majority of their charges. Schoenfeld (1988), for example, describes geometry classes where students are frustrated by what they see as an unnecessary emphasis on reproduction of the conventions of presentation of proofs at the expense of the logic (constitutive conventions) of the proofs. Similar phenomena must occur in sport. A coach or a commissioner can alienate players by emphasizing matters such as the conventions of uniforms or the appropriateness of haircuts, headbands, and behavior on the bench more than players think they should.

But constitutive conventions themselves can, like regulative conventions, vary across time, place, and person. Such variations might also be seen as involving variation in goods or criteria of success and beliefs about how to succeed. To catch such subtleties, we need to take the specifics of different activities seriously. The work of Scanlan (this volume and Scanlan, Stein, & Ravizza, 1989), for example, on the sources of enjoyment of figure skaters gives a rich picture of the meaning of that sport for elite participants. As well as ego-oriented satisfactions, for example, are others that seem unlikely to be found in the intellectual field.

In a similar vein is our study of college students' personal goals in writing and beliefs about what leads to success in writing (Silva & Nicholls, 1990). As in previous studies, we found rational relations between personal goals and beliefs about the causes of success. For writing, we found three dimensions of goals and beliefs about how to succeed. The first represented writing as an expressive and aesthetic activity. Loading on this factor were the goals of achieving a poetic form of expression and clarifying and enhancing one's personal values or priorities in life. Associated beliefs were that to write well one must be sensitive to poetic considerations, honestly express personal feelings and values, and be imaginative. The second dimension involved the goals of improving one's logical reasoning ability and one's knowledge of subject matter, and the belief that success in writing depends on flexibility of strategies for writing or writing to learn. The third dimension involved the goal of being methodical and correct in surface-level conventions (e.g., grammar, punctuation, and spelling), and the belief that successful writing requires a focus on correctness of surface conventions.

None of these dimensions of achievement goals were as obviously exogenous as ego orientation. Yet they seemed likely to vary in the degree to which they would make the experience of writing inherently valuable. In attempting to predict which dimension would be most associated with commitment to writing as an end in itself, we found current perspectives on motivation of little value. We turned instead to Dewey's (1916/1966) notion that the more an activity contributes to the broadening or total development of students, the more whole-hearted their engagement. In this light, we expected that the expressionistic cluster of goals and beliefs about the causes of success in writing would be most strongly related to commitment to writing as an end in itself. This was because, in this instance more than the others, writing involves one's intelligence, emotion, and values.

As predicted, this cluster was most highly associated with commitment. The more purely intellectual cluster of goals and beliefs was less related to commitment. Still less related (and not significantly) to commitment were the goals and beliefs concerning the importance of surface conventions. In summary, the more narrowly focused were goals and beliefs—the less inclusive of larger personal concerns—the less they were associated with the experience of writing as inherently valuable and as something students would want to continue with when they leave college.

The writing goals and beliefs described are obviously somewhat specific to writing. Yet the logic of the hypotheses could be applied to different sports. Sports that engage the whole person—the values, the social, emotional, aesthetic and intellectual as well as physical aspects of life—should (other things being equal) be more inherently satisfying, and should occasion more lasting commitment. Similarly, players whose goals and beliefs are more inclusive should be more satisfied and committed to their sport. Changes over time or across teams or coaches might also be thought of in terms of changes in the breadth of the human goals they satisfy. Changes in patterns of participation and satisfaction might follow. However, one cannot make a literal translation to sport activities of our writing goals and beliefs measures to test such hypotheses. New measures that reflect the unique features of the sports of interest would have to be developed.

Concluding Example: The Changing Meaning of Sport

In the game of rugby football, as in other sports, there is evidence for a recent increase in emphasis on scientific play: a more single-minded preoccupation with doing everything possible to increase the chances of winning. In Britain, rugby remains an amateur sport in that players are not paid. Yet, for those at the top levels, the orientation to the game is wholly professional in that it consumes their time and thoughts more than any other aspect of their lives (Dunning & Sheard, 1979). This is a far cry from earlier times when the game was characterized by a more truly amateur ethos. It was played for fun or excitement, and gentlemanly notions of fair play predominated. The change to a single-minded focus on dominance and increasing one's skill relative to others is manifest in many ways. For example, the recent moves toward tournaments provide clearer information (than do older organizations) about the relative standings of teams. These moves have long been stoutly resisted by proponents of the older amateur ethos. But the trend seems inexorable.

A comparable battle is being waged in college football in the U.S.A. where, despite an omnipresent preoccupation with national ranking, there is still no formal system for letting teams rather than pundits settle the question of who is number one. The voices of those who think major sports should play a more minor role in college life are heard faintly in the background. The trend to systematic, face-to-face competition is even evident in rock climbing which, for most of its history, has never seen anything like a tournament. This recent development can be seen as but part of a longer term and complex pattern of changes in the way the point of climbing is understood and in the ways it is done (Inglis, 1977).

Changes such as those described by Dunning and Sheard can be seen as involving changes in the constitutive rules of the game. Rugby's formal, constitutive rules have steadily been altered to increase the game's appeal to spectators. These changes are increasingly approved of by modern players. They, it seems, want spectators more than did the gentlemen amateurs of earlier times who were satisfied with a comradely sharing of the game with one another. These changes in formal rules were paralleled by changes in less formal constitutive rules that also help give the game its identity—that frame the point of the game. These include the implicitly accepted rules that define a "real rugby man." Nowadays this is a very masculine and rugged individual who is more determined to bury the opposition than, as in earlier times, to have a gentlemanly good time with like-minded fellows.

These formal and informal constitutive rules can be conceptually distinguished from the personal goals of individuals. Yet it is likely that changes in constitutive rules are responsive to and contribute to changes in the goals and beliefs of the participants. The changes in British rugby described by Dunning and Sheard appear to involve a steady increase in ego orientation and (though this is less certain) an increase in a rather solemn form of task orientation on the part of players. Presumably beliefs about the causes of success underwent parallel changes. But as our study of theories of composition suggests, finer grained description and measurement of goals and beliefs about success in rugby would capture more of the special features of the goals and beliefs of players. Such measures might be used to study future changes in the meaning of the game, as well as individual and team differences. They might also be useful for studying differences in motivation of players of other more and less "manly" sports. These measures could also be used to test hypotheses about the relationship of different theories (of individuals, or teams, or even sports) with satisfaction and continuing participation.

It would be interesting to go beyond simple associations and examine the impact of relationships between individuals' goals and beliefs and the ethos of teams or games as a whole. As Dunning and Sheard illustrate, a number of outstanding international rugby players prematurely drop out saying that they had become public property, had little time for the satisfactions of family and personal life, and found the pressure for constant peak performance meant the game was no longer fun. Though other outstanding players do not quit, it does not follow that they are having fun or that the game is as inherently satisfying for them as it was for the gentlemen participants of earlier times, who spent so much less time playing and thinking about the game.

We cannot administer measures of the sort I have been suggesting to players of earlier times. But we could use such measures to ask comparable questions in today's world of sport. If we do this, we will be on the way to generating a psychology of motivation in sport that is, in some respects, unique to sport. We might thereby construct a psychology and motivation in sport that would contribute to, as well as profit from, the work of sociologists such as Gruneau and Dunning and Sheard. These writers discuss the meaning that sport has for participants (and spectators), and the relationships between these meanings and larger social and economic processes. The latter are not the domain of the psychologist, but the problem of assessing the meaning of sport—the problem of assessing players' theories about their games—is.

If our theories of motivation encompass only variables such as self-efficacy, perceived ability, and attributions for success and failure, our work will have little bearing on questions such as the changing meaning of sport. The point of sport is much debated by spectators and players. The debate about amateurism in British rugby, richly described by Dunning and Sheard, is a case in point. Most current theories of motivation have nothing to contribute to such debates. Psychologists cannot settle such debates. They can, however, gather data that adds light to the heat of these debates.

If we assume that a win is success and a loss is failure, and if our analyses (like those of self-efficacy and attribution theory) are based on this assumption, we accept that winning is everything. Our work will then fit squarely into a contemporary, professionalized view of sport in which everything hinges on the record of wins and losses and on rank in a hierarchy of competence. If psychologists are to reflect on, rather than merely to reflect, the dominant ethos of their times, they will need more multifaceted, more obviously postmodern and pluralistic approaches to their subject matter. The rules of this game are waiting for players to constitute them.

Notes

[1]Some argue that motivation is important only to the extent that it influences action and accomplishment. A clear analysis of the nature of achievement concepts, theories, and goals is necessary before one can effectively examine the relations between these variables and behavior. In this chapter, I do not emphasize such "connections." This is partly because that has to be a second step. Even if this were not so, it would make little sense to study academic and sporting activities while ignoring the meaning of those activities for the participants.

Accomplishments themselves, whether they be Olympic records or new novels, are not important in any absolute sense. Such accomplishments only exist and have value to the extent that people construe them as accomplishments. It took recent European cultures, for example, to define climbing mountains as a meaningful sporting activity—which suggests that almost anything might become a meaningful accomplishment. The assertion that performance or accomplishment is important, and that meaning is not, is simply an assertion that one's own values are important. The meaning of achievement activities is no trivial matter here.

[2]It is common to find these and other matters conflated. Consider this assertion of Stipek and MacIver (1989):

According to the differentiated concept of ability, which Dweck refers to as an "entity" concept, ability is a stable *trait*, unaffected by effort. The more ability an individual has, the more *performance* is facilitated by effort. If two people exert the same amount of effort, the person with most ability will *perform* the best. (p. 523, italics added)

This passage starts out referring to the unchangeability of a trait and switches to unchangeability of performance. It explicates Dweck's concept of an "entity theory" with an inappropriate reference (in the second two sentences) to the conception of ability-as-current-capacity. Stipek and MacIver also assert that Miller's and my evidence on the development of this conception is evidence on the development of the entity theory. In our interview on the conception of ability-as-current-capacity, questions about whether ability can be changed are not asked, nor are subjects asked about the dimensionality of intelligence. But the entity theory implies that there is one dimension of intelligence and that it is unchangeable. Although they argue that children develop an "entity concept," Stipek and MacIver offer no evidence that bears on their claim. The same applies to Dweck and Elliott (1983) who introduced the notion of the entity concept. In support of their claim, they cite a review by Heckhausen (1982) who twice asserted that, at the time of his review, there appeared to be no evidence on the development of conceptions of the changeability of intelligence. At the time, Heckhausen was right. None of the evidence cited by Dweck and Elliott is about the changeability of intelligence. Despite the many declarations that the entity and incremental theories exist, there is still no evidence that they do—and some evidence to the contrary.

[3]In this second section, the focus is on individual and, later, historical variation in motivational orientations. As has often been noted, situations also vary in the tendency to promote task and ego involvement. There is, however, too much in this chapter already and it has been discussed elsewhere. (See Ames and Ames, 1984a; see also Ames, this volume; Duda, this volume; and Roberts, this volume.)

[4]The term *ego orientation* (and involvement) has, like most terms, been used in diverse senses. In the Freudian sense, the ego operates on the reality principle. In this Freudian sense, ego involvement means no more than involvement with reality. It implies no more than involvement in doing things. The term ego is redundant in this usage. This usage is also at variance with common usage as in egomania or egotist. *Performance goal* has been used in two ways: to imply ego orientation (Dweck & Elliott, 1983) and something closer to task orientation (Vealey, 1986). My reading of dictionaries suggests the latter is more consistent with established usage. The implication (of the former usage) that those in the performing arts are ego-oriented artists and, therefore, should perhaps not have performance as a goal also seems problematic. The task-oriented actor or player surely wants to perform; they could not be actors or players if they did not perform. Use of the term performance to describe an achievement goal creates confusion because, in the psychological literature, performance has long referred to how well individuals execute tasks. Any performance (in the sense of task execution) can reflect egotistic or task-intrinsic goals. As noted, competition is a defining feature of many sports. I'm for reducing egotism, but I'm not yet quite ready to advocate stopping competitive sports. Thus speaking of *competitive goals* as similar to egotism is problematic. For these and other reasons I have maintained the terminological and conceptual tradition of Asch, Ausubel, Crutchfield, and others (Nicholls, 1989).

[5]Despite this difference, many writers seem to find the present position nearly equivalent to that of Dweck and her associates. Though there are obvious similarities, there are also many empirically testable differences between these positions. (See Footnote 2 and the text discussion of lay achievement theories for but two other examples.) Dweck's predictions about performance and task choice are, as others in this volume note, similar to mine (which I have not discussed here). It is, however, misleading to label both social cognitive theories as if they are basically similar. This label could include Weiner's attribution theory. Theories are more than collections of predictions (Dennett, 1978). I derived my predictions of performance from the intentional stance (which is simultaneously cognitive and affective in basis) and evidence on the conception of ability-as-current-capacity (Nicholls, 1978, 1989). This means others can check, revise, or extend the logic on which predictions are based. If done well, systematic and explicit derivation of predictions makes for internal consistency—a property that distinguishes theories from collections of predictions. I am also puzzled that conceptions of the long-term changeability of intelligence should, in Dweck's position, be seen as influencing immediate performance. Conceptions of current capacity seem more relevant to immediate performance, which is why they play a crucial role in my theory of performance.

Motivation in Sport Settings: A Goal Perspective Approach

Joan L. Duda

Recent motivation research stemming from a social cognitive perspective has focused on a goal perspective analysis of motivational processes and behavioral patterns. The majority of this work has been directed toward the understanding of academic achievement and has been primarily based on the theoretical contributions of Nicholls (1984a, 1984b, 1989, this volume), Dweck (1986; Dweck & Elliott, 1983; Dweck & Leggett, 1988; Elliott & Dweck, 1988), Maehr (1984; Maehr & Braskamp, 1986), and Ames (1984a, 1984b, this volume; Ames & Archer, 1988). Although each might have his or her preferred nomenclature, issues of emphasis, and conceptual nuances, commonality exists among their theoretical frameworks with respect to the conception and role of goals in human motivation (see also Roberts, this volume).

In general, these theorists (Ames, 1984b; Dweck, 1986; Maehr, 1984; Nicholls, 1989) argue that a major focus in achievement settings is to demonstrate competence. Moreover, the psychological prominence of perceived ability is held to be the distinguishing feature of achievement motivation. When concerned with the study of motivation in nonachievement domains, perceptions of other personal attributes besides intellectual or physical skill and talent (e.g., honesty, kindness) are presumed to take on greater importance.

Contemporary social cognitive approaches to achievement motivation also assume that there are two major goal perspectives operating in achievement contexts. Nicholls (1984a, 1989, this volume), in particular, proposes that these goal perspectives are orthogonal and relate to how an individual construes his or her level of competence in a particular situation. In the first of these goal perspectives, perceptions of demonstrated competence are self-referenced, and the subjective experience of improving one's performance or mastering the demands of a task are the criteria underlying subjective success. According to Elliott and Dweck (1988, p. 5), the major question for someone who is focused on such a goal is "How can I best acquire this skill or master this task?"

With respect to the second goal perspective, improvement and/or personal mastery is not enough to occasion feelings of high ability. Perceptions of demonstrated competence are normative or other-referenced in this case, and subjective success is dependent on a favorable comparison of one's own ability with that of others. The question of whether an individual's ability is adequate is salient when he or she adopts this second goal perspective (Elliott & Dweck, 1988).

The terms *task involvement* and *ego involvement*, respectively, have been used by Nicholls (1984a, 1984b) to describe these two goal perspectives. These concepts have been introduced in earlier writings on motivation (e.g., Asch, 1952; Ausubel, Novak, & Hanesian, 1978; Crutchfield, 1962). Nicholls (1984a, 1984b) specifically argues that the two major goal perspectives relate to different ways of construing one's level of competence. Drawing from his developmental-based work (Nicholls & Miller, 1984), he suggests that ego and task involvement are based on a more or less differentiated conception of ability.

Other theorists (Ames & Archer, 1988; Elliott & Dweck, 1988) have developed different labels and slightly different conceptualizations of the two types of achievement goals. Dweck (1986; Dweck & Elliott, 1983; Dweck & Leggett, 1988), for example, refers to two classes of achievement goals. The first, learning goals, operate when individuals try to increase their competence and/or understand or master something new. The second type, performance goals, is focused toward gaining positive judgments of one's ability or avoiding negative perceptions of personal competence. Contrary to Nicholls (see Nicholls, this volume), Dweck assumes that these two classes of achievement goals are bipolar rather than independent dimensions.

Ames has adopted the concepts of mastery goals and ability goals in her work (1984b; Ames & Archer, 1988, p. 260). Respectively, the first type of goal perspective entails a "concern with being judged able, and one shows evidence of ability by being successful, by outperforming others, or by achieving success with little effort." The second major goal perspective places an emphasis on "developing new skills. The process of learning itself is valued, and the attainment of mastery is seen as dependent on effort." For the most part, Ames's research tends to focus on the antecedents and consequences of mastery versus ability goal-evoking environments (see Ames, this volume). For the purposes of conceptual clarity and consistency, the terms task and ego involvement will be utilized throughout the present text to represent the two distinct achievement goals.

A third point of convergence in the predominant goal-related theories of achievement motivation is that a person's goal perspective (or state of task or ego involvement) in a particular setting is held to be a function of situational factors and "individual differences in proneness to the different types of involvement . . ." (Nicholls, 1989, p. 95). According to Dweck and Leggett (1988, p. 269), dispositional differences in goal perspective "determine the a priori probability of adopting a particular goal and displaying a particular behavior pattern, and situational factors are seen as potentially altering these probabilities." In situations characterized by interpersonal competition, public evaluation, normative feedback and/or the testing of valued skills, a state of ego involvement is more likely to emerge. On the other hand, environments which place an emphasis on the learning process, participation, individualized skill mastery, and/or problem solving tend to evoke task involvement (Ames & Archer, 1988; Nicholls, 1989). Thus, situations may be considered more or less *task-* or *ego-involving* depending on the demands of the social environment.

In terms of individual differences in goal perspective, people are assumed to vary in task orientation and ego orientation (Maehr & Braskamp, 1986; Nicholls, 1989). It has been suggested that these dispositional goal orientations are independent and are a result of childhood socialization experiences (Nicholls, 1989; Nicholls, Patashnick, and Nolen, 1985).

A final point of agreement in the thinking of Nicholls (1989), Dweck (1986), Ames (1984b), and Maehr (1984) concerns the proposed interrelationships between goal perspectives, motivational processes, and behavior. An important tenet in recent theorizing on achievement motivation is that goals influence how we interpret and respond to achievement events. Specifically, it is suggested that an individual's goal perspective will affect self-evaluations of demonstrated ability, expended effort, and attributions for success and failure. In turn, these cognitions are assumed to impact achievement-related affect, strategies, and subsequent behaviors such as performance, task choice, and persistence (see also Roberts, this volume; Ames, this volume).

Dependent on whether one is task- or ego-involved, different achievement-related patterns are predicted. Task involvement, regardless of the level of perceived competence, is assumed to relate to the choosing of moderately challenging tasks, the exerting of effort, intrinsic interest in the activity, sustained or improved performance, and persistence (particularly following failure). Further, this goal state entails an attributional focus on effort.

In general, the desirable behaviors described are also predicted for ego-involved people—as long as they have high confidence in their level of ability. Perceptions of competence, however, are believed to be particularly fragile in ego involvement (Dweck, 1986). When ego involvement prevails and doubts about one's competence exist, a maladaptive pattern is expected. Such a behavioral pattern is labeled ''maladaptive'' because it is not conducive to long-term achievement and/or investment in achievement-related environments, however adaptive and rational the behaviors described are when considered in relation to the goal perspective being emphasized. It is assumed that ego involvement coupled with perceptions of low ability will result in the choosing of tasks that are too hard or too easy, in the rescinding of effort or devaluing of the task when success seems improbable, and in performance impairment and a lack of persistence (especially following failure). These predictions are predicated on the assumption that one is concerned with the adequacy of his or her competence when in a state of ego involvement. The attributional focus, in this case, is on ability.

An impressive body of research in the context of academic achievement has provided support for these assumptions (see Ames, this volume; Nicholls, this volume). This literature includes both classroom-based field studies as well as laboratory experiments involving cognitive tasks.

The purpose of this chapter is to review recent work which has adopted a goal-focused approach to the study of motivation in sport. First, research is described which has been directed toward the development of a sport-specific measure of task and ego orientation. Second, sport investigations are presented which have begun to test the assumptions embedded in social cognitive theories of achievement motivation. The studies highlighted in this chapter focus on three major issues, namely the relationship between goal perspectives and cognitive mediators of motivation such as perceived competence, causal attributions, and intrinsic interest; the potential impact of goal perspectives on behavior in sport settings; and the correspondence between goal perspectives and the broader concept of values in the sport domain. Third, similarities and distinctions between recent sport-specific studies and exercise motivation research based on a goal perspective approach are also briefly reviewed. Finally, the chapter concludes with suggestions for future work on the topic of goals and motivation in sport.

Measurement of Individual Differences in Goal Perspective

Past research in the sport domain has indicated that perceptions of demonstrated competence underlie perceptions of goal accomplishment or subjective success and failure (Kimiecik, Allison, & Duda, 1986; Roberts & Duda, 1984). Previous studies, employing both quantitative and qualitative techniques, have also suggested that sport participants do base their goals on personal improvement and task mastery as well as the demonstration of superior ability (Duda, 1985, 1986a, 1986b, 1988; Ewing, 1981). In general, the literature provides us with evidence for the existence and salience of task and ego involvement goal states in the specific achievement context of sport.

During the past decade, there has been considerable interest in determining individual differences in orientations to sport achievement (e.g., Gill & Deeter, 1988; Vealey, 1986). In particular, efforts have been directed toward developing measures of the tendency to be task- and ego-involved in the context of competitive sport. For example, based on Maehr and Nicholls's (1980) conceptualization of achievement goals, Ewing (1981; Pemberton, Petlichkoff, & Ewing, 1986) designed her Achievement Orientation Inventory to assess a sport-specific ability orientation and task orientation (as well as a social approval orientation). Balague and Roberts (1989) have recently worked on establishing the validity and reliability of an instrument which measures the emphasis placed on mastery and competitive achievement goals in sport.

Drawing from the scales designed to assess task and ego orientation in the classroom (Nicholls, 1989; Nicholls et al., 1985), John Nicholls and I recently developed the Task and Ego Orientation in Sport Questionnaire, or TEOSQ. When completing the TEOSQ, subjects are requested to think of when they felt most successful in a particular sport and then indicate their agreement with items reflecting task- and ego-oriented criteria. Version 1 of the TEOSQ contained 15 items and was initially administered to 286 male and female high school sport participants (see Duda, 1989c). Exploratory factor analysis (principal components analysis with both oblique and orthogonal rotations) revealed a two-factor solution with seven items loading on the Task Orientation factor and six items loading on the Ego Orientation factors. (It is interesting to note that the item "I feel most successful when I win," which was contained in Version 1 of the TEOSQ, tended to load on both the Task and Ego Orientation factors.) The two-dimensional factor structure was found to be stable across two subsamples in this initial study and in subsequent research involving samples of youth sport, and high school and college-age sport participants and nonparticipants (Boyd, 1990; Duda & Nicholls, 1989b). Consistent with what has been observed in the assessment of task and ego orientation in the classroom (Nicholls, 1989), the two scales are orthogonal.

In further studies of 10- through 12-year-old children, of adolescents, and of adults (Duda & Nicholls, 1989a; Duda, Olson, & Templin, 1991; White, Duda, & Sullivan, 1991), The Sport Task Orientation and Sport Ego Orientation scales have been found to be internally consistent (alpha = .81 − .86 and .79 − .90, respectively). Neither of the scales significantly correlate with social desirability, and both have acceptable test-retest reliability following a three-week period (r = .68 and .75, respectively). A listing of the items contained in the Sport Task and Ego Orientation scales (Version 2) can be found in Table 1.

Table 1   Items Contained in the Task and Ego Orientation in Sport Subscales

I feel most successful in sport when . . .

Task orientation	Ego orientation
I learn a new skill and it makes me want to practice more.	I'm the only one who can do the play or skill.
I learn something that is fun to do.	I can do better than my friends.
I learn a new skill by trying hard.	The others can't do as well as me.
I work really hard.	Others mess up and I don't.
Something I learn makes me want to go and practice more.	I score the most points/goals, etc.
A skill I learn really feels right.	I'm the best.
I do my very best.	

To address issues related to concurrent validity, the TEOSQ and Nicholls's (1989) classroom-specific Motivation Orientation Scales were administered to 205 high school students (Duda & Nicholls, 1989b). The presentation of the two instruments was counter-balanced. Significantly high positive correlations emerged between the Sport Task and Ego Orientation scale scores and their counterpart measures in the classroom ($r = .67$ and $.62$, respectively).

In a second validity study, we (Duda & Nicholls, 1989a) administered the TEOSQ, the Sport Orientation Questionnaire (SOQ; Gill & Deeter, 1988), and the Competitive Orientation Inventory (COI; Vealey, 1986) to a sample of undergraduate students. A further purpose of this investigation was to attempt to conceptually distinguish the concepts of task and ego orientation from seemingly similar constructs in the sport achievement goal literature.

The SOQ was developed as a "multidimensional, sport-specific measure of individual differences in sport achievement orientation" (Gill & Deeter, 1988, p. 191). The instrument is comprised of three separate but related factors which have been labeled Competitiveness, Win Orientation, and Goal Orientation. According to Gill and Deeter (1988):

> [The competitive factor assesses] the desire to enter and strive for success in sport achievement situations . . . The items . . . reflect a desire to enter sport achievement situations, to strive for success, to work hard, to master skills, and an eagerness to meet competitive challenges . . . The other two factors seem to reflect an orientation to the two major types of outcomes in sport achievement situations, specifically the desire to win in interpersonal competition in sport, and the desire to reach personal goals in sport. (p. 195)

As can be seen in Table 2, a much stronger positive correlation emerged between the competitiveness and win subscales scores and Sport Ego Orientation than what was observed between these two SOQ subscales and Sport Task Orientation. This result makes conceptual sense since a person high in ego orientation (particularly if she or he has high perceived competence) would be more likely to seek out competitive activities. The process of interpersonal competition is most conducive to judging the adequacy of one's ability relative to others. Further, it is also logical that an ego-oriented individual would tend to focus on competitive outcomes. Winning in interpersonal competition is an overt means to demonstrating superior ability.

An individual high in task orientation, on the other hand, seeks out and values competition only to the extent that this social process allows him or her to try one's best and improve skills. It is "how you play the game" rather than "whether you win or lose" which is most salient to a task-oriented person. In other words, task involvement means that one is primarily focused on the process of task mastery rather than on successful task outcomes. Although a task-oriented person may also be to some degree competitive, the very nature and meaning of the competitive challenge would contrast to what is assumed by an ego-oriented person. Thus, the concept of "competitiveness" seems obscure when analyzed from a goal perspective analysis.

Additionally, due to the ambiguity implicit in the concept of goal orientation, it was also not surprising that both the Sport Task and Ego Orientation scales would significantly and positively correlate with this particular SOQ subscale (see Table 2). In the case of both of these goal perspectives, it is likely that individuals will be concerned with setting goals, with working toward reaching those goals, and with performing to the best of their abilities. However, the critical conceptual distinction between task and ego orientation is

Table 2   Correlates of the Task and Ego Orientation in Sport Subscales

	Sport task orientation	Sport ego orientation
Sport Orientation Questionnaire (Gill & Deeter, 1988)	.25*	.53***
Competitiveness	.56***	.37***
Goal orientation	.14	.61***
Win orientation		
Competitive Orientation Inventory (Vealey, 1986)		
Performance orientation	.04	−.18
Outcome orientation	−.04	.21*

Note. Adapted from Duda and Nicholls (1989b).

*p < .05. ***p < .001.

how such people tend to construe their ability and judge subjective success (or goal accomplishment) in particular situations. That is, the very nature of the *goal* is different when one is in a state of task or ego involvement, and whether a person is in one of these states or the other is dependent on individual differences in task and ego orientation.

The Competitive Orientation Inventory or COI (Vealey, 1986) was developed to measure individual differences in the tendency to "strive toward achieving a certain type of goal in sport" (p. 222). In Vealey's view, the two goals upon which competitive orientations are based are playing well (performance orientation) and winning (outcome orientation). The format of the COI requires that the respondent weigh the importance of each goal simultaneously. Specifically, the respondent is requested to indicate his or her degree of satisfaction with 16 possible combinations of different game outcomes (i.e., easy win, close win, close loss, big loss) and levels of performance (i.e., very good, above average, below average, very poor).

The correlations between the sport-specific measures of task and ego orientations and Vealey's performance and outcome orientation scores are shown in Table 2. As predicted (Duda & Nicholls, 1989b), a significant and positive relationship emerged between outcome orientation and ego orientation. Once again, we would expect the outcome of a contest to be more salient to ego-oriented individuals as winning in sport typifies superior ability. Task orientation was not expected to correlate with outcome orientation, and this prediction was substantiated. It was also predicted that neither task orientation nor ego orientation would significantly relate to the emphasis placed on playing well or performance orientation. As I've pointed out previously (Duda, 1989a), the concept of "playing well" as measured by the COI is conceptually ambiguous. The meaning of playing well and the basis of such a judgment would vary dependent on whether task or ego involvement is prevailing. Moreover, as argued by Nicholls (this volume), both task- and ego-involved individuals would be concerned with "performance" or the execution of the task at hand.

In general, our initial research on the TEOSQ has indicated that established measures of competitiveness, of orientations to winning, and of the desire to reach personal goals in sport are not psychologically equivalent to task and ego orientation. Further, this research suggests that the determination of the importance placed on playing well in contrast to objective outcome in sport is not synonymous to a person's proneness for task or ego involvement in that context.

Previous classroom-based research has indicated that the assessment of individual differences in task and ego orientation provides us with considerable insight into how students interpret and respond to the academic environment (Nicholls, 1989). A valid and reliable measure of task and ego orientation specific to the sport domain would be invaluable to future studies examining the correlates of goal perspectives in sport. The preliminary psychometric work on the TEOSQ looks promising in this regard.

Goal Perspectives and
Motivational Processes in Sport

Research based on a social cognitive perspective of motivation in educational environments has indicated that students' goal perspectives relate to how they cognitively and affectively respond to classroom activities (Ames & Ames, 1981; Ames & Archer, 1988; Dweck & Leggett, 1988). In particular, studies have demonstrated that task and ego involvement impact causal attributions for performance, perceptions of competence, and subsequent intrinsic interest in the academic domain.

The generalizability of this literature to the sport setting has only recently begun to be examined. In ascertaining the potential impact of goal perspectives on motivational processes in sport, two research strategies have been adopted. One approach has been to determine the degree and direction of the relationships between task orientation, ego orientation, and the cognitions or related affects in question. A second strategy has been to manipulate the experimental situation so that it is more or less task- or ego-involving and then study the effect on subjects' subsequent cognitive and affective responses.

Attributions

Previous investigations in the academic context have revealed conceptually consistent relationships between goal perspectives and attributional focus (Ames, this volume; Ames & Ames, 1981; Nicholls, 1989). In general, this work indicates that ego involvement is linked to an emphasis on ability attributions (and/or downplaying the role of effort in performance), while task involvement corresponds to the employment of effort attributions.

Past sport research examining the attributions underlying goal orientations (e.g., Ewing, 1981; Whitehead, 1986) has supported the educational literature. This is exemplified by one of our recent studies which replicated classroom-based research by Nicholls and his colleagues (Nicholls et al., 1985; Nicholls, Cheung, Lauer, & Patashnick, 1989; Nicholls, Cobb, Wood, Yackel, & Patashnick, 1990). In the latter studies, the correspondence between task and ego orientation and students' beliefs about the causes of success in school was examined. Results indicated that students with a strong task orientation were more likely to believe that success in school stems from working hard, cooperating, being interested in one's work, and trying to understand rather than memorize. Ego orientation, on the other hand, was linked to the belief that success in school comes from being smart, trying to outperform other students, and knowing how to impress the teacher.

In our study (Duda and Nicholls, 1989a) in the sport domain, high school students were requested to complete the TEOSQ and then indicate their agreement with a series of reasons for success in sport. Factor analysis revealed four major beliefs, namely Motivation/Effort (e.g., players succeed if they work hard, try their best, and help each other), Ability (e.g., players succeed if they try to beat others, have the talent, and are naturally competent), Deception (e.g., players succeed if they cheat, know how to impress the coach, and know how to make themselves look better than they are), and External Factors (e.g., players succeed if they are lucky or have the right clothes and equipment). Consistent with what has been found in the classroom setting (Nicholls et al., 1985, 1989, 1990), task orientation was positively correlated with the belief that sport success is a function of motivational factors and hard work. Task orientation negatively related to the view that the ability to cheat and deceive the coach leads to sport success. Ego orientation, in contrast, was positively linked to the belief that being a more talented and skilled player results in sport success. These results can be seen in Table 3.

Our findings suggest that, in the achievement domain of sport, a person's dispositional goal perspective is logically consistent with his or her beliefs about how success is typically caused in the sport context. As proposed by Nicholls (1989, this volume), the observed patterns of relationships between goals and beliefs constitute individuals' personal theories of sport achievement.

Early work on sport attributions has indicated that causal attributional patterns vary depending on whether individuals are interpreting objectively (i.e., win/loss) or subjectively defined outcomes (McAuley, 1985b; Spink & Roberts, 1980). Further, this research reinforces the point that objective and subjective outcomes are not necessarily synonymous for all sport participants; in short, not everyone holds an ego-involved conception of success and failure in the sport setting. Researchers have only begun to specifically determine the effect of variations in conceptions of success and failure or, in other words, *differences in goal perspective* on performance-related attributions. Two such experimental studies will be described here.

Table 3   Correlations Between Task and Ego Orientation and Beliefs About the Causes of Success in Sport

	Task orientation	Ego orientation
Beliefs about sport success		
Motivation/effort	.50**	−.03
Ability	−.03	−.44***
Deception	−.33***	.16*
External factors	−.14*	.15*

Note. From Duda, Chi, and Nicholls (1989a).
*p < .05. **p < .01. ***p < .001.

Hall (1990) recently determined the effect of a task- versus ego-involving goal structure and perceived competence on ability and effort attributions among adult men performing a stabilometer task. Low-perceived-ability subjects performing under an ego-involving goal structure reported that they did not try as hard during the early trials as low-perceived-ability subjects in the task-involving situation or high-perceived-ability subjects in either condition. In the ego-involving condition, males with low perceived competence felt that their performance was *less* influenced by demonstrated ability than high-perceived-competence subjects or low-perceived-competence subjects in the task-involving condition. The implication of Hall's (1990) results on subsequent motivation are intriguing. In explicating these findings, it would appear that people who doubt their physical skill and are placed in an ego-involving situation may be more likely to diminish the role of effort and to sever the link between their competence and task performance. The latter might be a precursor to a learned helpless attributional pattern (Dweck & Leggett, 1988). The former, namely downplaying how hard one tried, surely would not lead to long-term achievement. When task-involved, on the other hand, people may be more likely to believe in the potential impact of effortful investment and demonstrated physical skill on performance, regardless of their level of perceived competence. Such an outlook should be conducive to positive achievement strivings over time.

In a field experiment, Duda and Chi (1989) examined the effect of a task- versus ego-involving game condition and objective outcome on performance attributions in basketball among college-age males. Seventy-nine students, who were enrolled in a physical education skill class, were assigned to play a one-on-one basketball game against an opponent of equal skill. In the ego-involving condition, the subjects played a competitive 12-point game. The first player to reach 12 points was declared the winner, and the outcome of the game was reported to the class instructor. To enhance the perceived importance and evaluative nature of the ego-involving condition, a referee was present to "call the game."

In the task-involving game, the subjects were asked to play one-on-one basketball for 10 minutes. They were told that there would be no winner or loser, to try their best, and to work on a specific offensive and defensive skill weakness which was identified by the class instructor. Unknown to the subjects in this condition, the score after 10 minutes of play (i.e., objective outcome) was recorded by an observer.

Immediately following the game, the subjects rated the degree to which they perceived their performance to be a function of how hard they tried, their basketball skill, the opponent's basketball skill, and lucky breaks. The results indicated that more winners than losers believed that their skill level had a greater effect on their performance. More losers than winners felt that their opponent's skill had a greater influence on their performance. The situational manipulation of goal perspective, however, had an impact on effort attributions among objective winners and losers. Specifically, consistent with the results of Hall (1990), losers in the ego-involving game were less likely to attribute their performance to the amount of effort exerted when compared to losers in the task-involving condition or to winners (see Figure 1). That is, ego involvement was linked to the tendency to downplay the role or impact of effort when faced with failure (or the possibility of demonstrating inferior ability).

Other results of this study indicated that in the task-involving situation, attributional patterns were best predicted by subjective outcome. Objective outcome (win/loss) was only pertinent to attribution ratings in the ego-involving condition.

In sum, initial sport research suggests that goal perspectives correspond to performance attributions and wider beliefs about the causes of success in a predicted manner. Based on this preliminary work, it appears that an awareness of the goals adopted by sport participants can provide us with an understanding of how they explain and interpret their sport experiences. Certainly much more systematic research on goals and attributions in sport is needed—research which examines short- and long-term variations in attributional patterns as a function of goal perspective, perceived ability, objective and sub-

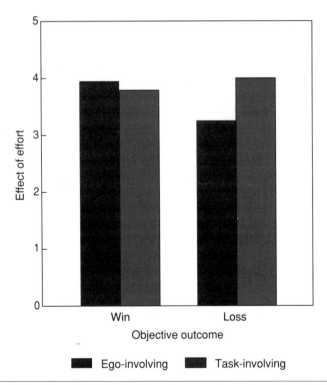

Figure 1.   Interaction effect of objective outcome and experimental condition on effort attributions.

jective sport outcomes, as well as the subject's history of success and failure in the activity.

Perceived Competence

Although sometimes known as perceived ability, self-efficacy, or confidence in various theoretical circles, the construct of perceived competence has played a central role in previous sport motivation research (Roberts, 1984). The predominant focus in this literature has been to ascertain the psychological and behavioral antecedents and consequences of varying levels of perceived competence in the sport domain (e.g., Feltz, this volume; Harter, 1978; Roberts, Kleiber, & Duda, 1981). Adopting a goal perspective approach to the study of perceptions of ability, however, underscores the relevance of how one's perceived competence is construed and the effects of such on subsequent feelings of competence.

Because the emphasis is on mastering the task, and perceptions of demonstrated competence are self-referenced, it is assumed that task involvement will foster the development of perceived ability. As pointed out by Elliott and Dweck (1988), the "focus of individuals who pursue learning goals or are *task involved* (whether they believe their ability to be high or low) is on improving ability over time, not on proving current ability" (p. 6). Ego involvement, on the other hand, entails a concern with the adequacy of one's ability level. When ego-involved, perceptions of demonstrated competence mean that one has outperformed others (or performed similarly with less effort). Consequently, it is proposed that ego involvement increases the probability of feeling incompetent (especially in the case of those who already doubt their ability).

Preliminary field studies in sport-related contexts support these predictions. Burton (1989b) determined the effect of a 5-month goal-setting program on self-confidence and post-meet ratings of perceived ability and subjective success among male and female intercollegiate swimmers. The goal-setting training was designed to encourage participants to base their competence on performance rather than outcome goals. Performance goals were focused on the attainment of challenging personal performance standards. Winning was considered to be the primary outcome goal operating in sport. Intercollegiate swimmers from a second university who did not receive goal-setting training served as the control. Swimmers who participated in the goal-setting program demonstrated higher perceived ability and felt more successful following competition than the swimmers who were not trained in personal performance-oriented goal-setting.

Similar findings emerged in a study by Newsham (1989) which examined the impact of a task-oriented physical education program on the perceived ability of elementary school children. The 12-week experimental program was designed to de-emphasize social comparison between the students and to focus the children on meeting personal performance goals. A control group participated in a 12-week traditional physical education class. Newsham found that the students who participated in the mastery-oriented physical education program were significantly higher in perceived sport competence and social acceptance than the controls.

Evidence supporting the predicted relationships between goal perspectives and perceptions of competence has also accrued from experimental research. In his study of the impact of a task- versus ego-involving condition on subjects performing a stabilometer task discussed above, Hall (1990) found that the experimentally-induced goal structure and perceived ability affected subjects' perceptions of competence before, during, and following task performance. Subjects who had low perceived ability and were placed in the ego-involving situation expected to perform worse during early trials than low-perceived-ability subjects in the task-involving condition or high-perceived-ability subjects in either condition. Interestingly, if performing under an ego-involving goal structure, even high-perceived-ability subjects began to doubt their ability and to expect that they would do less well during the later trials.

A similar pattern held for perceptions of confidence and demonstrated ability over trials as well as subjects' confidence regarding future success at the conclusion of the experiment. In each case, low perceived ability coupled with an ego-involving goal structure led to further decreases in the subject's sense of competence at the task.

Hall's (1990) research clearly indicates that ego involvement is not conducive to maintaining perceptions of high ability, particularly among individuals whose perceived competence is tenuous at best. Furthermore, this study implies that a declining sense of competence is unlikely when people are task-involved, regardless of their initial level of perceived ability.

In the field experiment described more previously, Duda and Chi (1989) determined the effect of pregame perceived competence, objective outcome, and a task- versus ego-involving game condition on post-performance ratings of perceived ability. In general, findings were consistent with the sport studies to date. The results indicated that, regardless of the objective outcome, low-pregame-perceived-competence subjects who were in the task-involving condition felt more able at the conclusion of a one-on-one basketball game than low-perceived-competence subjects who were in the ego-involving condition. Among the players who were objectively victorious, perceived competence was higher in the task-involving game than in the ego-involving game. Since perceptions of how well one played were not highly correlated with objective outcome in the task-involving condition (in contrast to what was observed in the ego-involving condition), it would appear that the task-involved subjects were using other criteria besides score to judge their post-game level of competence. The determination of the criteria used by people to judge their demonstrated ability in task- versus ego-involving situations is an important area for future inquiry (Ames & Ames, 1981).

In sum, the research to date suggests that task involvement fosters perceptions of ability in sport contexts when contrasted with ego involvement. An abundance of sport-related studies have demonstrated that perceptions of competence are important mediators of both performance (e.g., see Feltz, this volume) and persistence in the sport domain (Burton & Martens, 1986; Roberts, Kleiber, & Duda, 1981). Consequently, it would be interesting to examine the stability of the observed effects of goals on perceived competence and the behavioral consequences of the same over time.

Intrinsic Motivation

It has been suggested that "sports comprise one of the most pervasive sets of activities that people engage in for enjoyment" or intrinsic interest (Vallerand, Deci, & Ryan, 1988, p. 389). However, given the preponderance of extrinsic rewards in sport (e.g., trophies) and the point that people may participate to "prove themselves" rather than for the love of the game, intrinsic motivation may not always be at the forefront of sport involvement.

Contemporary social cognitive theories of achievement motivation suggest that goal perspectives should influence intrinsic motivation in achievement-related activities such as sport. Specifically, it is inferred that task involvement should foster intrinsic interest in an activity. In contrast, ego involvement is assumed to lead to a decrease in intrinsic motivation. According to Nicholls (1989), achievement strivings are experienced as a means to an end (i.e., the demonstration of superior ability) when one is ego involved. He argued that when an individual is task involved, an activity is experienced more as an end in itself. In a state of task involvement, therefore, our task-related strivings are more likely to be intrinsically satisfying. Using a similar line of reasoning, Dweck (1986) suggests that individuals who emphasize performance goals are primarily concerned about goal attainment and showing their superiority. Consequently, she proposes that a focus on performance goals will result in decreased intrinsic interest in an activity and less enjoyment from working hard at a task for it's own sake.

These predictions are aligned with the tenets of cognitive evaluation theory (Deci & Ryan, 1980; Plant & Ryan, 1985; Ryan, 1982; Ryan & Deci, 1989). According to Ryan (1982), ego involvement prevails when an individual's self-worth is contingent on good performance. The concept of ego involvement as addressed in cognitive evaluation theory is not exclusively focused on the demonstration of ability (Ryan & Deci, 1989). That is, Ryan and Deci assume that "people can be ego involved in matters of appearance, wealth, gender-consistent behavior, or any other outcome where failing to meet an internal standard is experienced as a threat to self-esteem" (p. 267). Task involvement, in contrast, is considered to be a state in which one's motivation to perform a task is derived from its intrinsic properties. It is argued that ego involvement represents a type of internal control or regulation. This "controlling" feature of ego involvement is assumed to foster an external perceived locus of causality; that is, the focus in this case is on meeting a performance standard rather than on the task at hand. Consequently, ego involvement is predicted to lead to a decrease in intrinsic motivation relative to task involvement.

In general, laboratory experiments have revealed a significant decline in intrinsic interest to engage in cognitive tasks when subjects are placed in evaluative and/or competitive environments, that is, ego-involving situations (Deci & Ryan, 1980; Koestner, Zuckerman, & Koestner, 1987; Plant & Ryan, 1985; Ryan, 1982; Ryan, Mims, & Koestner, 1983). The results of classroom-based studies, which have determined the impact of task- versus ego-involving evaluative feedback on intrinsic interest, are also consistent with theoretical predictions (Butler, 1987, 1988).

Recent sport research has examined the relationship between goal perspectives and intrinsic motivation. In general, this literature has concentrated on determining the possible influence of dispositional goal perspective or situationally induced goals on a variety of indices of intrinsic interest.

The correlations between task and ego orientation (as measured by the TEOSQ) and the degree of satisfaction, interest, and boredom experienced in the sport domain among high school students were determined by Duda and Nicholls (1989b). As can be seen in Table 4, a significant and positive relationship emerged between task orientation and the tendency to perceive playing sport as interesting and fun. Task orientation, on the other hand, was negatively correlated with the reported experience of boredom in sport. That is, students who were task oriented tended to disagree with such items as "I am usually bored when playing sport," "In sport, I often daydream instead of thinking about what I'm doing," and "When playing sports, I usually wish the game would end quickly."

Jackson (1988) examined the correspondence between goal perspective and the experience of flow in sport. As described by Csikszentmihalyi (1975),

Table 4 Correlations Between Task and Ego Orientation and the Degree of Enjoyment/Interest and Boredom Experienced in Sport

	All subjects		Females		Males	
	Task	Ego	Task	Ego	Task	Ego
Enjoyment/interest	.34**	.05	.58***	.32***	.30**	−.12
Boredom	−.28*	−.00	−.42***	−.12	−.19	.10

Note. Adapted from Duda and Nicholls (1989a).
*p < .05. **p < .01. ***p < .001.

flow is an intrinsically enjoyable experience that is typically autotelic in nature. In her study of college sport participants, Jackson found a positive relationship between task orientation and the frequency with which flow was experienced in competition. Ego-oriented individuals, particularly if they were low in perceived ability, experienced flow less frequently when competing.

The relationship between intrinsic motivation and individual differences in the proneness to be task- or ego-involved in sport was the focus of a study by Duda, Chi, and Newton (1990). In particular, we requested undergraduate students who were enrolled in a tennis skills class to complete the TEOSQ and the Intrinsic Motivation Inventory (IMI; Plant & Ryan, 1985; Ryan, et al., 1983) specific to the sport of tennis. The IMI assesses overall intrinsic motivation and five of the underlying dimensions of intrinsically motivated behavior (i.e., interest-enjoyment, effort, competence, pressure-tension, and perceived choice). Recent work by McAuley and colleagues (McAuley, Duncan, & Tammen, 1989; McAuley, Duncan, & Wraith, 1989) has provided evidence for the validity and reliability of the IMI when applied to sport and exercise settings.

Simple correlations revealed that task orientation was positively related to enjoyment, effort, and the composite intrinsic motivation score. A significant inverse relationship emerged between ego orientation, enjoyment, and overall intrinsic motivation. A canonical correlation analysis was used to determine the multivariate relationship between the two goal perspectives and the five dimensions of intrinsic motivation. As shown in Table 5, high task orientation and low ego orientation corresponded to greater perceived enjoyment of the tennis class.

Several experimental sport studies have examined the effect of task- versus ego-involving situations on intrinsic interest in the physical domain. Vallerand,

Table 5   Canonical Loadings: Goal Orientation and Dimensions of Intrinsic Motivation

	Standardized canonical coefficient
Goal orientation	
Task orientation	.754
Ego orientation	−.712
Intrinsic motivation dimensions	
Enjoyment-interest	.794
Competence	.137
Effort	.195
Pressure-tension	.156
Perceived choice	−.075

Note. From Duda, Chi, and Newton (1990).

Gauvin, and Halliwell (1986), for example, found that young boys spent significantly less time on task in a free-choice period if they were previously assigned to a competitive (i.e., focus placed on beating other children's scores), in contrast to a mastery-oriented (i.e., focus placed on trying one's best), condition.

Orgell and Duda (1990) determined the impact of task- versus ego-involving instructions on intrinsic interest in a sport activity. Male and female undergraduate students who were enrolled in a golf skill class were randomly assigned to one of two experimental conditions. In the task-involving situation, the subjects were requested to engage in a golf putting task which was being developed for future students to practice their skills. The subjects were told that they would not be scored on this task and to try their best at the activity. The subjects in the ego-involving condition were informed that the task had been designed to test putting skills in golf. Further, the subjects were told that their score would be recorded and compared to other students who had previously performed the task.

Intrinsic motivation was operationalized as the time spent engaging in the task during a subsequent 5-minute free-choice period. Results indicated that females spent less time-on-task in the ego-involving ($\overline{X} = 102.7$ sec) in comparison to the task-involving condition ($\overline{X} = 114.4$ sec). There was no significant condition effect on the time spent on task among the male subjects. Males spent more time-on-task during the free-choice period than females.

The tendency for evaluative environments to lead to a decreased intrinsic interest among females in particular has emerged in other sport research (Weinberg & Ragan, 1979). Further, given that the females in our study were significantly lower in perceived putting ability than the male subjects, we would expect that an ego-involving situation would be more detrimental to their level of intrinsic motivation.

In a study of Little League players, Boyd (1990) examined the effect of dispositional goal perspective (as measured by the TEOSQ) and win/loss on post-competition affective responses. The subjects in this investigation were members of four winning and four losing baseball teams. The players who were high in ego orientation reported that they enjoyed the game less than players low in ego orientation—regardless of whether they won or lost the contest. High ego-oriented players who lost the game, however, were less satisfied following the contest than high ego-oriented players who won the game. Among the low ego-oriented players, game outcome did not significantly effect their level of satisfaction.

In sum, preliminary correlational and experimental evidence in the sport domain supports recent theoretical predictions concerning the relationship between goal perspectives and intrinsic motivation. It seems that ego involvement can result in decreased intrinsic interest in and enjoyment of a sport activity. However, at the present time, there is more support for the proposition that task involvement tends to nourish intrinsic motivation in sport.

Goal Perspectives and Sport Behavior

The critical test of any theory of motivation is its ability to predict behavior. The behaviors which we assume reflect an individual's state of motivation include exerted effort, task choice, performance, and persistence (Maehr, 1984; Maehr & Braskamp, 1986; Roberts, this volume).

Effort Exerted

Exerting effort or *behavioral intensity*, particularly in the face of obstacles, has always been considered a hallmark of high motivation. In sport, we often speak in glowing terms of the individual who "hustles" or exerts effort, and we assume that such a person is highly motivated. Few investigations to date have examined the relationship between goal perspectives and the degree to which individuals work hard. In general, the research which has been conducted supports the theoretical predictions of Nicholls (1989), Dweck (1986), and Ames (1984b).

In my 1988 study, I found intramural sport participants who were high in task orientation reported that they practiced more in their free time. In a recent study of the predictors of adherence to athletic injury rehabilitation (Duda, Smart, & Tappe, 1989), task orientation was positively related to the effort exerted by athletes while completing their prescribed exercises. As indicated in the daily ratings provided by the assigned athletic trainer, athletes who were high in task orientation tended to push themselves and work hard during the exercise session. In contrast, low-task-orientation athletes were more likely to "walk through" their exercise protocol.

Trying hard as one performs certain sport-related skills or exercises is certainly a critical ingredient to improvement, to recovery from a setback such as physical injury, or to ultimate performance. Although behavioral intensity is not an easy variable to operationalize, much more work on the interdependence between goals and exerted effort in the physical domain is needed.

Task Choice

Nicholls (1984a, 1989) and Dweck (Dweck & Leggett, 1988; Elliott & Dweck, 1988) make elaborate predictions concerning the ways in which goal perspective and perceived ability impact patterns of task choice. Little sport research has been done on this issue. However, Nicholls (1989) interprets previous studies of risk taking, which used physical tasks to test the risk-taking predictions in Atkinson's (1964) theory of achievement motivation, in accordance with his theoretical framework (e.g., deCharms & Dave, 1965; Hamilton,

1974; Roberts, 1974). Because these investigations entailed the demonstration of a salient skill (i.e., physical ability among males) in a public arena, he suggests that the subjects were probably in a state of ego involvement. Nicholls also argues that the primary independent variable in such risk-taking studies (i.e., group differences in resultant achievement motivation scores) could be considered a measure of perceived ability. Congruent with social cognitive theories of achievement motivation, subjects in these investigations with low resultant motivation chose more extreme (i.e., very easy or very difficult) tasks. High-resultant-motivation subjects, on the other hand, tended to select a challenge of intermediate difficulty. It would appear that the systematic study of the effect of goal perspectives and perceived ability on subsequent task or activity choice is a promising area for future research.

Performance

Although this has been a point of contention, the field of sport psychology has focused much of its research on the prediction of sport performance. In terms of testing the performance-related predictions of recent social cognitive theories of achievement motivation, however, only a handful of investigations have been conducted at the present time.

A paucity of correlational studies specifically focus on the relationship of task and ego orientation to sport performance. Cross-sectional investigations using the SOQ (Gill, 1986; Gill & Deeter, 1988) and the COI (Vealey, 1986), though, have found high achieving sport players to have a higher goal or performance orientation, respectively, than their counterparts who have not demonstrated the same outstanding level of performance.

In a quasi field experiment previously described, Burton (1989b) examined the effect of a goal-setting program on the performance of intercollegiate swimmers. The purpose of this program was to teach the swimmers how to set accurate goals based on personal performance standards rather than outcome. Performance (time and race outcome) was assessed during a midseason dual meet and the league championship. The results indicated that trained swimmers who set accurate personal performance goals demonstrated higher performance when compared to a control group of trained swimmers who set inaccurate goals.

In another goal-setting study, Hall (1990) determined the effect of perceived ability, situational goal perspective, and success/failure feedback on performance. Perceived ability was manipulated by telling the subjects that they had performed well or poorly following a baseline measure of stabilometer performance. The subjects were then randomly assigned to either a task-involving (in which only personal performance feedback was given) or ego-involving (in which personal performance and normative feedback was given) experimental condition. Each subject completed six trials during which he was asked to achieve a goal of 60% improvement over baseline. Bogus feedback (i.e., the subject was told he reached or did not reach the target goal) was given at the conclusion of the second, fourth, and sixth trials. In support of contemporary social cognitive theories of achievement motivation (Ames, 1984b; Dweck & Leggett, 1988; Nicholls, 1989), subjects with low perceived ability who performed in the ego-involving condition displayed lower performance than low-perceived-ability subjects who were assigned to the task-involving condition.

To date, Hall's (1990) investigation has been one of the best experimental tests of the performance predictions embedded in recent goal-related theories of achievement motivation (see also Weinberg, this volume). Nicholls (1989), however, questions the possibility of producing a high state of task involvement in such laboratory experiments. He also distinguishes between the determination of factors influencing short- versus long-term performance. Laboratory experiments, in his view, tend to be oriented to the prediction of immediate, short-term performance. Nicholls (1989) maintains that the understanding and fostering of lifetime accomplishments (e.g., a scientific breakthrough, a stellar sport career) should be the major concern of motivation theorists. In that regard, he predicts that "task orientation is more likely to maintain the long-term involvement that such significant accomplishments demand" (p. 128).

Although preliminary research in sport-related contexts has been congruent with theoretical predictions concerning the impact of goal perspectives on performance, little is known about the mechanism by which goals influence task accomplishment. In particular, we have evidence at this point in time, in educational (e.g., Miller, 1985) and physical (e.g., Hall, 1990) environments, which reflects the potential performance debilitating effects of ego involvement. The major question which faces us, however, is *why* does this occur?

Nicholls (1989) argues that, in an ego-involving situation, "performance is impaired more by the expectation that failure will indicate one's lack of competence than by the mere expectation of failure to complete a task" (p. 119). He proposes that the expectation of looking incompetent might result in performance impairment in several ways. First, since individuals who are ego involved tend to be very concerned about demonstrating their competence, this goal perspective may push people into forming unrealistic aspirations. This proposition is consistent with the risk-taking literature briefly reviewed above.

Second, ego involvement may be linked to a conscious (or unconscious) willingness to withdraw effort when failure seems imminent. Although recent research has questioned the existence of this behavioral strategy in the academic context (Jagacinski & Nicholls, 1990), preliminary sport studies suggest that reduced effort may be a consequence of ego involvement in the sport domain (Duda & Chi, 1989; Hall, 1990).

An emphasis on ego-involved goals coupled with questions concerning one's level of competence may lead to alienation. That is, it is proposed (Nicholls, 1989) that ego-involved individuals with low perceived competence may eventually devalue or lose interest in an activity, and, consequently, performance will wane. In sport settings, we know that individuals who withdraw from sport often report that they had not been performing well and had lost interest in it (e.g., Burton & Martens, 1986). In research by Hall (1990), low-perceived-ability subjects performing under an ego-involving goal structure placed less importance on doing well on the (stabilometer) task than high-perceived-ability subjects in the same condition or low-perceived-ability subjects in a task-involving condition.

Finally, Nicholls (1989) suggests that ego involvement may result in impaired performance due to the debilitating effects of anxiety. Results of sport studies by Vealey and Campbell (1988) and Duda, Newton, and Chi (1990) are consistent with this hypothesis. In the latter investigation specifically, high precompetition state cognitive and somatic anxiety (and low state confidence) were primarily evident among tennis players who were high in ego orientation and did not expect to win the match.

Persistence

Researchers in the field of sport psychology have demonstrated considerable interest in identifying the predictors of dropping out of sport (Burton & Martens, 1986; Feltz & Petlichkoff, 1983; Gould, Feltz, Horn, & Weiss, 1982; Klint & Weiss, 1986). Drawing from this literature, we know that withdrawal from sport is linked to low perceived competence and less enjoyment of the sport experience.

Roberts (1984) was the first to attempt to assimilate work on dropping out (or a *lack of persistence*) in sport within social cognitive theories of achievement motivation. In particular, he argued that individuals with high ego involvement will not persist in sport if their high ability goals are not met.

To date, the majority of research on goal perspectives and persistence in the sport domain has been correlational in nature. For the most part, these correlational studies have revealed a positive relationship between task orientation and persistence. Aligned with Roberts's (1984) predictions, ego involvement has been negatively linked with continued involvement in sport.

Ewing (1981), in her research on 14- to 15-year-old adolescents, found ability-oriented subjects (or adolescents who were high in ego orientation) to be most likely to have dropped out of sport. In a study of intramural sport participants, recreational participants who were higher in task orientation were found to have continued involvement in their chosen sport for a longer time (Duda, 1988).

The relationship between goal perspectives and participation and persistence in sport among high school students was examined in a second study by Duda (1989b). The students were divided into five groups in this investigation. Group One was presently involved in both interscholastic and recreational sport programs. Group Two participated in organized sport only, and Group

Three was comprised of recreational sport only participants. Those students who had dropped out of sport were included in Group Four. Group Five included students who had never been regularly involved in sport. The results indicated that those students who were presently involved in sport endorsed a mastery-based conception of success more than did those who had ceased participation or students who had never been involved. Further, dropouts were found to be most troubled (as indicated in a preference rating) by a sport failure experience in which an individual demonstrated lower ability in relation to his or her peers. This latter finding is consistent with research by Whitehead (1989) who observed dropouts in British sport clubs to be more concerned than youngsters who have persisted about demonstrating superiority over their peers.

A recent study by Weitzer (1989) nicely linked perceptions of competence with goal perspectives in an attempt to predict involvement in physical activity among male and female fourth grade children. The results indicated that boys and girls who emphasized mastery (i.e., task-involved) goals, regardless of their level of perceived ability, tended to participate in physical activities such as sport. Children who stressed outcome (or ego-involving goals) and perceived their competence to be low were less likely to still be active when compared to low ego-oriented children who had high perceived competence.

In a laboratory experiment, Rudisill and her colleagues (Rudisill, Meaney, McDermott, & Jibaja-Rusth, 1990) examined the effect of goal-setting orientations on children's perceived competence and persistence. Nine- through twelve-year-old children were requested to perform three different motor tasks (i.e., throwing for accuracy, standing long jump, sit and reach) under one of four experimental conditions:

1. A task-mastery goal condition in which the children were asked to set performance goals which were 20% higher than their own previous performance
2. A competitive goal condition in which the children were asked to set normatively based goals
3. A self-goal condition in which the children were asked to set their own goals for performance
4. A control group condition in which the children were not instructed to set goals

Persistence was defined as the time the children spent practicing the motor skills during a free-time period following the test trials. Perceived motor skill competence did not significantly change pre- to post-trials as a function of experimental condition. However, consistent with theoretical predictions and previous correlational sport research, children who were assigned to the task-involving mastery group persisted longer at the long jump and flexibility tasks than those assigned to the other three goal-setting conditions.

In an attempt to explain the observed negative relationship between ego involvement and persistence, I have argued that a prevailing ego orientation provides less opportunity for subjective success in competitive sport environments marked by uncertain outcomes and constant challenges to one's ability (Duda, 1989b). As subjective success is based primarily on personal improvement when task-involved, the reproduction of successful sport experiences seems more secure in this case. Consequently, we would expect task involvement to positively correspond to persistence in sport. In support of this argument, Hall (1990) found subjects assigned to an ego-involving condition reporting lower levels of subjective success over performance trials than those assigned to a task-involving condition. Moreover, the research reviewed concerning the differential relationship of task and ego involvement to attributions, perceived competence, and intrinsic motivation in sport is consistent with this thesis. The cognitions and achievement-related experiences associated with ego involvement do not set the stage for long-term investment in an activity. The opposite appears to hold for task involvement.

Research testing the predictive utility of recent social cognitive theories of achievement motivation in terms of sport-related behaviors is in its infancy. However, an examination of the literature at this juncture reveals findings which are consonant with what is theoretically proposed.

Goal Perspectives and Views About Sport

Adopting an ecological perspective on social cognition, Nicholls (1989) argues that "different motivational orientations are not just different types of wants or goals. They involve different world views" (p. 102). Specifically, he proposes that an individual's goal perspective tends to be consistent with the person's views or philosophy about the wider purposes of the achievement activity itself, and his or her opinions concerning what is acceptable behavior in that arena. In regard to the former, studies in the academic domain have found that an ego orientation is linked to the belief that education should result in extrinsic ends such as wealth and status. Task orientation, however, corresponded to the view that school should enhance one's commitment to society, understanding of the world, and desire to keep learning (Nicholls et al., 1985; Thorkildsen, 1988).

Sport has been assumed to be a vehicle for the socialization of prosocial values (Kleiber & Roberts, 1981). The presumed positive relationship between sport involvement and character development has not been strongly supported in the literature. Drawing from Nicholls's (1989) thinking, an examination of participants' goal perspectives might provide us with a better understanding of the positive or negative attitudes and values which have been linked to the sport experience.

Replicating work done in the academic domain, I (Duda, 1989c) recently examined the relationship between goal perspectives and the perceived wider purpose of sport involvement among high school sport participants. The subjects were administered the TEOSQ and the 60 item Purpose of Sport Questionnaire. The items contained in the latter questionnaire were generated from three sources: relevant questions contained in the Purposes of Schooling Questionnaire (Nicholls, 1989), previous literature on the values and benefits associated with youth sport involvement, and open-ended responses provided by high school students in a pilot investigation. A factor analysis of the sport questionnaire revealed seven beliefs about what sport should accomplish, namely that

1. sport should teach the value of mastery and cooperation;
2. sport should show people how to be physically active for life;
3. sport should make good citizens;
4. sport should make people competitive;
5. sport should help individuals obtain a high status career;
6. sport should enhance self-esteem; and
7. sport should show people how to ''get ahead'' and increase their social status.

A conceptually coherent relationship emerged between task and ego orientation and the seven purposes of sport. As can be seen in Table 6, individuals high in task orientation tended to believe that sport should enhance our cooperative skills and investment in personal mastery. Task orientation negatively related to the view that sport should improve an individual's social status. In total, task orientation was linked to an endorsement of the intrinsic dimensions and prosocial consequences of the sport experience.

A strong ego orientation, on the other hand, corresponded to beliefs about sport reflecting the extrinsic benefits and personal gains aligned with athletic

Table 6 Canonical Loadings: Goal Perspectives and Purposes of Sport

	Standard canonical coefficient Function 1	Standard canonical coefficient Function 2
Goal orientation		
Task orientation	.937	.350
Ego orientation	−.381	.925
Purpose of sport		
Mastery/cooperation	.443	.009
Active lifestyle	.124	.260
Good citizen	.244	−.386
Competitiveness	.191	.337
High status career	.063	−.092
Enhance self-esteem	.051	.628
Enhance social status	−.773	.350

Note. From Duda (1989c).

involvement (Duda, 1989c). Specifically, the stronger the ego orientation, the stronger the belief that sport should increase one's sense of self-importance and make one popular. Further, ego orientation positively related to the view that sport should build a competitive spirit and the desire to get ahead in the world, and negatively related to the belief that sport should foster good citizenship. Clearly, the broader conception that sport involvement is a means to some end appears to coincide with an ego-oriented goal perspective in the sport setting.

The premise that an individual's goal perspective will correspond to his or her view of an activity as a means to some outcome or as an end in itself also presupposes a logical relationship between task and ego orientation and what a person would do to achieve his or her goal. In Nicholls's words (1989),

> a preoccupation with winning (beating others) may well be accompanied by a lack of concern about justice and fairness. . . . When winning is everything, it is worth doing anything to win. (p. 133)

In the context of interscholastic sport specifically, I and my colleagues (Duda, Olson, & Templin, 1991) examined the link between goal perspectives and the behaviors perceived as acceptable to secure victory. More specifically, we determined among male and female basketball players the relationship of task and ego orientation (as measured by the TEOSQ) to sportsmanship attitudes and perceptions of the legitimacy of intentionally injurious acts. With respect to the assessment of sportsmanship attitudes, players indicated their degree of approval of three types of behaviors. The first were actions that entailed stretching the rules so that one's team could have an unfair advantage (e.g., allowing an ineligible star player to play, turning up the heat in your gymnasium when playing a faster team, faking an injury to stop the clock). These actions were labeled "unsportsmanshiplike/cheating" behaviors. The second class of behaviors were those that were more strategic in nature (e.g., faking a charge on defense, trying to distract the opposing free throw shooter). The third type of behaviors reflected what we might consider to be good sportsmanship in basketball (e.g., admitting to touching a ball knocked out of bounds, helping an opposing player up from the floor).

As shown in Table 7, task orientation was negatively related to the endorsement of cheating behaviors. Simple and multivariate analyses also indicated that task orientation corresponded to a greater approval of sportsmanlike actions.

A modified basketball-specific version of the Continuum of Injurious Acts or CIA (Bredemeier, 1985) was also completed to assess the players' legitimacy judgments. The revised CIA consisted of six written scenarios depicting aggressive acts in basketball with intended consequences that become increasingly more serious, that is, nonphysical intimidation, physical intimidation, miss a few minutes, miss the rest of the game, miss the rest of the season, and permanent disability. Following the presentation of each scenario, the players were requested to answer the following question: Is this OK (legitimate) to do

Table 7 Canonical Loadings: Goal Orientation and Sportsmanship Attitudes

	Standardized canonical coefficient
Goal orientation	
Task orientation	−.825
Ego orientation	.482
Sportsmanship attitudes	
Unsportsmanlike play/cheating	.848
Sportsmanlike play	−.427
Strategic play	−.024

Note. Adapted from Duda, Olson, and Templin (1991).

if it was necessary in order to win the game? As can be seen in the results presented in Table 8, ego orientation related to higher legitimacy ratings of non-physical intimidation, injuring an opponent so that she or he misses a game, and injuring an opponent so that she or he misses the entire season.

These findings, focused on the relationship between goal perspectives and ratings of the legitimacy of intentionally injurious acts, were replicated among high school and college-level football players (Huston & Duda, 1990). Further, the football players' adopted goal perspectives were found to be a better predictor of legitimacy judgments than competitive level (i.e., high school versus college) or the reported years of involvement in competitive football.

Previous sport research has indicated that values such as the importance of fairness, of playing by the rules, of the gracious acceptance of victory and

Table 8 Canonical Loadings: Goal Orientation and Legitimacy Judgments

	Standardized canonical coefficient
Goal orientation	
Task orientation	.239
Ego orientation	.997
Legitimacy judgments	
Nonphysical intimidation	−.651
Physical intimidation	.308
Miss a few minutes	−.049
Miss game	−.810
Out for season	−.569
Permanently disable	.195

Note. Adapted from Duda, Olson, and Templin (1991).

defeat, and of respect for one's opponent tend to be inversely related to competitive sport involvement (e.g., Allison, 1982; Blair, 1985; Kleiber & Roberts, 1981; Silva, 1983). The studies described here, however, suggest that it is not competitive involvement per se but the goal perspective that is adopted by sport participants that impacts their broader view of what sport is all about. Participants who tend to be ego- or task-involved in sport seem to have very different conceptions of the long-term value of sport involvement and of what is considered acceptable or fair behavior within the sport arena (see Nicholls, this volume). Based on initial research in this area, it appears that players who are high in ego orientation focus on two questions, namely "What's in it for me?" and "What do I need to do to win?"

Tentative Conclusions

At the present time, the limited research which has been conducted in the sport realm is consistent with the academic literature and the theoretical arguments of Nicholls (1989), Ames (1984b; Ames & Archer, 1988), and Dweck (1986; Dweck & Leggett, 1988). In particular, conceptually coherent relationships have emerged with respect to the interdependencies between goal perspectives and motivational processes, achievement-related behaviors, and values and beliefs in the sport domain.

This consistency in findings across academic and sport environments might be due to the fact that both are clearly achievement situations. In each context, the demonstration of competence, the standards of excellence, and the evaluation of performance are salient and apparent (Roberts, 1984; Scanlan, 1978b). Consequently, one might assume that theories which focus on the motivational dynamics of achievement behavior in the classroom setting might readily generalize to sport. However, results from one of our recent studies suggest an additional reason for the convergence in research findings (Duda & Nicholls, 1989a). Specifically, it appears that goal perspectives and the corresponding beliefs about the causes of success generalize across sport and the classroom.

In this particular study, parallel scales assessing motivational orientation and beliefs about the causes of success in both the classroom and sport were administered to high school students. Each situation-specific motivational orientation assessment included four scales, namely a measure of task orientation, ego orientation, work avoidance, and cooperation. For example, "I feel really successful when I can goof off," and "I feel really successful when my friends and I help each other improve" are typical items reflecting work avoidance and cooperation motivation orientations, respectively. The four context-specific beliefs about the cause of success were motivation/effort, ability, deception, and external factors.

A factor analysis of the scale scores was conducted and four factors emerged. As shown in Table 9, the first indicated that work avoidance was a motivational strategy that transcended situation. The second factor suggested that an emphasis on learning and personal improvement (i.e., task orientation), the belief that success is due to effort, and the importance of helping others generalizes across the two achievement domains. As reflected in the third factor, the salience of outdoing others and the view that success is dependent on superior ability (i.e., ego involvement) also appears not to be situationally dependent. Finally, the fourth factor indicates that the tendency to perceive that deceptive tactics and external factors result in success in the classroom coincides with a similar belief system in sport.

In sum, this preliminary data implies that people operate in accordance with implicit transsituational motivation theories (Dweck & Leggett, 1988). Such theories entail a systematic interplay between goal perspective, cognitive mediators such as attributions, and behavioral patterns. Roberts (this volume) argues that a convergence of recent social cognitive theories of achievement motivation may provide a strong, conceptual framework for our further

Table 9   Factor Analysis of Sport (S) and Classroom (C) Goal Orientation and Beliefs About Success Subscales

	Factor 1 Work avoidance	Factor 2 Task orientation	Factor 3 Ego orientation	Factor 4 External/ deception
Work avoidance (C)	.920			
Work avoidance (S)	.861			
Effort attributions (C)		.813		
Task orientation (S)		.809		
Task orientation (C)		.798		
Effort attributions (S)		.767		
Cooperation (C)		.751		
Cooperation (S)		.718		
Ego orientation (S)			.912	
Ego orientation (C)			.864	
Competence beliefs (C)			.561	
Competence beliefs (S)			.547	
External beliefs (C)				.857
External beliefs (S)				.824
Deception beliefs (C)				.748
Deception beliefs (S)				.637
Eigenvalue	4.62	3.22	1.57	1.25
Percent of variance	28.9	20.2	9.8	7.8

understanding of sport and exercise. Our findings (Duda & Nicholls, 1989a) suggest that an understanding of goal perspectives may be at the forefront of the development of a general theory of motivation in achievement contexts.

Goal Perspectives in the Exercise Domain

The possible relevance of variations in goal perspectives to motivational processes and behavior in the exercise context has begun to be considered in recent research (e.g., Kimiecik, 1990). The majority of the work in this area has been conceptually based on the personal investment theory (Maehr & Braskamp, 1986). Personal investment theory is a comprehensive social cognitive theory of motivation which assumes that one's behavioral investment in a situation is a function of the meaning of the situation to the person. *Meaning* is held to be comprised of three interrelated components, namely *personal goals or incentives, sense-of-self characteristics*, and *perceived behavioral options*.

Similar to contemporary social cognitive theories of achievement motivation (Ames, 1984b; Dweck, 1986; Nicholls, 1989), personal investment theory, or PIT, holds that task and ego involvement are two major goal perspectives that individuals can adopt in a particular situation. There are important differences, however, between these former theoretical perspectives and Maehr and Braskamp's (1986) theory of motivation. First, PIT assumes that there are other salient goal perspectives or *personal incentives* which serve as the focus of motivated behavior. Because the PIT is not specific to achievement settings, it acknowledges that people can strive to demonstrate other attributes besides competence (e.g., power incentives). Further, this theoretical perspective recognizes that individuals may emphasize the social consequences (e.g., affiliation or social recognition incentives) of one's involvement in an activity, rather than the experience of learning or beating others.

Second, the theory of personal investment holds that other *sense-of-self variables* besides perceived competence impact an individual's behavioral investment. According to Maehr and Braskamp (1986), a person's tendency to set and to try to achieve goals (i.e., *goal directedness*), degree of *self-reliance*, and sense of *social identity* (or perceived social group membership) are also believed to determine behavioral patterns.

Third, PIT maintains that an individual's *perceived behavioral options* will also affect his or her investment in a particular context. This more situationally based factor refers to whether a person views a specific action as an attractive and realistic alternative. Such a concept is not specifically addressed in contemporary social cognitive theories of achievement motivation (Ames, 1984b; Dweck, 1986; Nicholls, 1989).

Finally, PIT differs from the theoretical perspectives proffered by Ames (1984b), Dweck (1986), and Nicholls (1989) because the theory of personal investment tends to be more descriptive in nature. That is, in its present stage of development, the interrelationships between personal incentives, sense-of-self variables, and behavioral options have not yet been clearly delineated at either a theoretical or empirical level. The PIT predicts that these three dimensions of meaning will predict behavior. How and why personal incentives, perceptions of self, and behavioral options interact to result in different behavioral patterns in specific settings has not yet been systematically addressed.

In contrast to the PIT, other contemporary social cognitive theories of achievement motivation focus on goals as the critical determinant of behavioral variation (Ames, 1984b; Dweck, 1986; Nicholls, 1989). It is assumed that one's goal perspective interacts with perceived competence "to set in motion a sequence of specific (cognitive) processes that influence, in turn, task choice, performance, and persistence" (Elliott & Dweck, 1988, p. 11).

I have been involved with both students and colleagues in a series of studies focused on determining the predictive utility of personal investment theory with respect to exercise behavior. The first major step of this work, of course, entailed the operationalization of the concepts embedded in the PIT specific to the exercise domain. Our recent investigations have involved a variety of populations and exercise-related contexts (Chen & Duda, 1990; Duda, 1989a; Duda & Tappe, 1988, 1989a; Duda, Tappe, & Savage, 1990; Tappe & Duda, 1988; Tappe, Duda, & Ehrnwald, 1990). At this point in our work, two findings stand out: (a) Task involvement, in contrast to ego involvement, seems to be a salient ego perspective in the exercise domain (see also Roberts, this volume), and (b) consistent to what has been observed in the classroom and sport settings, task involvement has been predictive of positive motivated behaviors (e.g., intensity of participation, persistence). Similar results have been reported by Kimiecik, Jackson, and Giannini (in press) in a study of adult exercisers.

Recent research has indicated that one's degree of task orientation can impact the experience of exercise in and of itself (Duda, Sedlock, Noble, Cohen, & Chi, 1990). Specifically, we determined the effect of a task- versus ego-involving condition on perceived exertion ratings (RPE) and affective response among high task-/low ego-oriented and low task-/high ego-oriented college students. Task and ego orientation was assessed before the start of the experiment by the TEOSQ (Duda & Nicholls, 1989b). The task was a 6-minute submaximal cycle ergometer exercise at an intensity equal to 70% of maximum oxygen uptake. Perceptions of overall exertion were assessed in addition to effort perceptions specific to the legs and cardiorespiratory system using the Borg (1962) scale. Affective response (i.e., how the subject felt at a specific moment in time) was indicated on an 11-point bipolar feeling scale with +5 being extremely positive and −5 being extremely negative (Rejeski, Best, Griffith, & Kenney, 1987). Both the RPE and affective response measures were obtained during the last minute of exercise.

Subjects completed this exercise bout in one of two experimental conditions. In the task-involving condition, subjects were informed that the purpose of the task was to determine individualized physiological responses to the exercise. They were told that they should "try your best" and "try to enjoy the exercise." Subjects assigned to the ego-involving condition, on the other hand, were informed that the exercise was a test of physiological capacity. It was emphasized to these subjects that their responses would be compared to other students of the same age and sex.

The results indicated that high task-/low ego-oriented subjects tended to perceive their exertion level to be lower and reported more positive affect than did low task-/high ego-oriented subjects. Although not statistically significant, it is interesting to point out that the two groups of subjects were best distinguished in the ego-involving condition. That is, in contrast to the task-involving condition, high task-/low ego-oriented subjects tended to perceive that the exercise was less demanding in the ego-involving condition. The reverse was true for subjects who were low task-/high ego-oriented.

It has been proposed in previous work that motivation has an important impact on RPE and affective responses during exercise (Mihevic, 1981; Pandolf, 1983; Rejeski, 1985). In this regard, our preliminary research suggests that if a person emphasizes skill acquisition and improvement (i.e., task involvement) and de-emphasizes social comparison (i.e., ego involvement) during exercise testing, she or he tends to respond to the exercise experience with a more positive outlook. Such an individual seems to report more of a "feel good" response and appears less likely to focus on the discomfort associated with moderately demanding physical activity. Further, based on the lower RPE values obtained from the high task-/low ego-oriented subject, it would appear that she or he could work much harder if necessary. That is, the exercise did not seem to be as fatiguing to such an individual. On the other hand, individuals who are high ego-/low task-oriented and are placed into an ego-involving exercise setting seem to be more aware of the distress associated with physical exertion. In any regard, the potential impact of goal perspective on perceptions during exercise appears to be an intriguing topic for further study.

Future Directions

Initial sport-related research based on contemporary social cognitive theories of achievement motivation provides support for these theories' relevance to the sport domain. Much more work is needed in the sport realm, however, to examine systematically the tenets of these theoretical perspectives. As we forge ahead in such efforts, there are several important directions for future research based on a goal perspective approach to the study of sport behavior. In concluding this chapter, I would like to propose that sport motivation researchers begin to

1. develop ways by which we can assess perceived situational goal perspective and determine the effect of these perceptions on sport participants (see also Ames, this volume);
2. study specific ways in which practitioners can create a task-involving sport climate (see also Ames, this volume);
3. examine the socialization processes by which individuals become disposed to being more task- or ego-involved in sport (see also Roberts, this volume); and
4. investigate the impact of developmental change on goals, conceptions of ability, and related cognitive mediators of behavior (see also Roberts, this volume).

As emphasized by Nicholls (1989), Ames (1984b), and Dweck (Dweck & Leggett, 1988), the understanding and determination of situational demands as they relate to goal perspectives is an important area of study. Ames and Archer (1988) and Nicholls (1989) have demonstrated that students clearly perceive the goal perspective which is prevailing in a particular classroom. The perceptions of the degree to which a classroom is task- or ego-involving relate to the students' beliefs about success and use of effective learning strategies.

Do athletic participants differentiate sport environments with respect to task- and ego-involving dimensions? If yes, what are the major cues which are used by participants to distinguish the sport climate with respect to the predominant goal perspective (Ames & Archer, 1988)? Such questions would provide the basis for most interesting sport motivation research.

As mentioned, previous classroom-based studies and laboratory experiments have supported the predictions stemming from recent social cognitive theories of achievement motivation (Ames, 1984b; Dweck & Leggett, 1988; Nicholls, 1989). Although this line of work is in its infancy, sport research as highlighted in this chapter has also been consistent with these theoretical perspectives. In general, both bodies of literature seem to point to the significance of task involvement in regard to adaptive motivational processes and behavioral patterns.

Based on this literature then, we are faced with a practical issue that needs our careful attention. If task involvement is so desirable from a motivational standpoint, how can those who are out in the fields, gymnasiums, and ballparks (e.g., coaches and physical education teachers) create and maintain a task-involving sport situation for their players/students? The enhancement of task involvement might be viewed as a particular challenge as the sport world is so overtly competitive and outcome-oriented. To begin to address this issue, there is a need for applied studies that implement and test the practical implications of recent goal-related research in real-life sport settings. An excellent model for such research is the work of Smith and Smoll (Smith, Smoll, & Curtis, 1978; Smith, Zane, Smoll, & Coppell, 1983; Smoll & Smith, 1984) on coaching effectiveness within the youth sport context. As has been suggested by Chaumeton and Duda (1988), the behavioral guidelines for effective coaching developed by Smith and Smoll can be considered to be the building blocks for a task-involving environment. It would seem that this type of work would provide sound theoretically-based guidelines for the practitioner in terms of how to foster "equality of motivation" (Nicholls, 1989).

Because there appears to be individual differences in the proneness to be task- or ego-involved in sport (Balague & Roberts, 1989; Duda & Nicholls, 1989b), the issue of how people are socialized to favor one goal orientation over the other also becomes important. Previous classroom (Eccles, Midgley, & Adler, 1984) and sport (Chaumeton & Duda, 1988) research has suggested that both environments are characterized by greater evaluation and emphasis on performance outcomes as children progress through the system (i.e., from grade to grade, or from one competitive sport level to the next). Based on these investigations and other work (e.g., Scanlan, 1978a), this increase in the ego-involving dimensions of the classroom and sport setting should relate to a corresponding increase in ego orientation among students and sport participants, respectively. Recent cross-sectional research in the sport domain by White et al. (1990) is compatible with this premise. They found male and female intercollegiate sport participants to be significantly higher in ego orientation (as measured by the TEOSQ) than college-age recreational sport participants or high school-level competitors.

Of course, when we speak of variations in the self-perceptions and behaviors of children as they continue their involvement in sport, the potential impact of cognitive as well as motoric developmental change must be considered. The relevance of developmental differences in children's conceptions of ability, intelligence, effort, luck, and task difficulty in academic environments has played an important role in the development of contemporary social cognitive theories of achievement motivation (e.g., Dweck, 1986; Nicholls & Miller, 1984; Nicholls, 1989). To date in the sport motivation literature focused on children, however, we have virtually ignored possible age-related changes in psychological processing and physical development, or we have generalized from work conducted in the academic domain (Duda, 1987; Roberts, 1984; Weiss & Bredemeier, 1983). One notable exception to this state of affairs is research by Whitehead and Dalby (1987). Future investigations stemming from a developmental perspective are critical to furthering our knowledge of achievement motivation in sport.

Summary

In summary, this chapter has reviewed the ways in which recent classroom-based theories of achievement motivation have begun to be tested in the sport setting. Preliminary findings suggest that the determination and analysis of goal perspectives are pertinent to our understanding of how people experience, respond to, and interpret sport. Further, it appears that this approach has the potential to offer us much insight into behavioral patterns within the sport domain and the exercise setting as well. I hope that the studies discussed and ideas espoused in this chapter will be a catalyst for future motivation research on the antecedents and consequences of goal perspectives in the physical domain.

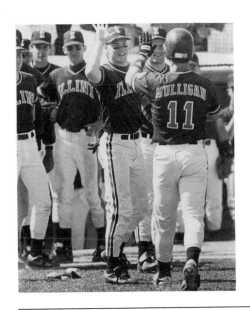

Understanding Motivation in Sport: A Self-Efficacy Perspective

Deborah L. Feltz

The adage, "You can do it if you just have a little confidence," is very familiar to coaches and sport participants. In fact, self-confidence—or self-efficacy as it is being used here—is one of the most frequently cited psychological factors thought to affect sport performance and is a primary focus of research by sport psychologists. The most extensively used theory for investigating self-confidence in sport and motor performance has been Bandura's (1977a) theory of self-efficacy. This chapter focuses on the nature of the relationship

Note. Some sections of this chapter include revised and expanded material from Feltz, D.L., "Self-confidence and sports performance." In K.B. Pandolf (Ed.), *Exercise and Sport Sciences Reviews* (Vol. 16). Copyright © 1988 American College of Sports Medicine. Adapted with permission of Macmillan Publishing Company.

between self-efficacy and sport motivation and performance. A brief theoretical overview is presented followed by a discussion of the nature of the relationship between self-efficacy and sport including research examples and suggestions for future research.

Theoretical Overview

Self-efficacy theory, developed within the framework of a social cognitive theory (Bandura, 1986), poses self-efficacy as a common cognitive mechanism for mediating people's motivation, thought patterns, and behavior (see also McAuley, this volume). Self-efficacy beliefs, defined as people's judgments of their capability to perform at given levels, are a product of a complex process of self-persuasion that relies on cognitive processing of diverse sources of efficacy information (Bandura, 1989). These sources of information include performance accomplishments, vicarious experiences, persuasion, and physiological states.

- *Performance accomplishments.* Performance accomplishments provide efficacy information through one's own mastery experiences and, therefore, provide the most dependable source of information. One's mastery experiences affect self-efficacy judgments through cognitive processing of such information. If one has repeatedly perceived these experiences as successes, efficacy expectations will increase; if these experiences are perceived as failures, expectations will decrease. The influence that performance experiences have on perceived efficacy also depends on the perceived difficulty of the task, the effort expended, the amount of physical guidance received, and the temporal patterns of success and failure (Bandura, 1986). Performance accomplishments on difficult tasks, tasks attempted independently, and tasks accomplished early in learning with only occasional failures carry greater efficacy value than easy tasks, tasks accomplished with external aids, or tasks in which repeated failures are experienced early in the learning process.

- *Vicarious experiences.* Efficacy information can also be obtained through a social comparison process with others. Although vicarious sources of efficacy information are generally weaker than performance accomplishments, their influence on self-efficacy can be enhanced by a number of factors. For instance, the less experience people have had with a task or situation, the more they will rely on others to judge their own capabilities. In addition, the effectiveness of modeling procedures on the self-efficacy of individuals has been shown to be enhanced by perceived similarities to the model in terms of performance or personal characteristics (Gould & Weiss, 1981).

- *Persuasion.* Persuasive information includes verbal persuasion, self-talk, imagery, and other cognitive strategies. Efficacy expectations based on this type of information are also likely to be weaker than those based on one's own accomplishments. In addition, persuasive techniques are effective only if heightened appraisal is within realistic bounds. The extent of persuasive influence on self-efficacy also depends on the credibility, prestige, trustworthiness, and expertise of the persuader.

- *Physiological states.* One's physiological state or condition can also provide efficacy information through cognitive appraisal such as associating physiological arousal with fear and self-doubt or with being psyched up and ready for performance. Bandura (1986) notes that physiological sources of self-efficacy beliefs are not limited to autonomic arousal. People use their levels of fatigue, fitness, and pain in strength and endurance activities as indicants of physical inefficacy (Feltz & Riessinger, 1990).

These four categories of efficacy information are not mutually exclusive in terms of the information they provide, though some are more influential than others. Efficacy judgments that are based on these principal sources of information determine people's levels of motivation, as reflected in the challenges they undertake, the effort they expend in the activity, and their perseverance in the face of difficulties. Bandura points out, however, that self-efficacy is a major determinant of behavior only when proper incentives and the necessary skills are present. People's self-efficacy beliefs also affect certain thought patterns that also influence motivation (Bandura, 1986). For instance, self-efficacy beliefs influence people's success/failure imagery, worry, goal intentions, and attributions.

Bandura (1977a) also emphasized that the relationship between efficacy expectations and performance accomplishments is reciprocal: "Mastery expectations influence performance and are, in turn, altered by the cumulative effect of one's efforts" (p. 194). Bandura (1989) has emphasized the reciprocal nature of the relationship between self-efficacy and thought patterns as well. The relationship between the major sources of efficacy information, efficacy expectations, and behavior/thought patterns as predicted by Bandura's theory is presented in Figure 1.

Bandura (1977a, 1986) distinguishes judgments of personal efficacy from response-outcome expectations. Self-efficacy is a judgment of one's ability to perform at a certain level, whereas outcome expectancy pertains to one's judgment that certain behaviors will lead to desired outcomes. For example, a woman may believe that running a marathon in less than two hours will lead to social recognition, money, and self-satisfaction (outcome belief), but may question whether she can actually run that fast (efficacy belief). Similarly, a woman may believe that karate self-defense techniques will deter assault, but may doubt her capability to be effectively aggressive against a powerful assailant. Although behavior is best predicted by considering both outcome and self-efficacy beliefs, Bandura (1986) contends that when people's self-efficacy beliefs are controlled for, this accounts for much of the variance in the kinds of outcomes people expect. Thus, self-efficacy beliefs predict performance much better than expected outcomes.

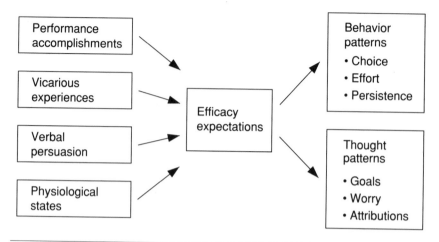

Figure 1. Relationship between major sources of efficacy information, efficacy expectations, and behavior and thought patterns as predicted by Bandura's theory. *Note.* From Feltz, D.L., "Self-Confidence and Sports Performance." In Pandolf, K.B. (Ed.), *Exercise and Sport Sciences Reviews* (Vol. 16). Copyright © 1988 American College of Sports Medicine. Adapted with permission of Macmillan Publishing Company.

In terms of measuring self-efficacy, Bandura (1977a) advocates a microanalytic approach for testing propositions about the origins and functions of perceived self-efficacy (see McAuley, this volume). This requires a detailed assessment of the level, strength, and generality of perceived self-efficacy. According to Bandura (1986), this method permits a microanalysis of the degree of congruence between self-efficacy and action at the level of individual tasks.

Self-Efficacy in Sport and Physical Activity

There have been over two dozen studies conducted on the topic of self-efficacy in sport and physical activity since Bandura's article was published in 1977(a). Much of this research has focused on examining the effect of various treatment methods for increasing self-efficacy beliefs and sport performance, and on examining the relationship between self-efficacy and performance. These studies have typically based various treatment techniques on one or more of the four major sources of efficacy information outlined by Bandura (1977a). This research is described under each of these sources of information.

Research Based on Enactive Efficacy Information

As stated previously, performance accomplishments provide the most dependable source of information upon which to base self-efficacy judgments because they are based on one's mastery experiences. The research in sport and physical activity has shown techniques based on performance accomplishments to be effective in enhancing both self-efficacy beliefs and performance (Brody, Hatfield, & Spalding, 1988; Feltz, Landers, & Raeder, 1979; Hogan & Santomier, 1984; McAuley, 1985a; Weinberg, Sinardi, & Jackson, 1982). Studies have also supported the superiority of performance-based information over other sources of efficacy information (Feltz et al., 1979; McAuley, 1985a; Weinberg et al., 1982). For instance, participant modeling, which involves a model's demonstration plus guided participation of the learner, has been shown to produce superior diving performance and stronger expectations of personal efficacy than either live modeling or videotaped modeling techniques (Feltz et al., 1979).

Research Based on Vicarious Efficacy Information

Information gained through vicarious experiences has been shown to influence perceived efficacy in muscular endurance performance (Feltz & Riessinger, 1990; Gould & Weiss, 1981; Weinberg, Gould, & Jackson, 1979; Weinberg, Gould, Yukelson, & Jackson, 1981), gymnastic performance (McAuley, 1985a), and balancing performance (Lirgg & Feltz, 1991). These techniques have included modeling (Gould & Weiss, 1981; Lirgg & Feltz, 1991; McAuley, 1985a) and social comparison (Feltz & Riessinger, 1990; Weinberg et al., 1979, 1981). Weinberg and his colleagues (1979) manipulated subjects' efficacy expectations about competing on a muscular endurance task by having them observe their competitor (a confederate), who either performed poorly on a related strength task and was said to have a knee injury (high self-efficacy), or who performed well and was said to be a varsity track athlete (low self-efficacy). Results indicated that the higher the induced self-efficacy, the greater the muscular endurance. Subjects who competed against an injured (perceived as relatively weaker) competitor endured longer than those who competed against a varsity athlete.

Modeling provides efficacy information through a comparative process between the observer and the model. Gould and Weiss (1981) demonstrated that a model who was similar to observers in gender and physical ability and who made positive efficacy statements enhanced observers' efficacy beliefs and endurance performance over a dissimilar model. McCullagh (1987) also found that subjects performed better after watching a model whom they perceived to be similar than after one they perceived as dissimilar, though she did not find corresponding differences in efficacy judgments. In addition, Lirgg and Feltz (1991) found that subjects decreased their efficacy judgments to a greater extent when they observed a model whom they perceived to be competent but who performed in an unskilled manner, compared to subjects who observed the model perform skillfully.

Research Based on Persuasory Efficacy Information

The role that cognitive strategies play in influencing performance in sport and physical activity has become a central focus in sport psychology research. Cognitive strategies are typically based on persuasion to influence self-efficacy, though most studies on this topic have not explored this influence. The few studies that have investigated persuasive techniques such as positive self-talk (Weinberg, 1985; Wilkes & Summers, 1984), imagery (Feltz & Riessinger, 1990; Wilkes & Summers, 1984), performance deception (Fitzsimmons, Landers, Thomas, & van der Mars, in press), and reinterpreting arousal (Yan Lan & Gill, 1984) as a source of efficacy information have reported mixed results. Weinberg (1985) found no effects on endurance performance with the use of dissociation and positive self-talk strategies, and Yan Lan and Gill (1984) found that providing subjects with bogus feedback and the suggestion that elevated arousal levels were indicative of good performance did not induce higher self-efficacy. On the other hand, Wilkes and Summers (1984) found confidence and arousal persuasions to influence strength performance, but efficacy-related cognitions did not seem to mediate the effect. Fitzsimmons and her colleagues (in press) found that false positive feedback increased self-efficacy judgments and future weight-lifting performance. In addition, Feltz and Riessinger (1990) found significant effects on endurance performance using mastery imagery with corresponding effects on self-efficacy.

One explanation for the equivocal findings in these studies may be the differences in the extent of persuasive influence of their techniques and the extent of their subjects' personal experience on the task. In the study by Weinberg (1985), subjects were not told that the cognitive strategy they were to employ would enhance their performance. There was no attempt at persuasion. In comparison, Wilkes and Summers (1984) instructed subjects to persuade themselves that they were confident, or to persuade themselves that they were charged up.

The extent of persuasive influence also depends on the believability of the persuasive information. Yan Lan and Gill (1984) tried to lead subjects to believe that they had the same heightened pattern of physiological arousal as good competitors. However, there was no manipulation check that the subjects believed this information. Fitzsimmons et al. (in press), on the other hand, used pilot data to insure that the deceptive feedback given was believable.

In addition, lack of effects may have been due to confounding with actual performance. All of these studies used multiple performance trials; therefore, subjects' perceptions of their performance experience may have overshadowed much of the influence that the treatment variable had on self-efficacy. This explanation was supported by Feltz and Riessinger (1990); we found that the significant effect for endurance performance and self-efficacy was short-lived after subjects experienced performance failure.

In our study (Feltz & Riessinger, 1990), treatment subjects were exposed to a positive-oriented imagery strategy after losing to a confederate on a related task, then they were told to perform two trials in back-to-back competitions in which the confederate always won by 10s. Self-efficacy was measured in two ways: comparative to the opponent (ego-oriented), and self-referenced (mastery-oriented). Although subjects experienced an increase in self-efficacy and comparative efficacy after receiving the imagery treatment, the experience of failure decreased both types of efficacy expectations to below pretreatment levels. Subjects were also asked an open-ended question regarding the information on which they based their efficacy beliefs in order to determine the information sources of those beliefs. Examination of subjects' sources of efficacy beliefs also demonstrates how difficult it is to change efficacy beliefs in the face of performance experience: Results revealed that the sources for the majority of subjects did not correspond to the imagery treatment to which the subjects had been exposed. Most subjects continued to base their beliefs on either their own experiences or comparisons to their competitor.

Research Based on Physiological States

Few sport studies have investigated the influence of physiological or emotional states on self-efficacy (Feltz, 1982, 1988a; Feltz & Mugno, 1983; Kavanagh & Hausfeld, 1986). In my work on diving, I found that although actual physiological arousal did not predict self-efficacy expectancies, perceived autonomic arousal was a significant predictor, but not as strong a predictor as previous performance accomplishments. Kavanagh and Hausfeld (1986), however, found that induced moods (happiness/sadness), as measured by self-report, did not alter efficacy expectations in any consistent manner using strength tasks.

Research on the Relationship Between Self-Efficacy and Performance

At least 17 studies have examined the relationship between self-efficacy and performance across a number of sport tasks and physical activities (Feltz, 1988b). These correlational results do not necessarily demonstrate a causal relationship between self-efficacy and performance, however.

A few studies in the sport and physical activity area have been conducted to investigate the causal relationships in Bandura's theory (Feltz, 1982, 1988a; Feltz & Mugno, 1983; McAuley, 1985a). Using path analysis techniques, these studies found that although self-efficacy was indeed a major determinant of performance, direct effects of treatment on performance (McAuley, 1985a) and direct effects of past performance on future performance (Feltz, 1982, 1988a; Feltz & Mugno, 1983) were also present.

For instance, in my studies on back-diving approach behavior (Feltz, 1982, 1988a; Feltz & Mugno, 1983), I examined the influence of self-efficacy as a common cognitive mechanism mediating approach/avoidance behavior. The self-efficacy path model predicted that self-efficacy would be the major predictor of back-diving behavior over the course of four trials compared to past accomplishments and physiological arousal. It also predicted a reciprocal relationship between self-efficacy and back-diving behavior. Results provided little support, however, for the complete network of relationships in the path model. Self-efficacy was the major predictor of behavior on the first of four diving attempts. After Trial 1, however, performance on a previous trial was the major predictor of performance on the next trial. Furthermore, although a reciprocal relationship between self-efficacy and diving behavior was evidenced, they were not equally reciprocal. As subjects progressed over trials, diving behavior became a stronger influence on self-efficacy than self-efficacy became on diving behavior. These results indicate that performance-based treatments affect behavior through other mechanisms as well as through perceived self-efficacy. Although the findings suggest that self-efficacy, as a common cognitive mechanism, cannot account for all behavior change in motor performance, self-efficacy has been found consistently to be an important and necessary cognitive mechanism in explaining behavior in physical activity and sport.

Research in Sport and Competitive Settings

Few studies have been conducted specifically to investigate the relationship of self-efficacy to performance with participants in actual sport situations (Barling & Abel, 1983; Feltz, Bandura, & Lirgg, 1989; Gayton, Matthews, & Burchstead, 1986; Lee, 1982; McAuley & Gill, 1983; Weiss, Wiese, & Klint, 1989) or with subjects in laboratory experiments under competitive conditions (Feltz & Riessinger, 1990; Weinberg et al., 1979). The field studies have shown that the higher the perceived self-efficacy, the better the sport performance. For example, Weiss and her colleagues (1989) found that the correlation between self-efficacy and performance was $r = .57$ for young gymnasts competing in a state gymnastics tournament. In addition, when self-efficacy is manipulated in a laboratory, research has supported the findings in the field (e.g., Weinberg et al., 1979, $r = .68$). Although ego-involved conceptions of ability were probably operating among subjects in these studies, efficacy expectations still significantly predicted performance. Most correlations were above $r = .50$.

Much of the research on self-efficacy beliefs in sport and competition has been confined to the individual level of performance. In most sports, however, individuals perform as members of teams rather than as independent competitors. Thus, many of the challenges and difficulties participants face reflect team problems requiring team efforts to produce successful performance.

Drawing from Bandura's (1986) concept of collective efficacy, perceived team efficacy should influence what participants choose to do as a team, how much effort they put into it, and what their staying power is when team efforts fail to produce results. The belief that one's team may be able to produce the required performance may be just as important to performance success as the belief in one's own capabilities.

Thus far, there has been only one research study to investigate the concept of team efficacy (Feltz et al., 1989). In this study, we were interested in comparing the relationship of self-efficacy to team performance and team efficacy to team performance with seven collegiate ice hockey teams across a 32-game season. Players completed questionnaires on perceived team rankings, team efficacy, and individual efficacy no more than 24 hours before each game. Efficacy items were developed in consultation with coaches, through a conceptual analysis of the most important subskills needed for successful performance in hockey. These items were tied closely to explicit indices of group performance as suggested by Bandura (1986).

Preliminary results suggested that, in hockey, team efficacy was only slightly more related to team performance than was individual efficacy. However, players' perceptions of their team's rank in the league were more predictive of team performance than team or individual efficacy. Perceived team ranking may be a better measure of perceived ability than our team efficacy measure because it may be less susceptible to response distortion.

Future Directions

Research on self-efficacy in sport and physical activity has been confined primarily to laboratory studies examining the effects of various methods used to increase the strength of self-efficacy beliefs, and to studies examining the relationship between self-efficacy and performance rather than the motivated behavior and thought patterns specified by the theory. This section describes the research needed in areas such as team efficacy; in motivational behavior (e.g., persistence); the resiliency of self-efficacy beliefs; in the generalizability of self-efficacy beliefs; and the relationships between self-efficacy beliefs and thought patterns.

Team Efficacy

More research is needed on efficacy beliefs as they relate to team performance in sport. Bandura (1989) has suggested that the relative predictiveness of team and individual efficacy may vary depending on the degree of task interdependence of the sport. Future research may determine whether players' perceptions of their team's ability are more relevant to team performance in sports that require high interdependence (e.g., hockey), than in sports that do not require high interdependent effort (e.g., swimming), or in teams that are high in cohesion versus low in cohesion. Similarly, there may be differences in the relevance of team efficacy in professional teams as compared to collegiate or high school teams. The confidence that a team has in a key player (e.g., a goal tender, a quarterback, or a pitcher), or in its coach may also have an important impact on team performance. In addition, coaches' perceived efficacy may have an important impact on team performance. Evidence that managerial self-efficacy affects organizational performance is especially relevant to this issue (Wood & Bandura, 1989). Furthermore, Bandura (1989) has also suggested that a performance slump, especially by a key player or leader on the team, could also influence the sense of efficacy of other players.

Influence of Self-Efficacy on Motivational Behavior

Much of the research on sport and physical activity has examined self-efficacy in relation to performance in terms of skill rather than in terms of the motivated behavior actually specified by the theory—such as persistence or mastery attempts, choice of activities or skills, and effort expended (see Nicholls, this volume; Roberts, this volume). These behaviors are certainly contributors to skillful performance and should be given more attention in the study of self-efficacy in sport and physical activity. Some of my work has examined choice behavior in terms of approach/avoidance to a motor task (Feltz, 1982, 1988a; Feltz & Mugno, 1983), and the research examining muscular endurance may be construed as persistence, although people are limited somewhat by their physical strength. More research is needed, however, to examine the nature of the relationship between self-efficacy and motivational behavior.

In addition, future research must control for people's incentives to participate and persist in an activity. As I mentioned earlier in this chapter, Bandura points out that self-efficacy is a major determinant only when proper incentives and the necessary skills are present. Most of the efficacy research in sport and physical activity has assumed the presence of proper incentives rather than assessing and controlling for this factor.

Resiliency of Self-Efficacy Beliefs

Bandura (1986, 1989) has suggested that people must have a resiliency of self-belief to sustain perseverant effort in the face of failure. Experience with setbacks and difficulties is needed to develop this robust sense of self-efficacy. How this robust sense of personal efficacy is developed, how different patterns of success and failure affect it, and what the perseverant effort that follows awaits further research (see also Nicholls, this volume). In addition, although according to Bandura (1986, 1989) an optimistic sense of personal efficacy is advantageous to continued effort and persistence, substantial overestimates of one's efficacy beliefs provide a dangerous basis for action (Baumeister,

1989). Research is needed to determine the optimal distortion necessary to foster the persistence needed for mastering various sport tasks.

When self-doubts set in after failure, some individuals recover from their perceived inefficacy more quickly than others (Bandura, 1989). Knowing why some people recover from self-doubts more quickly than others would also be valuable information for coaches and sport psychologists.

Generalization of Self-Efficacy Beliefs

In terms of the generality of self-efficacy, examination of the relative contributions of generality, level, and strength to overall performance would help determine where to focus intervention studies. For instance, is a moderate level of confidence in all aspects of golf more influential to performance than a strong sense of confidence in just driving and putting? Can self-efficacy about a physical skill generalize to nonmovement domains of functioning, such as psychological skills?

Only a couple of studies have examined the issue of generalizability of self-efficacy beliefs about physical tasks (Brody et al., 1988; Holloway, Beuter, & Duda, 1988). Brody and his colleagues found that self-efficacy beliefs that were enhanced regarding the skill of rappeling generalized to other high risk activities but not to a psychomotor task. Holloway and her colleagues found that the increases in self-efficacy of adolescent girls through strength training generalized to more general dispositional attitudes and confidence levels about their bodies and general self-esteem. Future research may help to determine if some tasks have more generalizability effects than others.

Relationships Between Self-Efficacy and Thought Patterns

As I stated early in this chapter, people's self-efficacy beliefs affect certain thought patterns as well as behavior. The self-efficacy research in sport and physical activity has given scant attention to this aspect of Bandura's theory. Two thought patterns of particular interest to the study of motivation in sport and physical activity are goal intentions, which operate on motivation anticipatorily through the exercise of forethought, and attributions, which operate on motivation through retrospective reasoning (Bandura, 1989).

Self-efficacy beliefs influence personal goal-setting and mediate the relationship between goal intentions and cognitive motivation (see Weinberg, this volume). Research outside of sport has shown that the stronger people's self-efficacy beliefs, the higher the goals they set for themselves, and the firmer their commitment is to them (Locke, Frederick, Lee, & Bobko, 1984). In addition, cognitive motivation based on goal intentions, according to Bandura (1989), is mediated by three types of self-reactive influences: (a) affective

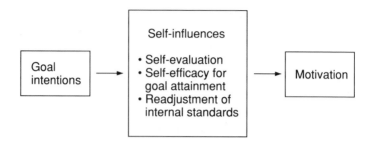

Figure 2. Schematic representation of Bandura's (1986) conception of cognitive motivation based on goal intentions. *Note*. From Feltz, D.L., "Self-Confidence and Sports Performance." In Pandolf, K.B. (Ed.), *Exercise and Sport Sciences Reviews* (Vol. 16). Copyright © 1988 American College of Sports Medicine. Adapted with permission of Macmillan Publishing Company.

self-evaluation (satisfaction/dissatisfaction), (b) perceived self-efficacy for goal attainment, and (c) adjustment of personal standards. Figure 2 schematically summarizes Bandura's conception of cognitive motivation based on goal intentions.

Bandura predicts that in the face of negative discrepancies between personal goals and attainments, those who have high self-efficacy beliefs will heighten their level of effort and persistence, whereas those who have self-doubts will quickly give up. The interrelationships among this self-evaluation component, self-efficacy beliefs, and internal standards readjustment could provide further insight into the goal-setting research within sport and physical activity (see also Duda, this volume; Nicholls, this volume; Roberts, this volume).

Bandura (1986, 1989) also suggests that self-efficacy beliefs bias causal attributions. Those who hold high self-beliefs of efficacy have been shown to attribute failure to lack of effort, whereas those who hold low self-beliefs of efficacy ascribe their failures to lack of ability (Collins, 1982). Studies using causal analyses also indicate that the effects of causal attributions on performance are mediated through self-efficacy beliefs (Schunk & Gunn, 1986; Schunk & Rice, 1986). Therefore, attributional and self-beliefs involve bidirectional causation.

Within the sport and physical activity literature, only one attempt has been made to examine specifically the complex relationships that Bandura (1986) proposes between efficacy cognitions and causal attributions. McAuley, Duncan, and McElroy (1989) found self-efficacy cognitions to be significantly related to perceptions of success on a competitive bicycle ergometer task, and to stable and controllable attributions. Their results suggest that efficacy cognitions play an important role in forming causal attributions independent of one's perception of the achievement outcome. Further research is required to address the efficacy-attribution linkage and to examine the reciprocal causation relationship proposed by Bandura.

Additional areas that deserve attention regarding the relationship between self-efficacy and thought patterns are how self-efficacy affects imagery, control over intrusive thoughts such as ruminations over mistakes, control over other distractions that affect attention and concentration, and control over the pain and discomfort that comes with many sport activities. Imagery, attention/concentration, and other psychological skills pertinent to sport performance are undoubtedly influenced by one's self-efficacy beliefs, but to what extent these beliefs influence these cognitive skills awaits further research.

Conclusion

Although Bandura's theory of self-efficacy is not without its criticisms (see Feltz, 1988b; Roberts, this volume), research on self-efficacy in numerous sport and physical activity settings has shown a consistent significant relationship between self-efficacy and performance. Contrary to Roberts's view (this volume), where self-efficacy has not been shown to be a reliable predictor of sport performance, it has probably had more to do with the way in which performance was measured (nonmicroanalytic) than with the conceptual soundness of self-efficacy theory. Further research will help to uncover the relationship between self-efficacy and other motivational behaviors in sport and physical activity. However, self-efficacy, if considered as a common mechanism mediating behavior, should not be expected to fully explain human behavior (Bandura, 1984), particularly the complex behavior of sport performance (Vealey, 1984).

Understanding
Exercise Behavior:
A Self-Efficacy Perspective

Edward McAuley

In the past two decades the United States Public Health Service (1979, 1980) has developed a preventive orientation in public health policies, promoting exercise and physical fitness as a behavioral orientation expected to reduce morbidity and mortality. Habitual physical activity is purported to influence positively a broad range of health conditions, both physiological and psychological. Physiological benefits reported have included reduced symptomology in osteoporotics and Type II diabetics (Siscovick, LaPorte, & Newman, 1985) and decreases in such coronary risk factors as obesity, hypertension, and elevated blood lipids (Bonnano & Lies, 1974; Cooper, 1968; Paffenberger, 1986). Although the evidence is less compelling, psychological benefits reported have typically included reductions in anxiety and depression as well as increases in percepts of psychological well-being (Dishman, 1982; Taylor, Sallis, & Needle, 1985).

Although the benefits of exercise in health terms appear to considerably outweigh the risks, the participation rates of North Americans in exercise and fitness regimens is not particularly impressive. Epidemiologists report that less than 20% of the 18- to 65-year-old population exercise at sufficient levels of intensity, frequency, and duration to accrue positive health and fitness benefits (Powell, Spain, Christenson, & Mollenkamp, 1986). An additional 40% of this age group report participation in some form of leisure activity, but at insufficiently taxing levels to benefit physiologically. The remaining 40% of the adult population lead a sedentary lifestyle. More importantly, many individuals who engage in organized fitness or exercise programs withdraw before any health benefits have been realized. Indeed, the statistics are well-documented regarding the alarming attrition rate in exercise programs, which approximates 50% within the first six months (Dishman, 1982; Morgan, 1977; Oldridge, 1982). Those who do adhere seldom comply with the prescribed exercise intensity, frequency, and duration necessary to achieve and to maintain health benefits. This failure to adhere to exercise regimens parallels the compliance dilemma in modern medicine, one of the most serious problems encountered in disease control and health promotion (Epstein & Cluss, 1984).

Although the benefits of habitual exercise and physical fitness are well-documented, the mechanisms that underlie successful adherence to exercise regimens are less well-understood. Early adherence research was largely atheoretical, and it is only recently that researchers have begun to employ theoretical frameworks to explain and comprehend the adherence/attrition phenomenon. Unfortunately, few of these models have resulted in consistent predictions, and many of the findings have been equivocal (Dishman, 1986). I direct interested readers to Dishman (1986, 1988) and Martin and Dubbert (1985) for extensive reviews of the exercise adherence literature.

Some theoretical models that have focused on self-perceptions as important mechanisms mediating exercise behavior have been employed to determine which factors underlie the pursuit or avoidance of exercise behavior. For example, Sonstroem (1976, 1978; Sonstroem & Morgan, 1989) has proposed that self-perceptions affect adoption of physical activity through the mediation of attraction to the activity, perceived capability with respect to physical activity, and the percepts of self-esteem developed as a function of these variables and participation. Although successful in predicting adoption of physical activity in some populations, Sonstroem's model has met with little success in the prediction of continued activity beyond the adoption stage. Recent developments by Sonstroem and Morgan (1989) have led to a more complex model of self-esteem and exercise that may be more successful in attempting to explain prolonged exercise behavior. However, this model remains to be fully tested.

Self-Efficacy Theory

One theoretical approach to understanding behavior that holds considerable promise for the exercise and physical activity domain is self-efficacy theory (Bandura, 1977a, 1986). Self-efficacy theory is a social cognitive approach to behavioral causation that posits behavior, physiological and cognitive factors, and environmental influences to operate as interacting determinants of each other (Bandura, 1986). Self-efficacy theory focuses on the role of self-referent thought on psychosocial functioning, and provides a common mechanism through which people demonstrate control over their own motivation and behavior. Self-efficacy cognitions are broadly defined as the beliefs that one has in one's capabilities to engage successfully in a course of action sufficient to satisfy the situational demand. Percepts of efficacy have been consistently shown to be important determinants of physical activity and sport behavior (see Feltz, 1988b, this volume), as well as social, clinical, and health-related behaviors (see O'Leary, 1985 for a review). For a more extensive overview of the underpinnings of self-efficacy theory, I refer the reader to the chapter by Deborah Feltz in this volume.

Measurement of Self-Efficacy

Bandura (1977a, 1986) has argued that the measurement of self-efficacy cognitions should be conducted in a microanalytic fashion by assessing efficacy along three dimensions: level, strength, and generality. *Level* of self-efficacy concerns the individual's expected performance attainment or the number of tasks that he or she can perform leading up to the target behavior. For example, indicating that one can walk or jog a quarter mile in three minutes, a half mile in six minutes, a mile in 12 minutes, and so forth, demonstrates successive levels of efficacy.

Strength of self-efficacy determines the certainty with which the individual expects to successfully attain each of the component tasks or levels. For example, one might feel very confident about being able to successfully complete half a mile in the requisite time period, but might feel considerably less confident about being able to complete the mile distance, especially in the early stages of exercise regimens for sedentary or untrained individuals. Strength of efficacy is customarily assessed on a 10- to 100-point scale at 10-point intervals. These intervals are representative of the percentage of confidence in the subject's belief that he or she can successfully complete each of the levels (Bandura, 1977a). Overall strength of self-efficacy is determined by summing the confidence ratings and dividing by the total number of items comprising the target behavior.

Generality refers to the number of domains in which individuals consider themselves efficacious. Thus, someone who has high self-efficacy with respect to exercise may feel quite comfortable about his or her capabilities in jogging, biking, calisthenics, and so forth. Some evidence exists in the sport and exercise literature to support this notion of self-efficacy cognitions generalizing across events (Brody, Hatfield, & Spalding, 1988; Holloway, Beuter, & Duda, 1988; McAuley, Courneya, & Lettunich, 1991). However, this particular aspect is not as well-substantiated as other tenets of self-efficacy theory.

Assessments of self-efficacy are generally developed with a view to tapping what Bandura (1986) terms the "generative capabilities" (p. 397) with respect to a task, rather than to singular acts that collectively constitute the task. In other words, if one is interested in assessing subjects' efficacy with respect to exercise frequency, it is necessary to determine their confidence in being able to exercise at the prescribed regimen in the face of potential barriers or obstacles to attendance. Such obstacles might include schedule conflicts, lack of apparent progress, or perceived lack of attention or support from the exercise leader. Simply asking, "How confident are you in attending exercise classes on a regular basis?" is insufficient because it fails to address the many components that are relevant to judging one's efficacy with respect to exercise frequency.

Somewhat in contrast to such recommendations, Ryckman, Robbins, Thornton, and Cantrell (1982) have developed the Physical Self-Efficacy Scale, a measure of the individual's perceived physical self-confidence. This scale consists of 22 items assessing two subscales: the individual's perceived physical ability, and the individual's physical self-presentation confidence. Together, the two subscales represent a measure of physical abilities (e.g., speed, strength, reaction time, and so forth). Although applied in a variety of physical tasks in a laboratory (Ryckman et al., 1982), marathon running (Gayton, Matthews, & Burchstead, 1986), and competitive gymnastics (McAuley & Gill, 1983), this global measure has been shown to be less predictive of skilled performance than of task-specific measures (McAuley & Gill, 1983). This theory supports Bandura's (1986) assertion that particularized, or task-specific, measures of self-efficacy are more predictive of behavior and offer more explanatory power than do more generalized measures. However, the perceived physical ability subscale has recently been shown to be predictive of measures of exercise intensity (ratings of perceived exertion) in adult beginning exercisers (McAuley, in press).

Although efficacy cognitions have been shown to mediate motor skill and sport performance (see Feltz, this volume; Roberts, this volume) it is only recently that researchers have begun to examine the potential value of efficacy cognitions in explaining and predicting exercise behaviors. However, a significant body of literature exists within the fields of health psychology and behavioral medicine to suggest that efficacy cognitions mediate preventive behaviors leading to improved health and functioning. For example, self-efficacy has been demonstrated to mediate attrition from a weight loss program and continued weight loss over a 6-month period (Bernier & Avard, 1986). Godding and Glasgow (1985) have shown perceptions of self-efficacy to predict smoking behaviors over time, and Beck and Lund (1981) revealed self-efficacy to be significantly related to preventive dental hygiene patterns.

Self-Efficacy and Exercise
as Primary and Secondary Prevention

Of central import in this review is the premise that self-efficacy is a conceptually valid theoretical model within which to understand and explain exercise behavior. In considering this relationship, there are a number of approaches that can be pursued. I propose to consider self-efficacy from both the antecedent and consequence perspectives. That is, how has or can self-efficacy influence such exercise behaviors as adoption, adherence, and maintenance of activity (antecedent), and how has or can exercise be employed to enhance individuals' perceptions of personal capabilities (consequence)? It goes without saying, that to demonstrate these relationships effectively, the construct of interest needs to be appropriately defined and accurately measured. As we shall see, this has not always been the case.

It has been previously indicated, here and elsewhere, that the failure of individuals to follow prescribed regimens, whether exercise or medical, constitutes a major health problem. Exercise can play two distinct roles as a health habit insomuch that it can be prescribed as either primary or secondary prevention modality. *Primary prevention* is concerned with taking the appropriate courses of action to assail risk factors before morbidity begins to develop. There are two approaches to primary prevention (Taylor, 1986). One is focused on alteration of problematic behaviors, whereas the second approach is designed to prevent detrimental health habits from ever developing. Although the second approach is preferable, few successful efforts, with respect to exercise, have been forthcoming—as evidenced by the large portion of the adult population identified as being sedentary or engaging in insufficient activity to accrue health benefits (Powell et al., 1986). Therefore, those studies reported with respect to primary prevention deal with the relationship between self-efficacy and exercise in populations (adults) who, for the most part, employ exercise as a preventive measure against the onset of possible disease.

Secondary prevention involves the adoption of or active engagement in preventive behaviors once morbidity or presence of disease is diagnosed as having developed. For example, individuals involved in cardiac rehabilitation embark on an exercise regimen in an effort to reduce the likelihood of a second episode of myocardial infarction or coronary artery disease. Exercise and physical activity as secondary prevention measures are discussed in terms of symptomatic populations such as sufferers of postmyocardial infarction, coronary artery disease, chronic obstructive pulmonary disease, diabetes, and chronic pain.

Self-Efficacy, Exercise, and Primary Prevention

The following sections are predominately designed to reflect some of the work that has been conducted in the exercise psychology field examining the consistency of self-efficacy as an influential variable over exercise behavior. To this end, the literature in this area will be reviewed from the perspectives of studies that focus upon (a) the adoption or adherence of exercise behavior as a function of self-efficacy, and (b) the role efficacy plays in aspects of exercise performance.

Adoption and Adherence

Self-efficacy theory predicts that highly self-efficacious individuals are more likely to adopt or engage in a greater number of like behaviors than are their counterparts whose personal efficacy has been impaired (Bandura, 1977a, 1982, 1986). Where exercise is concerned, those who perceive themselves to be more efficacious with respect to their physical capabilities are more likely to adopt and maintain a lifestyle in which exercise plays an important role. In a recent study of the behavioral epidemiology of physical activity, Sallis, Haskell, Fortmann, Vranizan, Taylor, and Solomon (1986) examined variables considered to be predictors of adoption and maintenance of physical activity in a large community sample of adults. This direction enables one to understand better the etiology of exercise behavior. They reported different patterns of behavior for predicting the adoption and maintenance of exercise across varying degrees of activity intensity. Self-efficacy was a significant predictor of adopting vigorous exercise and maintaining moderate activity, as well as predicting exercise change activity within both categories of activity. Such findings are in accord with Bandura's (1986) theoretical approach that suggests that as the desired behavior becomes more difficult, self-efficacy plays a more important role.

Several studies exist that document the mediational role played by perceived efficacy in subjects' adhering to prescribed exercise programs and maintaining activity after program termination. Although not without their individual flaws, the studies do provide some support for the contention that self-efficacy mediates exercise behavior. Desharnais, Bouillon, and Godin (1986) attempted to predict adherence to an 11-week adult exercise program that employed the self-efficacy framework. As compared to outcome expectations assessed as the product of the extent to which exercise would result in certain beneficial outcomes and in value placed on those outcomes, self-efficacy was shown to be more capable of discriminating between subjects classified as adherers and those classified as dropouts. Although interesting, the findings are confounded by a number of factors. First, the classification of subjects based on the author's attendance criteria ignores the obvious possibility that subjects may be exercising even though they are not attending class (Dishman, 1986). Second, there is some concern with the measurement of self-efficacy by a one-item question tapping whether or not the subjects believed they were capable of attending the complete program. Efficacy assessments should be conducted in terms of one's generative capabilities. Consequently, assessing whether one could adhere in the face of increasingly difficult barriers to participation, or assessing whether one could continue to work out vigorously for succeeding periods of time may both be more appropriate methods for the microanalysis of the construct of interest. Similar problems exist with a study conducted by Corbin, Laurie, Gruger, and Smiley (1984) that employed a single-item measure of general self-confidence in sport and physical activity to examine the effects of vicarious information influencing confidence, commitment, and involvement in physical activity. If efficacy cognitions are to be assessed, they must be measured accurately!

McAuley (1990a) and McAuley and Jacobson (1990) have recently employed the self-efficacy model to determine its role in the exercise behavior of college females and sedentary adult women, respectively. McAuley (1990a) utilized structural equation modeling to examine the relationships among self-efficacy, intention to engage in other aerobic activity, and exercise behavior during and following an aerobic dance program. Although self-efficacy prior to the program influenced attendance and perceptions of performance, only the latter variable and intention to engage in other activity predicted self-efficacy at the end of the program. These are theoretically relevant relationships with efficacy influencing the behavior in question, and past performance information influencing subsequent percepts of personal capabilities. Finally, efficacy expectations at the end of the program successfully predicted a composite index of exercise behavior (self-reported frequency and intensity of exercise) at three-month postprogram termination. These findings are encouraging in terms of identifying efficacy as an active ingredient in the maintenance of exercise behavior. However, future studies might contribute further by venturing beyond the self-report nature of exercise behavior and beyond reliance on attendance as the sole indicants of activity. More rigorous quantification of adherence is called for (Dishman, 1988; Epstein & Perkins, 1988). The employment of alternative behavioral measures, assessment of intensity through instructor evaluation or physiological measurement, and utilization of perceptual measures of exercise behavior such as ratings of perceived exertion are all potential indices of exercise behavior that would present a more complete representation of exactly what the individual is doing during exercise.

McAuley and Jacobson (1990) studied the exercise behavior of 58 middle-aged sedentary females enrolled in a low-impact aerobic exercise program. Our subjects were categorized as good or poor attenders and good or poor exercisers based on median splits of their attendance records and daily logs of all aerobic activity, respectively. Subsequent analyses compared these groups on biometric, self-efficacy, and postprogram perception measures. Multivariate analyses revealed good attenders to be significantly lighter and to lose weight over the course of the program, whereas poor attenders were heavier and actually gained weight during the program. There were no significant multivariate differences between the attendance groups on pre- and postprogram efficacy measures, although the means were in the theoretically proposed direction. However, subjects classified as good overall exercise participants on the basis of their exercise logs perceived themselves to be significantly more capable of exercising in the face of barriers to exercise following program participation than did poor participants. As expected, good attenders perceived their condition to have improved, enjoyed the program more, perceived their performance as more successful, and achieved their personal exercise goals more so than poor attenders at postprogram evaluation. Finally, multiple regression analyses revealed the modest but significant ability of self-efficacy to predict attendance to the program and exercise behavior at two-month follow-up.

Our (McAuley & Jacobson, 1990) findings support self-efficacy theory but must be interpreted with caution. The exercise program only lasted for two months, thus it is difficult to gauge the true effects of self-efficacy. Moreover, the measures of exercise behavior (attendance, self-report) are limiting. However, this study did attempt to overcome the problem, inherent in many studies, of nonattendance being considered synonymous with nonactivity by having participants keep daily logs of any aerobic activity of greater than 15-minute duration.

McAuley (in press) examined further the utility of self-efficacy in predicting exercise behavior in a prospective study of sedentary, middle-aged males and females over a 5-month period. Self-efficacy was able to predict exercise frequency and intensity at 3 months but past exercise behavior was the best predictor of exercise behavior at 5 months. Such findings suggest that the determinants of exercise participation differ with the respect to the stage of exercise being studied. For example, in the early adoption and adaptation stages of exercise, a strong sense of belief in one's capabilities to continue exercising appears important. However, when the environment places less demand on one's resources, that is, as one becomes accustomed to exercising, then efficacy cognitions are less important.

Two recent studies by Dzewaltowski, (1989; Dzewaltowski, Noble, & Shaw, 1990), report data that compare the relative merits of self-efficacy theory and attitudinal models of behavior change, specifically, the theory of reasoned action (Fishbein & Ajzen, 1974) and Ajzen's (1985) theory of planned behavior, in explaining physical activity behaviors in college undergraduates. In both studies, self-efficacy was a significant predictor of exercise behavior whereas the reasoned action and planned behavior models failed to add any further unique variance.

Long and Haney (1988) have examined the effects of self-efficacy on adherence to a jogging program in a community sample of males and females. These researchers were unable to demonstrate any significant relationship between self-efficacy and adherence. Although this finding appears at odds with the other results reported and with self-efficacy predictions, it can easily be explained by their measurement of self-efficacy. Long and Haney (1988) employed Coppel's (1982) trait measure of general self-efficacy, which should not be a particularly good predictor of such a specific behavior as jogging. Once again, the essence of appropriate efficacy measurement is the microanalytic assessment of generative capabilities rather than general tendencies (Bandura, 1977a, 1986; McAuley, 1990b; McAuley & Gill, 1983).

Long (1984, 1985) has also examined the ability of stress inoculation training (Meichenbaum, 1977) and aerobic exercise to reduce stress and enhance self-efficacy. At the end of the program and at a 15-month follow-up, these treatment modalities were found to have increased self-efficacy significantly but not differentially. Once again, however, Long's measurement of efficacy cognitions was suspect; it employed the Self-Efficacy Scale (Sherer, Maddux, Mercandante, Prentice-Dunn, Jacobs, & Rogers, 1982), a measure of general self-efficacy. Therefore, it is not surprising that the two treatment modes, both designed to reduce stress, had similar effects on perceptions of general self-efficacy.

Godin and Shephard (1985) employed the Physical Self-Efficacy Scale (Ryckman et al., 1982) to examine gender and age differences in exercise perceptions among 45- to 75-year-olds. Although there were no age differences, males were reported generally to be more physically self-efficacious and to have higher perceived physical ability than females. These differences were explained from a cultural bias perspective rather than a biological one, with the authors arguing that women of this age group were simply not encouraged to exercise earlier in their lives. Once more, these results say something about a very general relationship between self-efficacy and exercise from a gender perspective but fail to focus on the microanalytic approach that self-efficacy theory stipulates as necessary for its postulates to be tenable.

The studies documented in this section provide some support for the mediational role played by the perceptions of personal efficacy in predicting the adoption of, and adherence to, exercise regimens. In spite of the diverse populations studied, the often inadequate operational definition of exercise behavior, and the varied methods of assessing self-efficacy expectations, the relationship between personal convictions of capability and the exercise of personal agency with respect to this domain of functioning remains remarkably consistent. Although the relationship is modest, if, through appropriate interventions, fitness and exercise leaders can enhance efficacy cognitions and thereby influence adherence to exercise regimens, then self-efficacy should be considered a vital component in the constellation of elements that influence this complex behavior.

Effects of Efficacy on Exercise Performance

Although a host of studies examine the role that self-efficacy has played in the performance of motor skills (see Feltz, this volume), relatively few studies exist that report how parameters associated with exercise performance (e.g., effort, work output, etc.) employ asymptomatic populations. The few that have been reported present a similarly consistent picture of the dependent variables related to exercise being positively influenced by self-efficacious demeanors.

In an important study examining the relationships among goals, self-efficacy, and self-evaluation, Bandura and Cervone (1983) employed a bicycle ergometer task to assess effort, the dependent variable in the study. At issue here was the tenet of self-efficacy theory that posits goal systems to be sources of motivation only in the presence of self-efficacy and self-evaluative mechanisms. The latter systems are presumed to be launched into operation through cognitive comparison (Bandura, 1982). To test this postulate, subjects were assigned to ergometer performance with either goals plus performance feedback, goals alone, feedback alone, or with no goals or feedback conditions. Consistent with predictions, goals affected performance only when high dissatisfaction with performance was combined with high self-efficaciousness for goal attainment resulting in more vigorous effort. The effects that efficacy cognitions have on exercise behavior through the mediation of goal-setting have gone largely unexplored. Interestingly, one of the probable mechanisms that is in effect in the dynamic process of exercise is the goal mechanism. How efficacy information impacts exercise directly and indirectly through goals needs further exploration. Recent work by Bandura and Wood (1989) suggests these two effects upon behavior to be quite considerable.

McAuley, Duncan, Wraith, and Lettunich (1991) recently assessed efficacy expectations regarding exercise behaviors (walking, biking, sit-ups) in a sample of middle-aged (45 to 65 years) adults prior to and following submaximal bicycle ergometer work. Efficacy cognitions were raised significantly from pre- to posttesting for all three aspects of exercise behavior; this evidences support for self-efficacy theory's contention that positive past performance information leads to enhanced personal efficacy. Self-efficacy was also significantly correlated with a number of physiological work indices. In all measures of efficacy there were significant gender differences, with males evidencing stronger perceptions of physical capabilities. However, analyses of the change in efficacy over time were nonsignificant with females raising their perceptions proportionately as much as males. Indeed, after a 20 week training period females were as efficacious as males in all domains. Such findings have implications for how expectations of personal efficacy must be considered in terms of facilitating continued exercise behavior. That is, if exercise leaders consider males and females to be equally confident in their exertion capabilities, the likelihood of increasing recidivism in females may be fostered by placing unrealistic demands on the exerciser at an early stage. Once early progress is made and initial barriers are overcome, efficacy cognitions should be sufficiently robust to cope with incremental physical demand.

Holloway, Beuter, and Duda (1988) have reported that participation in a strength training program resulted in significant changes in self-efficacy over time for both specific efficacy related to lifting and to more general behaviors such as self-defense and ability to withstand confrontations. Although hampered by some methodological limitations, this study provides an exciting point of departure for future research examining the generalizability of certain capabilities to other settings and the mediating role played by self-efficacy.

There is some evidence, therefore, to suggest that various aspects of exercise behavior, that is, adoption, adherence, effort, and persistence, are influenced by the mediation of self-efficacy in normal (asymptomatic) populations. These relationships are consistent but, admittedly, modest. There is a need to determine under which conditions and in concert with which other cognitive, environmental, and physiological parameters self-efficacy is most potent. For example, it has been suggested that goal orientations (Duda, this volume) and the motivational climate (Ames, this volume) may have important implications for understanding, explaining, and predicting exercise and sport behavior. How or if these approaches parallel or interact with self-efficacy theory necessitates exploration (see Roberts, this volume). Furthermore, at this point we lack any evidence to suggest that exercise-related efficacy-enhancing interventions can boost exercise participation and reduce attrition. If such empirical evidence can be made manifest, then optimizing self-efficacy should become one of the focal points of every exercise program.

Efficacy Cognitions and Exercise as Secondary Prevention

The emphasis of the following sections is on the role played by percepts of personal efficacy in exercise behavior prescribed for diseased populations. For many maladies of the human condition, and particularly in cardiac rehabilitation, exercise within prescribed ranges is considered to have beneficial effects. A growing body of literature in health psychology offers considerable support for the theoretical postulate that one's perceptions of physical capabilities are more accurate predictors of subsequent physiological functioning and adherence to treatment (in this case exercise) regimens than are actual physical capabilities. I will now present some of the empirical support for this statement.

Self-Efficacy, Exercise, and Cardiovascular Disease

Researchers at the Stanford Cardiac Rehabilitation Program initiated a series of studies that examined the role played by self-perceptions in recovery from acute myocardial infarction (MI). Recognizing the importance of restoring perceived physical efficacy following a heart attack, these researchers sought to establish a link between efficacy and various physical activities during stages of coronary artery disease (CAD) and cardiac rehabilitation.

Ewart and his associates (Ewart, Stewart, Gillilan, & Kelemen, 1986; Ewart, Stewart, Gillilan, Kelemen, Valenti et al., 1986; Ewart, Taylor, Reese, &

DeBusk, 1983; Taylor, Bandura, Ewart, Miller, & DeBusk, 1985) present some compelling data underscoring the role played by psychosocial variables in the adoption of, adherence to, and performance of exercise-related activities in this population. The initial study in the series (Ewart et al., 1983) employed a variety of self-efficacy scales assessing such behaviors as walking, jogging, lifting, static exertion, stair climbing, and sexual activity in early acute post-myocardial infarction patients. Testing the basic tenets of self-efficacy theory, Ewart et al. were able to establish that self-efficacy was able to predict tread-mill performance with posttest efficacy cognitions increasing as a function of that performance. Supporting the specificity notion of self-efficacy theory (Bandura, 1977a, 1986), it was established that these relationships were stronger for the measures that more closely approximated dynamic large muscle group activity (i.e., walking, jogging, stairs) than for dissimilar tasks (sexual activity, static effort, lifting). More importantly, the post-treadmill cognitions were better predictors of subsequent home activity than was actual treadmill performance, suggesting that what one thinks one is capable of is more important than one's actual physical capabilities (Bandura, 1986).

The recovery period associated with such a traumatic event as myocardial infarction is not solely a physiological process. Rather, it is a social process in which various agents in the diseased individual's social environment play important roles in terms of provision of supportive behaviors contributing to the eventual healing of the heart and the resumption of normal activity (Bandura, 1986). The role played by these various social support agents can be positive, wherein they offer encouragement to comply with the prescribed treatment regimen. Conversely, they can be negative, insomuch that the social support advocates or encourages inactivity and an overly protective lifestyle.

Exploring these notions, Taylor, Bandura, et al. (1985) used the exercise setting as a vehicle to enhance patient and spousal confidence in the cardiac capabilities of postmyocardial infarction patients. Patients' spouses (all female) were assigned to one of three groups: (a) waiting outside the laboratory during graded exercise testing, (b) observing their husbands participate in the graded exercise testing, and (c) actually participating in the exercise testing for three minutes at a similar peak workload to that attained by their husbands. Self-efficacy assessments of general physical efficacy and cardiac efficacy were collected from both the patients and their spouses prior to and after testing. Following testing, each couple met with a cardiologist who counseled them with respect to interpretation of the test results. Subjects were then assigned, by a nurse, to a home physical activity regimen.

Statistical analyses indicated complete divergence prior to testing between patients' and spouses' perceptions of what the patient was capable. Uniformly, wives perceived their husbands to be less physically capable and to have deficient cardiac capacity. Treadmill testing significantly increased the patients' posttest perceptions of their cardiac efficacy, but only the wives who actually participated in the treadmill testing evidenced significant increases in their perceptions of their husbands' physical and cardiac efficacy. Moreover, the change in perceived efficacy also influenced the persuasiveness of the medical counseling following exercise testing. Thus, once more we have confirmatory support for the ability of past performance accomplishments to positively influence percepts of personal agency.

Subsequent correlational analyses indicated that perceptions of a robust heart were associated with higher treadmill workloads which, in turn, enhanced posttest efficacy. Of greater consequence, however, was the finding that a composite index of the patients' cardiac capabilities combining patients' and wives' perceptions proved to be the best predictor of subsequent treadmill performance at 11 and 26 weeks posttesting.

Although correlational in nature, these findings emerge as important markers with respect to how cognitive interpretations of personal competencies are related to physical activity in secondary prevention environments. Of equal importance is the effect that differential types of information can have on those individuals who play crucial roles in cardiac rehabilitation from the social support perspective, namely the spouse. Although, Taylor and his colleagues do not interpret their findings from the perspective of social support theory (e.g., Cohen & Syme, 1985; Sarason & Sarason, 1985), the ties between social support, self-efficacy, and behavior appear clear. These data would suggest that social support, rather than having a direct effect on health behavior, acts in an indirect manner through the mediation of self-efficacy. Duncan (1989; Duncan & McAuley, 1991) has recently reported such a sequence of relations. However, more comprehensive testing of this relationship is required. Equally important is the necessity of determining whether there are specific aspects of social support, on the part of the spouses, that have a greater impact upon efficacy and subsequent recovery.

The remaining two studies in the series explore the mediation of efficacy cognitions in gains of strength in patients with CAD (Ewart, Stewart, Gillilan, & Kelemen, 1986), and the employment of self-efficacy to predict noncompliance to prescribed exercise (Ewart, Stewart, Gillilan, Kelemen, Valenti, et al., 1986). In the strength gains study, more evidence is presented to support the concept that self-efficacy assessments are best conducted in terms of specificity to the task of interest. Efficacy for lifting was highly correlated with arm strength but unrelated to endurance. Baseline efficacy was also a significant predictor of posttraining strength when pretraining strength was statistically controlled. These results offer some conservative support for self-efficacy theory but were unable to demonstrate as pronounced efficacy changes as those reported in the post-MI patients.

Although exercise is often advised for patients suffering from CAD, it is recommended within a prescribed range. That is, over or underexertion can have deleterious health effects. Consequently, compliance to prescribed regimens is of paramount importance. Ewart, Stewart, Gillilan, Kelemen, Valenti, et al. (1986) reported the utility of self-efficacy and the patients' ability to monitor heart rate in the prediction of noncompliant (over or underexertion) exercise behavior. Patients were randomly assigned to either jogging or circuit weight training with noncompliant behavior defined as the number of minutes they exercised above or below their prescribed range during 20-minute exercise sessions. Subjects were also defined as under or overachievers if they exercised for 10 minutes under or over their minimum or maximum recommended heart rates respectively, when randomly assessed by electrocardiography.

Self-efficacy proved to be a more potent predictor of adherence to prescribed exercise regimens than did previous treadmill performance or other psychological measures. Low and medium self-efficacious patients tended to underachieve (exercise below minimum target heart rate), whereas highly efficacious individuals tended to overachieve (exercised above). Moreover, patients who overestimated their heart rate tended to undercomply in terms of the intensity of their prescription. That noncompliance was related more to self-perceived capabilities than to actual physical capabilities suggests that self-efficacy may influence activity levels across incremental phases of health improvement (Ewart, Stewart, Gillilan, Kelemen, Valenti, et al., 1986).

This group of studies represents an important contribution to our understanding of how self-perceptions may play instrumental roles in health regimens, specifically exercise and physical activity, that are prescribed for individuals following myocardial infarction. More specifically, as with the asymptomatic populations previously discussed, efficacy perceptions appear to influence not only physical activity performance but also the more vital component of adherence. Furthermore, it appears that efficacy cognitions may be influenced by, and mediate the effect of, socially supportive influences thought to directly effect behaviors (Duncan, 1989). What the direct and indirect paths and relationships of such variables are needs to determined. As previously suggested, more sophisticated testing of these relationships, their direction, and which effects mediate exercise behavior needs to be further established.

Self-Efficacy, Exercise, and Other Disease States

As well as recovery from or secondary prevention of cardiovascular disease, there remain a number of other diseases in which exercise is often prescribed as part of the treatment; but, it is invariably difficult for the diseased individual to adopt, adhere to, and maintain such a regimen.

Chronic Obstructive Pulmonary Disease (COPD).   Sufferers of COPD have been reported to garner considerable relief from symptomology as a function of maintaining and adopting physical activity; however, the poor adherence rates in this population are often the result of physical activity incurring the onset of shortness of breath, wheezing, and fatigue (Kaplan, Atkins, & Reinsch, 1984).

Atkins, Kaplan, Timms, Reinsch, and Lofback (1984), following the recommendations of Martin and Dubbert (1982a), employed behavior modification (Kazdin, 1981), cognitive modification (Ellis, 1962), and cognitive behavior modification (Meichenbaum, 1977) in an attempt to increase adherence to exercise and to influence self-efficacy in patients with COPD. A combination of the three treatment groups produced greater adherence than did attention and no-treatment control groups to a walking program; cognitive behavior modification provided the greatest levels of adherence. The treatment conditions also served to influence changes in self-efficacy over the course of the program.

Whether such cognitions as self-efficacy and health locus of control (Wallston, Wallston, & DeVallis, 1978) mediated exercise compliance was reported by Kaplan, Atkins, and Reinsch (1984). Efficacy cognitions for various aspects of exercise in COPD patients were correlated positively with exercise tolerance at three months and self-reported compliance, whereas health locus of control was not. However, correlations between exercise behavior and efficacy were significant for subjects with an internal health locus of control, but not for externals. Although this might suggest that efficacy expectations may be stronger for those who hold a generalized belief that there is a relationship between health and behavior, Sallis, Priski, Grossman, Patterson, and Nader (1988) were unable to substantiate such a claim in a recent study of undergraduate students.

Diabetes Mellitus.   Sufferers of diabetes mellitus are often prescribed exercise and frequently have problems adhering to such activity. Crabtree (1987) explored the possibility that self-efficacy might influence such behaviors as general self-care, medication self-care, and exercise behavior in diabetes patients. With respect to the latter, only self-efficacy was a predictor among other psychosocial and demographic variables assessed, and it accounted for approximately 35% of the explained variance in exercise. However, these results should be viewed cautiously given that the measurement of self-efficacy really did not assess confidence in patients' ability to carry out self-care behaviors. Actually, it is difficult in Crabtree's scale to differentiate between self-care behaviors and self-efficacy for these behaviors.

Chronic Pain.   Finally, Dulce, Crocker, Moletterie, and Doleys (1986) detailed the role self-efficacy played in predicting treatment outcomes in patients suffering from chronic pain. Self-efficacy was consistently shown to be related to follow-up measures of exercise behaviors, supporting Bandura's (1977a, 1986) basic contention that self-efficacious individuals are able to persevere with activities in the face of aversive or stressful stimuli and Litt's (1988) findings that self-efficacy expectations mediate pain control.

Summary

As has been verified thus far, there is considerable documentation to support the proposed theoretical relationship between self-efficacy and miscellaneous aspects of exercise behavior in the prevention of secondary onset and recovery from diseased conditions. However, similar to the primary prevention literature, the findings must be considered with some caution. In many cases, the samples studied are restrictive with respect to size, race, and sampling techniques. As will be subsequently suggested, the most insightful and revealing applications of self-efficacy theory might be from the perspective of employing it to link, understand, and embellish other theoretical lines of thinking associated with exercise as a causal entity in health behavior.

Future Applications of Self-Efficacy Theory to Exercise Behavior

In order to lead a healthy lifestyle, it is necessary to take control of one's health habits and to counteract negative environmental conditions that have deleterious influences on the physical condition. As many of us realize, our health lies largely within our own grasp (Bandura, 1986). The adoption and maintenance of a physically active lifestlye has been identified as a possible mechanism to combat the onset and ravages of certain diseases, especially those of a cardiovascular nature. Although the vast majority of those who are neither incapacitated nor infirm are capable of engaging in physical activity or exercise programs from which health benefits might be accrued, they do not. This is not because those individuals do not possess the skills or because the activity is so physiologically demanding that it becomes an improbable task.

For effective behavior change to take place, one must optimally exercise self-regulatory behavior. Beliefs in one's capabilities to exercise control over one's self and one's environment represent one of the most potent mechanisms of human agency (Bandura, 1986). The difference between successfully adopting and maintaining an exercise regimen long enough to cause physiological and possibly psychological change, and failing to regularly exercise or discontinuing entirely may well lie in the strengths of one's efficacy cognitions. High self-efficacy often results in prolonged effort and perseverance, prerequisites to successful outcomes in the face of challenging environments.

Evidence was presented earlier to suggest that the relationship between exercise behavior and percepts of efficacy is tenable. Efficacy has been demonstrated to play a role in the adoption of (Sallis et al., 1986) and adherence to (McAuley, 1990a, 1991; McAuley & Jacobson, 1990) exercise regimens in asymptomatic adults. In the area of secondary prevention, Ewart and his colleagues (Ewart, Taylor, Reese, & DeBusk, 1983; Ewart, Stewart, Gillilan, & Kelemen, 1986; Ewart, Stewart, Gillilan, Kelemen, Valenti, et al., 1986; Taylor, Bandura, Ewart, Miller, & DeBusk, 1985) present some compelling data to underscore the role played by self-efficacy in the exercise behaviors of patients suffering from cardiovascular disease. However, in the majority of the cases reported, the strength of the association is modest. This is not to undermine the potentially important role that self-efficacy can play in exercise and physical activity behaviors. Rather it serves to lead us into a discussion of (a) how we might better test the self-efficacy model in this domain and (b) how we might identify other models that have been linked to exercise but may, in actuality, be driven by the mediation of the self-efficacy construct.

More Effective Tests for the Self-Efficacy Model

It appears that the relationship between efficacy and exercise is strongest when there are considerable barriers, real or perceived, to be successfully surmounted. Resumption of activity following myocardial infarction (Taylor, Bandura, et al., 1985), when having to endure the chronic pain of fibrositis (Klug, McAuley, & Clark, 1990), or when suffering from an incurable state such as chronic obstructive pulmonary disease (Kaplan et al., 1984) forms a real barrier. In such instances, a staunch sense of personal agency is required to engage successfully in activity, and the relationship between self-efficacy and behavior may well be more resilient and robust. However, engaging in an activity class as an undergraduate student may be more forcefully driven by other mechanisms such as mandatory attendance (absenteeism results in a failing grade), convenience (the gymnasium is across the road from the dormitory room), or social reasons (friends participate together). In order to determine whether self-efficacy is an active mediating variable in the process of exercise behavior, it makes some fundamental sense to examine the construct in the context of the environments or activities that are meaningful, present challenge, and require substantial effort on the part of the participant to be successful. I refer the reader to Nicholls, this volume, and Roberts, this volume, for further discussion of the importance of considering the significance of the environments or activities in question.

This brings us to how one should operationalize and measure self-efficacy and exercise behavior. From the perspective of efficacy, it is of paramount importance to employ assessment strategies composed of referents that adequately approximate the behavior in question. It would be expected that some degree of association would be present between a general measure of physical efficacy and some exercise criterion. However, the predictive magnitude of self-efficacy is likely to be considerably amplified if the measure in question more closely resembles the types of subskills required to successfully execute the behavior. That is, if the intensity of activity, the convenience, time management, and social or work obligations are likely to influence one's involvement in exercise, then they should be assessed.

Recent efforts by Sallis and his colleagues (Sallis et al., 1986) have undertaken the problem of developing self-efficacy scales for diet and exercise behaviors. Their exercise scale is composed of two factors labeled *resisting relapse*, which identifies items reflecting the ability to stick with or adhere to exercise, and *making time for exercise*, which is self-explanatory. Although these efforts are a more representative and accurate method of assessing the construct than general measures (e.g., Ryckman et al., 1982; Sherer et al., 1982), it should be remembered that self-efficacy, like exercise, is a dynamic process that is continually adjusted as a function of behavioral, cognitive, and environmental information (see also Roberts, this volume). It is therefore necessary to complete multiple assessments of self-efficacy over time that may better reflect different aspects of the behavior in question. For example, in the early stages of exercise adoption, muscle soreness, stiffness, and minor injury may prove to be irritants or barriers of sufficient magnitude to mediate attrition. However, if one is able to successfully surmount these barriers, they become less salient as the body physiologically adapts to training and endurance, and musculature becomes more fully developed. At this point, other barriers such as work and family commitments may become more prominent, and being sufficiently efficacious to overcome *these* barriers rather than others may prove to be the cognition of importance at that time.

Traditionally, efficacy measures have been composed of hierarchical items reflecting the generative subskills necessary to execute the behavior in question. This approach is not always appropriate, and in the case of exercise it may prove difficult to identify hierarchies, especially when some items may take on more or less importance at different times. One approach to the dilemma is to tap the subjects' phenomenology in ascertaining what aspects of exercise represent adoption, adherence, and maintenance of activity (McAuley, 1990b; Meichenbaum & Turk, 1987). In essence, this demands an attributional approach to the construction of the measures, involving the subject as an active agent in the process, and tapping cognitions that are more accurate and representative of the behavior in question (McAuley & Duncan, 1990).

McAuley, Poag, Gleason, and Wraith (1990) have taken such an attributional approach recently in an attempt to better understand an individual's reasons for attrition from exercise programs. Moreover, McAuley (in press) has employed this method to determine items that reflect barriers to exercise in sedentary adult populations.

Interaction of Other Models and Self-Efficacy

This section suggests that some other models of behavior change that might be useful in understanding exercise have at their foundations self-referent thought (McAuley, 1990a). The remainder of this section is devoted to exploring some of those other systems, their theoretical underpinnings, and of more importance, how these systems may be studied from the perspective of their interaction with self-efficacy.

Lest one be accused of theoretical myopia, let it be stated that other models might be equally well-suited, may interact with, or better explain the process of exercise behavior. Indeed, the authors of other chapters in this volume ably advocate a variety of theoretical approaches, which Roberts (see this volume) suggests may represent convergent aspects of a more general theory. To some extent this is what Bandura (1986) proposes in his social cognitive framework.

Positive Reinforcement

Positive reinforcement, often in the form of goal-setting and self-monitoring procedures, is considered to be an important influence on exercise behavior (Knapp, 1988; see also Weinberg, this volume, for a review of the goal-setting research in sport). The basic premise of goal-setting theory is that cognitions serve to regulate purposive behavior (Locke, 1968). Some evidence exists to suggest that goal-setting mechanisms can influence exercise behavior (e.g., Keefe & Blumenthal, 1980; Martin et al., 1984; Olson & Zanna, 1982). However, little effort has been made to determine what might influence goal-setting behavior or what mediates goal-setting. Bandura and Cervone (1983) have previously shown goal-setting to be potent only in the presence of high self-efficacy and self-evaluative systems. Recent work by Bandura and Wood (1989), in a managerial decision-making context, suggests that strong beliefs in one's capabilities have a direct effect on performance and an indirect effect through the mediation of personal goal-setting and analytic strategies. Poag and McAuley (1991) have also reported data linking goals, efficacy, and perceived exercise achievement in community exercisers. It is probably not an inaccurate statement to say that goal-setting is applied in exercise environments carte blanche with little notion of what makes it work. However, the challenge for sport and exercise psychologists is to determine if such goals influence exercise behavior through the mediation of efficacy and other perceptions (e.g., Hall & Byrne, 1988) and how those perceptions influence the goals that we set.

Social Support

Social support has also been identified as a variable likely to influence adoption of and adherence to exercise regimens (e.g., Heinzelmann & Bagley, 1970; Wankel, 1985). The influence of social groups, in particular spousal or significant other influences, has been widely implicated in health behaviors (e.g., Cohen & Syme, 1985; Sarason & Sarason, 1985). However, the exercise research is methodologically and theoretically suspect in this area. For the most part, social support has been defined as a positive attitude by significant others toward the subject engaging in physical activity. However, it is not as simple as this. Social support is currently viewed as being a multidimensional construct (e.g., Cobb, 1976; Cohen & Syme, 1985; Kahn, 1979), and it is not possible to generate hypotheses with respect to the psychological variables social support might influence until its functions are clearly delineated (Cutrona & Russell, 1987). Furthermore, once functions are identified, reliable and valid measures of the construct need to be employed.

The previously discussed work of Taylor, Bandura, Ewart, Miller, and DeBusk (1985) suggests a link between socially supportive behavior and self-efficacy in the mediation of exercise behavior. Self-efficacy cognitions provide one mechanism through which individuals are able to cope with stressful environments (Bandura, 1977a; 1982). Obtaining support from significant members of one's social environment serves to provide the individual with information pertinent to one's capabilities, and, consequently, self-efficacy is enhanced. Therefore, it is suggested that the effects of social support on exercise behavior are not direct but rather indirect through perceptions of personal efficacy. Although there is some evidence to suggest that efficacy mediates the effects of social support on depression (Cutrona & Troutman, 1986), the proposition still needs to be fully tested. Duncan (1989; Duncan & McAuley, 1991) has recently presented data to suggest that efficacy mediates the social support effects on the exercise behavior of middle-aged males and females. The challenge now for exercise researchers interested in such mediators is to establish how social support affects exercise behavior and, if it does so, to determine whether self-efficacy mediates this relationship. As well as establishing the exact relationships among self-efficacy, social support, and exercise, it is necessary to determine whether certain aspects of social support are more important under certain conditions than are others.

Relapse Prevention Model

Another model of substance that identifies self-efficacy as playing an important role in the maintenance of health behavior is Marlatt and Gordon's (1985) relapse prevention model. In its most basic form, the model posits self-efficacy to mediate between coping or non-coping responses in high risk or pressure situations and the subsequent decrease or increase in the probability of relapse. Although developed as a framework within which to understand and predict relapse in addictive behaviors, it has potential value for exercise behavior. Two early studies (King & Frederickson, 1984; Martin et al., 1984) employed the relapse prevention model in exercise settings, but both suffered from methodological weaknesses. A more recent application to exercise by Belisle, Roskies, and Levesque (1987) examined the model to predict adherence to a 10-week exercise program and at three-month follow-up. Belisle et al. were able to show that relapse-prevention treatment resulted in greater adherence as compared to a control group. However, they neglected, or chose not to assess, the underlying component of self-efficacy that Marlatt and Gordon (1985) suggested to mediate coping responses. The relapse prevention model, if applied correctly and assessed accurately, holds considerable promise in helping us better understand exercise behavior.

Conclusion

It has been submitted that perceptions of personal capabilities, or self-efficacy, with respect to exercise and physical activity are influential agents in the mediation of exercise behavior. Evidence from both primary and secondary prevention perspectives has been presented that demonstrates considerable consistency in the patterns of findings. That is, self-efficacy is influenced by information based on previous exercise/physical activity performance; it influences adoption of and adherence to such activities; and, by implication, it plays an important role in the effects of and effects on goal-setting, social support, and coping responses. A consistent criticism of the exercise psychology and, in particular, the adherence literature has been its predominantly descriptive nature and lack of theoretical focus (Dishman, 1988). Self-efficacy provides such a theoretical framework to understand better and to predict behavior. The interactive role that efficacy cognitions play with other social cognitive variables, detailed by authors elsewhere in this volume, offers the potential to further enrich our understanding of the exercise process. That is, self-efficacy might be more beneficially understood by studying it in concert with other supposedly potent influences on exercise behavior such as goal orientations, coping strategies, goal-setting, motivational climate, and social support mechanisms.

Acknowledgment

The preparation of this chapter was facilitated by a Public Health Service grant to the author (#AG07907) awarded by the National Institute on Aging.

Motivation for Exercise Behavior: A Critique of Theoretical Directions

W. Jack Rejeski

There is increasing evidence that exercise is an important behavior within the realm of public health (Dishman, 1988). In fact, as early as 1982 the Department of Health and Human Services (National Office of Disease Prevention and Health Promotion) published exercise objectives for citizens of the United States that were very aggressive. By the year 1990, this federal agency desired to have over half of the adults in this country (60%) and most children (90%) involved in a regular program of vigorous physical activity. In 1985, Dishman, Sallis, and Orenstein concluded from an extensive review of the literature that dropout rates for vigorous physical activity continued to hover around the 50% level, a disturbing figure when you consider that current estimates place only 10 to 20% of the 18- to 65-year-old population in programs of physical activity that are sufficiently vigorous to yield improved fitness (Powell, Spain, Christenson, & Mollenkamp, 1986). It is disappointingly clear that levels of physical activity in the United States have increased very slowly, if at all, despite a rapidly expanding data base that underscores the wisdom inherent in national exercise objectives.

Epidemiological data have confirmed that physical activity reduces the incidence of cardiovascular disease (Paffenbarger & Hyde, 1988) and may prove valuable in the fight against essential hypertension (Paffenbarger, Wing, Hyde, & Jung, 1983). Research has linked exercise to the normalization of carbohydrate and fat metabolism (Rosenthal, Haskell, Solomon, Widstrom, & Reaven, 1983; Seals, Hagberg, Hurley, Ehsani, & Holloszy, 1984), and Brownell (1982, 1989) has repeatedly emphasized that exercise is a critical link to the enormous health risk posed by obesity. In yet other developments, exercise therapy has shown promise in ameliorating certain forms of bone mineral loss reported with aging (Siscovick, Laporte, & Newman, 1985), particularly among post-menopausal women (Krolner, Toft, Nielsen, & Tandewold, 1983). There is also accumulating evidence that exercise can enhance psychological well-being. Acute bouts of physical activity improve mood (Berger, Friedmann, & Eaton, 1988; Morgan, 1987; Thayer, 1987), whereas chronic levels of physical activity have been reported to lower physiological reactivity to mental stressors (Crews & Landers, 1987) and to reduce depression (McCann & Holmes, 1984).

Although continued research is needed to explore the components of exercise prescription that are necessary for specific health effects, an equally pressing concern is motivation. How can we increase the public's intention to exercise, what must be done to convert intent into action, and how do we maintain exercise behavior once it is initiated? The position adopted in this chapter is that the identification of effective interventions is closely tied to the theoretical perspectives we espouse. With this assumption in mind, the initial objective is to establish the value of theory. Although this may seem rudimentary, a review of the available literature on exercise motivation suggests that theory is either ignored or misunderstood (see also Nicholls, this volume; Roberts, this volume). As a corollary to the merits of theory, a second objective is to provide a set of criteria to be used in selecting or designing a theory. Assuming that all theories do not have equal worth, what qualities should we look for?

As we pursue the third objective, which is a critical examination of theories employed in the area of exercise motivation, it will become apparent that some theories have been inappropriately applied or misrepresented. However, in other instances the problem has been more serious—there are design flaws in the theory that are destined to produce failure. I arrive at a simple conclusion: Whether one's objective in selecting a particular theory is research or application based, the implementation of a theoretical perspective in and of itself does not guarantee success. Rather, as the final section of this chapter demonstrates, understanding the criteria of a sound theoretical perspective is essential to grasping knowledge, conducting research, and utilizing state-of-the-art intervention protocols.

Intervention Research in Exercise: The Merits of Theory

The absence of a theoretical perspective is one of the major criticisms of research in exercise compliance (Dishman, 1982; Godin, Valois, Shephard, & Desharnais, 1987), yet little or no rationale is typically offered for such a weakness. What have been the consequences of "shotgun empiricism"? How will theory resolve the dilemmas created?

Delimitation

Exercise, like many other behaviors, is enormously complex. Thus a question that surfaces is: Where do we begin our study of motivation? One response has been to select variables that have intuitive appeal and to determine whether or not they discriminate between subjects who adhere and do not adhere to some predefined criterion. Commonly used measures of compliance have been frequency of involvement over a specified unit of time and dropout. For example, in the late 1970s and early 1980s, three studies were published from a large Canadian project that dealt with exercise and the heart. The first investigation, published in 1978 (Oldridge, Wicks, Hanley, Sutton, & Jones, 1978), used a subsample of the total Canadian project, and it reported that those who left the program tended to be Type A, were inactive in their leisure time, had had at least two previous heart attacks, and were smokers.

In 1979, Andrew and Parker published dropout data on the entire Canadian project, which employed a 13-page questionnaire with items that targeted the physical facilities, personal convenience factors, attitudes toward the program personnel, motives for joining, work-related issues, and family attitudes. These investigators found that in comparison to compliers, dropouts lacked enthusiasm for the program, experienced more post-exercise fatigue, found it difficult to arrive at sessions on time, felt their job interfered more with the program, perceived less spouse support, and doubted the purported benefits of exercise. In 1981, Andrew and his colleagues (Andrew et al., 1981) generated a third paper which was an elaboration and statistical refinement of the 1979 data. As in 1979, they found variables from three main categories to be associated with high dropout: convenience of the exercise center, perceptions of the exercise program, and family/lifestyle factors.

Although there is much to learn in the descriptive data provided by these investigations, it is difficult to understand why in 1978 Oldridge and his associates elected to use one set of variables, whereas in 1979 and 1981 the dependent measures changed. These studies are not unique in this regard; other investigators have elected to adopt a similar shotgun strategy (e.g., Bruce, Frederick, Bruce, & Fisher, 1979; Massie & Shephard, 1971). The important point here is that this lack of structure is directly relevant to the argument for theory-based hypothesis testing, because one of its primary functions is delimitation. In other words, theory prevents "the observer from being dazzled by the full blown complexity of natural or concrete events" (Hall & Lindzey, 1970, p. 14). It does so by directing the attention of investigators to specific variables. Without some delimitation in the area of exercise motivation, there is little hope for order, and the inclusion of specific constructs will largely be a function of intuition.

Organizational Function

A second purpose of theory is organizational in nature. Theories provide a conceptual framework for grouping research findings into logical units. The value of this function in the area of exercise interventions is readily apparent in Martin and Dubbert's (1984) review of cognitive/behavioral research. In this paper, major headings include: reinforcement control, stimulus control, behavioral contracting, cognitive strategies, generalization training, reinforcement fading, and self-control techniques. This approach neatly ties together over 25 investigations in the area of exercise and leaves the reader with a coherent picture of available empirical data relevant to exercise motivation.

Yet another positive feature of the organizational structure provided by theory is that it standardizes the operation of terminology and assists in identifying gaps in knowledge. A consistent definition of terms is critical to the integration of information and represents a problem that has plagued research on exercise motivation. For example, Dishman (1982), in a comprehensive review of the exercise adherence literature, concluded that "attitudes toward physical activity have not predicted who will eventually adhere or drop out of an exercise program" (p. 240). He cited work by Andrew and Parker (1979), Dishman and Gettman (1980), and Sonstroem and Kampper (1980) to support his position. The problem is that Andrew and Parker (1979) did not use a psychometrically sound measurement approach to the study of attitudes, whereas Dishman and Gettman (1980) as well as Sonstroem and Kampper (1980) employed the Physical Estimation and Attraction Scale (PEAS). Notwithstanding the fact that the PEAS was constructed within a social learning framework rather than conventional attitude theory, Sonstroem himself has indicated that failure of the PEAS to predict adherence "may be related to the method of construct measurement rather than to serious inadequacy of the model itself" (1982, p. 5). The major point here is that in the absence of a theory-driven science, conclusions reached are often erroneous.

A final benefit provided by the organizational function of theory in exercise motivation research is that it provides a structure, by way of systematic definitions, for determining the conditions that are necessary for observing specific effects. This can resolve many inconsistencies that appear in the literature. The best example that comes to mind in the exercise motivation area is research that has employed Rotter's social learning theory of personality (Rotter, Chance, & Phares, 1972). The most basic tenet of this theoretical position is that behavior is jointly determined by expectancies (i.e., control) and reinforcement value. Thus, if I believe that aerobic exercise will reduce muscular tension, and I really want to find a way to reduce this somatic symptom of stress, then there is a good chance that I will jog or perform some other act of aerobic activity. Additionally, generalized expectancies of control represent a higher order construct in the theory (a personality trait) that can mediate specific expectancies. In short, some people are optimistic (internals) about their behavior producing effects, whereas others are more pessimistic (externals).

Without assessing the reinforcement value of exercise (e.g., Slenker, Price, & O'Connell, 1985), one shouldn't expect locus of control to predict exercise behavior. Stated differently, why would people exercise if they did not value the outcomes of the behavior? Control in and of itself is not a strong predictor of behavior. Furthermore, in attempting to predict compliance, a number of researchers have used generalized measures of control in combination with an assessment tool for evaluating the value associated with exercise (Dishman & Gettman, 1980; Long & Haney, 1986; Sonstroem & Walker, 1973). However, a frequently overlooked proposition of social learning theory is that generalized control only predicts behavior in novel or ambiguous situations. Close examination of the samples employed and contexts studied reveals that these investigations have not provided an adequate test of the theory.

Systematic and Heuristic Effects on Research Directions

A third and final purpose of theory is what Hall and Lindzey (1970) term the systematic and heuristic generation of research. In general, the unsystematic quality of extant empirical study has been the primary complaint of reviewers who criticize the compliance literature for being atheoretical. That is, with few exceptions (e.g., Godin, Valois, et al., 1987; Martin et al., 1984; Valois, Desharnais, & Godin, 1988), there has been little step-by-step building of knowledge in exercise motivation. Often the only common denominator linking research studies is the title, and as is true of the attitude area, without agreement on operation of terms, the same words often have multiple meanings.

The heuristic function of theory implies that an inherent quality is its ability to stimulate activity that is novel and not necessarily a logical extension of existing structure. For example, Valois, Desharnais, and Godin (1988) recently contrasted the abilities of Fishbein and Ajzen's (1975) theory of reasoned action and Triandis's model (1977) to predict exercise intentions. Both of these theoretical positions espouse an Expectancy × Value framework; however, each represents a unique refinement of early propositions. In other words, the expectancy construct and an empirical law of effect have influenced thinking in psychology for decades (Atkinson, 1964; Tolman, 1934).

Criteria for Sound Theory

Although theory testing has far more value than shotgun empiricism, there is considerable variation in existing theories. In examining the adequacy of a theory for intervention research in exercise motivation, it is important to address two broad concerns: First, was the theory developed for the application intended? And second, does the theory have desirable attributes?

Application

Although the appropriateness of a theory for a specific application is rarely given explicit attention, violations of this principle are legion, particularly in the prediction of behavior. Consider if you will contemporary attribution theory, which offers an explanation for how people make sense of the world in which they live. The mother theory originally proposed by Heider (1958) had no formal theoretical structure that would make it useful in the prediction of behavior. In fact, it was originally a theory of interpersonal perception. Whereas the heuristic function of the theory has resulted in expanding the principles of attribution theory to self-perception, and research has tied the causal dimensions of attributions to expectations and emotion (Rejeski & Brawley, 1983), by themselves attributions predict behavior very poorly. I cannot help but recount a recent experience that serves to emphasize this point.

A neighbor of mine began regularly scheduled Nautilus workouts at the YMCA, but she quit within the first two weeks. When asked why, she indicated that the workouts were making it difficult for her to do errands or pick up the children after school, a cause that was quite reasonably beyond her control. Several efforts by my wife to remedy the problem failed. Although it was clear that the assistance was appreciated, the simple fact remained that the Y's program just wasn't worth the aggravation. As a point of fact, my neighbor had become bored and disinterested in Nautilus training. Interestingly, from the very beginning the only real reward for her was that the program offered a time-out when she could socialize with my wife. She had no idea from the onset that the cost of the physical work would be so great. Perceived control had absolutely nothing to do with her noncompliance. The barriers were self-constructions that permitted her to rationalize her actions.

This scenario does not rule out the possibility that attribution theory could be important in understanding cognitive processes involved in exercise motivation; however, causal attributions constitute only one piece of the puzzle. Throwing attributional data into a mathematical equation in an attempt to discriminate compliers from noncompliers would make little sense. In this regard, it is important to recognize that theories are developed for specific applications. Moreover, those responsible for the creation of different theoretical perspectives have assumptions and targets in mind that may not fit well with the social reality of exercise behavior. Unfortunately, these assumptions are not always explicitly stated, nor are they always considered by individual researchers (see also Nicholls, this volume; Roberts, this volume).

Relevant Structural Criteria

The second test that I propose for evaluating the adequacy of theory is to examine the characteristics that the theory possesses. Does it have desirable attributes? As a means of formally evaluating theory, I am going to draw heavily from the writings of Rotter (1954) and Rychlak (1968) as well as from personal interactions that I had with Julian Rotter. The criteria to be considered include: (1) levels of inclusion and levels of construction, (2) process versus content orientation of constructs, and (3) systematization and operationality.

Levels of Inclusion and Construction

In the early 1980s, Dishman and his colleagues (Dishman, Ickes, & Morgan, 1980) introduced the Self-Motivation Inventory (SMI) as a dispositional measure of behavioral persistence. In initial research, the SMI predicted compliance of women to crew training and was valuable in discriminating between dropouts and adherers in organized fitness/rehabilitation programs (see Dishman, Ickes, & Morgan, 1980; or Dishman & Ickes, 1981). Ward and Morgan (1984) subsequently found that, as part of a psychobiological model, the SMI contributed to the identification of healthy adult compliers engaged in a structured fitness program; yet, it did not assist in classifying those who eventually dropped out. Furthermore, Wankel (1984) has reported on two investigations in which neither SMI main effects nor SMI × treatment interactions were related to attendance.

What has troubled this research paradigm? Are there any explanations for the inconsistencies across studies? For our purposes, let's ignore methodological differences and focus on the criteria raised in this section. Does the theory underlying the SMI possess adequate levels of inclusion and construction? To evaluate these criteria, we can pit the SMI against current empirical knowledge. Most important, it is well recognized that trait theory, as represented in this instance by the SMI, is too restrictive. Behavior is determined by the joint contribution of both personal and situational factors (Rotter et al., 1972). Thus, the SMI fails the test of inclusiveness. Also, because the SMI relies on a single core construct, there are no lower levels of construction. For example, does self-motivation necessarily result in a singular behavioral style that is equally predictive of persistence across varied situations? Such a pattern is highly unlikely.

Dishman and his associates should be commended for bringing the concept of self-motivation into focus for the scientific community; however, as presently conceptualized, it is largely a construct that exists independent of an integrated theoretical structure.

Process- Versus Content-Oriented Constructs

Of particular importance to intervention research in exercise motivation is the extent to which the constructs of a given theory are process and/or content oriented. Process-related constructs help to explain why behavior occurs and how it is changed. On the other hand, constructs that are strong on content provide a description for individual differences. For example, trait theory is strong on content; it offers a system for classifying individuals on a variety of dimensions. Yet, such theory offers no clue as to how behavioral change can be effected. At the other extreme are theories such as operant conditioning in which constructs are exclusively process oriented.

Although the availability of process-oriented constructs is critical to intervention, the absence of constructs that describe the content of individual differences poses a serious limitation. The effects of this theory imbalance between content- and process-oriented constructs have existed in health care settings for some time. For example, there are a number of programs that have employed principles of behavior modification to enhance weight loss and/or increase activity levels. While the initial impact of these programs is frequently very promising, long-term outcomes are disappointing. That is, the influence of behavior therapy on lifestyle change appears effective for a certain subgroup of clients, yet fails to yield the desired behavior patterns for many others. The simple fact is that the theory does not offer any content-related constructs to explain differential responses to modification of reward structures.

A somewhat different dilemma is faced by programs that operate from psychological data provided by theories of types and traits such as MMPIs, 16PFs, and similar measures. They have elaborate content descriptions of their clients, but lack mechanisms for effecting change (Blumenthal, Williams, Wallace, Williams, & Needles, 1982). While the logical solution might be to combine theoretical approaches that are strong on either content or process, such an amalgamation rarely works in practice. Underlying assumptions of theories differ, there is discord in operation of terms, and there is no empirical basis on which to anchor clinical judgments.

Systematic and Operational Definitions

In previous discussion, I identified systematization and operationality as two important functions of theory. Unfortunately, not all theories represent healthy systems, nor are the constructs involved operational. Moreover, it is also true that investigators often violate the internal standards provided by theory (see also Roberts, this volume).

Perhaps the most critical feature of systematization is the link that it provides between propositions in a theory. In other words, there should be explicit systematic definitions. In the ideal case, every variable in a theory would be interrelated with every other. This enhances both predictability and the process-oriented features of constructs and serves as a catalyst for generation of experimental hypotheses. For example, in Rotter's (1954) social learning theory, expectancy is defined as the belief that a specific reward will follow a given behavior. This definition ties together two major constructs: expectancy and reinforcement value. When the expectancy construct is employed in research, the operational definition must reflect its relationship to reinforcement value. Failure to do so will yield an inappropriate test of the theory.

For example, McCready and Long (1985), in an introduction to their research on social learning theory and adherence, commented on the weaknesses of past research. More specifically, they cited a dissertation by Noland (1981) that was responsible for the development of an exercise locus of control scale. In an astute analysis, they noted that the items in this scale assessed perceptions of what controlled subjects' exercise behavior, rather than expectations regarding reinforcements. A mismatch existed between the systematic definition in theory and the experimental operation of the construct. Note how the use of well-designed theory encourages precision in methodology.

Summary

The major goal of this deliberation on the criteria of sound theory has been to emphasize the confusion that can be created either by improperly applying a given theoretical perspective or using a theory that is seriously lacking in structural integrity. For certain, the term "atheoretical" does not describe adequately the problem that exists in research on exercise motivation. Furthermore, without thoroughly understanding a particular theory, it is nearly impossible to judge the veracity of empirical data. I would also argue that sound theory is the only sensible way to proceed with clinical evaluations and interventions (see Rejeski & Kenney, 1988). Without such a framework, the practitioner is as helpless and error prone as the shotgun empiricist.

An Analysis of Theory-Based Intervention Research

Having discussed the merit and criteria of good theory, the purpose of this section is to summarize and critique exercise motivation research that has been theory based and that has direct implications for intervention. The review will include investigations conducted within a theoretical framework that possess process-oriented constructs. These include self-efficacy theory, the health belief model, Rotter's social learning theory, the theory of reasoned action, Triandis's model of interpersonal behavior, Bandura's social cognitive theory, and the general paradigm reflected in cognitive/behavioral modification.

Self-Efficacy Theory

In the past decade there has been a growing interest in the relationship between self-efficacy theory and exercise behavior. Because Edward McAuley (this volume) offers a detailed review of this research, I will restrict my comments to six investigations that have been cited as self-efficacy studies with relevance to intervention research in exercise motivation. In doing so, my purpose is to emphasize that research associated with this theory requires a great deal of scrutiny. In several instances, the theory has been represented inappropriately, and there are limitations to this approach that are rarely considered.

Davis and colleagues (Davis, Jackson, Kronenfeld, & Blair, 1984) and Shephard in conjunction with his colleagues (see Shephard, 1985) have provided data pertaining to initial involvement with organized fitness programs. The investigation spearheaded by Davis was designed to identify psychosocial variables that might predict participation in health promotion programs. These investigators hypothesized that dissatisfaction with current level of fitness and intent to change are related to eventual exercise behavior. Their results suggested that workers with low personal efficacy reported more dissatisfaction with their level of fitness and had a greater desire to change their physical self than those with high personal efficacy. In apparent contrast, Shephard and co-workers found that those who were successfully recruited to a corporate fitness program exhibited stronger beliefs in their ability to improve health— high self-efficacy.

From the perspective of self-efficacy theory, a critical shortcoming of these studies is that neither provided an appropriate operational definition of the construct. That is, in the study by Davis et al. (1984) three questions were used to define personal efficacy. They were as follows:

1. When I am exercising or playing sports I feel self-conscious about the way I look.
2. I am the kind of person who does not get enough exercise.
3. It's kind of hard for me to find time in a day to get some exercise. (p. 369)

Only Number 3 even vaguely resembles the self-efficacy construct. The work by Shephard and his colleagues (see Shephard, 1985) assessed generalized perceived control over health. This is more akin to health locus of control than self-efficacy theory.

A second group of studies, conducted with symptomatic populations, had the intent of determining whether exercise accomplishments influence self-efficacy, and whether or not self-efficacy is linked to changes in physical parameters as well as compliance to exercise therapy. Ewart, Taylor, Reese, and DeBusk (1983) found that treadmill testing of cardiac patients following an infarction improved their self-efficacy in a variety of physical activities. Interestingly, improvements in self-efficacy as a result of the test also correlated with positive changes in physical activity during a subsequent three-day period.

Kaplan, Atkins, and Reinsch (1984) studied a group of patients with chronic obstructive pulmonary disease. These individuals were randomly assigned either to one of three experimental conditions designed to enhance compliance, or to an attention placebo group. After three months of exercise training, those who had received the behavioral intervention had improved compliance (Atkins, Kaplan, Timms, Reinsch, & Lofback, 1984) and enhanced self-efficacy (Kaplan et al., 1984). Kaplan et al. (1984) also reported that the three-month self-efficacy scores were positively related to tests of exercise tolerance. The implication in these data is that increasing compliance with behavioral strategies results in improved self-efficacy that should serve as a stimulus for increased motivation toward further physical activity. In fact, there is some evidence for the proposed relationship between self-efficacy and subsequent motivation. Ewart, Stewart, Gillilan, and Kelemen (1986) found that the self-efficacy of cardiac patients was related to strength gains achieved in a circuit training program, whereas Gillilan et al. (1984) have shown that high self-efficacy subjects with coronary disease are inclined to exceed prescribed levels of exercise intensity, and those low in self-efficacy fail to achieve desired heart rate ranges.

Although these data on symptomatic populations are promising, it should be recognized that the incentive value of exercise in such groups is likely to be higher than in individuals who are asymptomatic. This point raises an interesting question regarding the need for additional constructs in self-efficacy theory (see also Roberts, this volume). Specifically, wouldn't the predictive value of the theory improve with the inclusion of an incentive-related construct? And will researchers eventually find the need for content-oriented constructs to define individual differences? There is little question that self-efficacy plays a role in exercise motivation (see McAuley, this volume); however, by itself, it is highly unlikely that self-efficacy will be a potent predictor of behavior.

Health Belief Model

Figure 1 provides an illustration of the two major dimensions of the health belief model (HBM) that presumably determine compliance with preventive health behavior (Becker, 1974). To my knowledge, Lindsay-Reid and Osborn (1980) were the first investigators to apply this theoretical approach to exercise. The study population consisted of firefighters who volunteered to engage in self-directed exercise programs for a 6-month interval. Questionnaire items that addressed three components of the readiness dimension were used prospectively

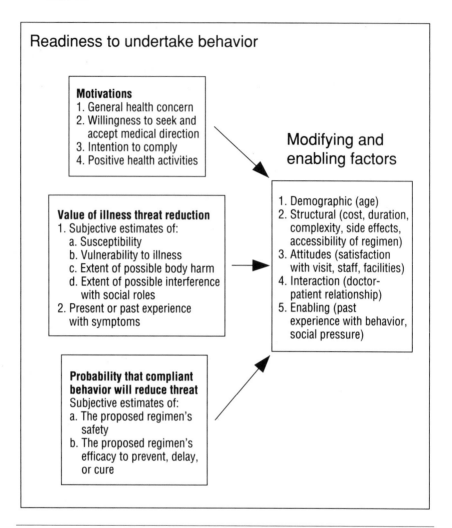

Readiness to undertake behavior

Motivations
1. General health concern
2. Willingness to seek and accept medical direction
3. Intention to comply
4. Positive health activities

Modifying and enabling factors

Value of illness threat reduction
1. Subjective estimates of:
   a. Susceptibility
   b. Vulnerability to illness
   c. Extent of possible body harm
   d. Extent of possible interference with social roles
2. Present or past experience with symptoms

1. Demographic (age)
2. Structural (cost, duration, complexity, side effects, accessibility of regimen)
3. Attitudes (satisfaction with visit, staff, facilities)
4. Interaction (doctor-patient relationship)
5. Enabling (past experience with behavior, social pressure)

Probability that compliant behavior will reduce threat
Subjective estimates of:
a. The proposed regimen's safety
b. The proposed regimen's efficacy to prevent, delay, or cure

Figure 1.   Determinants of compliance to health behaviors. Adapted from Becker et al., 1977.

to contrast two distinct groups: those who reported "no exercise" versus individuals who reported "regular physical activity." The components consisted of a heart disease risk index, an illness probability index, and an efficacy index (i.e., Will specific health behaviors reduce the risk of heart disease?). Unfortunately, the results were disappointing. Contrary to expectations, it was those who perceived a lower risk for heart disease who became more physically active. The illness probability index was unrelated to reported activity level and the efficacy index only predicted regular activity in older adults (aged 51 to 60 years).

In 1984, two additional studies of the HBM appeared in the literature. Slenker, Price, Roberts, and Jurs (1984) examined the ability of a comprehensive HBM, including components from both the readiness and motivating/enabling dimensions, to discriminate between joggers and nonexercisers. They found that the theoretical tenets of the HBM accounted for 61% of the variance between the two groups. In contrast to joggers, nonexercisers indicated that barriers such as competing activities, lack of desire, and unsuitable weather were apt to keep them from running; variables that accounted for 40% of the total between group variance. Also, joggers manifested a stronger general health motivation, perceived more social benefit from exercise, and were slightly more inclined to perceive greater severity in potential health problems than nonexercisers. It is also worth noting that a number of the variables in the HBM shared substantial common variance. This is undesirable since variables in a theory should have minimal overlap (Rotter, 1954).

The second investigation reported in 1984 involved participation in a corporate fitness program at General Foods (Morgan, Shephard, Finucane, Schimmelfing, & Jazmaji, 1984). This study involved an analysis of the HBM in predicting both initial involvement as well as level of physical activity in those who enrolled for the program. In general, those who enrolled were more physically active than those who chose not to enroll in the program (an enabling factor in the HBM). Also registrants had a stronger belief in the ability of exercise to prevent heart attacks and evidenced a stronger general health motivation than nonparticipants. A unique finding in the subsample of women was that enrollment correlated inversely with perceived health status: Those with poorer health were more likely to join the program. After 20 months of the program's operation, two groups of registrants were identified: those who attended a minimum of 2 sessions per week for 20 minutes or more ("active"), and a group that was labeled "physically inactive." Analogous to the Lindsay-Reid and Osborn study (1980), males who were "active" reported a higher level of initial perceived health, a finding that runs counter to predictions from the model. Males who adopted exercise also had more realistic expectations of the program than males who were physically inactive. No clear differences emerged in the health beliefs of women who were identified as "active" or "inactive."

Investigators have to question seriously the theoretical merit of the HBM. First, while it does have a delimiting function, the limits defined by the motivating and enabling dimension are ambiguous, and considerable error variance is created from one study to another by the multiple meaning given to terms. Second, the HBM does not specify any systematic definitions, nor is attention given to concrete individual differences such as health locus of control. Third, an obvious shortcoming is failure of the model to address delay of gratification and hierarchy of needs. Social learning theory has identified the problem that exists in getting people to take immediate steps toward long-term rewards. The simple fact of the matter is that most people are not motivated by the delayed consequences associated with health outcomes. They seek immediate gratification. Also, health behaviors are frequently in competition with work and leisure pursuits. These considerations are not well-delineated in the current model. And fourth, a major assumption in employing the HBM is that the primary driving force for exercise behavior is concern over physical health. To the extent that other exercise motives exist (see Duda, this volume), they will reduce the predictive power of the model.

Rotter's Social Learning Theory

The major constructs in Rotter's social learning theory (1954) are expectancy and reinforcement value. It is Rotter's position that people act in a particular way because they *expect* that the behavior will produce some *desired outcome*. Important to research in exercise is the construct termed generalized locus of control. Rotter proposed that through social learning we develop generalized expectancies concerning our ability to control reinforcements in our lives. As mentioned previously, some individuals are optimistic (manifesting an internal locus of control), whereas others are more pessimistic (exhibiting an external control orientation). The importance of generalized control to behavior is that when faced with novelty or ambiguity, it is these generalized expectations that will guide behavior. However, once we have experience with a particular behavior, specific expectancies may run counter to generalized beliefs. Stated otherwise, an individual could be very pessimistic about his or her ability to control reinforcements in general, yet feel very much in control over his or her physique.

Interestingly, most research involving social learning theory and exercise motivation has incorporated some generalized control measure and Kenyon's (1968) attitude scale as an index of incentive. For example, using Rotter's Locus of Control Scale (LCS) Bonds (1980) found that elderly men and women who were internal reported more recreational exercise each week than those who were external. Sonstroem and Walker (1973), studying college males, found that internals on the LCS who had a positive attitude toward physical activity ran a 600-yard run faster and reported more vigorous physical activity than internals whose attitudes toward physical activity were more negative, or than externals who expressed either a positive or negative attitude toward physical activity.

A second approach has been to employ a Health Locus of Control Scale (HLCS) as opposed to a more generalized measure. The reasoning here is that the increased specificity in expectations should increase prediction. Unfortunately, this logic has produced mixed results. The HLCS has not predicted activity level (Blair et al., 1980; Laffrey & Isenberg, 1983), nor has it been useful in distinguishing between compliers and dropouts in formal exercise programs. In a retrospective study, O'Connell and Price (1982) did find that compliers to a corporate fitness program were more internal on a revised HLCS than dropouts, whereas Slenker, Price, and O'Connell (1985) using the same measure found that exercisers were more internal than nonexercisers. It is also worth mentioning that Dishman and Gettman (1980) reanalysed their data to explore an interaction between the HLCS and value for health and fitness. Those subjects with an internal locus of control who placed a high value on health and fitness were more likely to adhere to structured exercise than those who were external and exhibited low scores on value for health and fitness.

Finally, recent research has explored the merit of an exercise specific locus of control scale combined with a revised version of Kenyon's attitude scale to predict women's initiation of exercise (Long & Haney, 1986) and their adherence to structured exercise programs (McCready & Long, 1985). Again the data have been disappointing. Long and Haney (1986) found that an Internal Locus of Control × Value interaction accounted for only 5% of the variance in initial involvement. In the McCready and Long (1985) study, Exercise Locus of Control × Value did not predict adherence. In contrast, when they substituted the exercise scale for a generalized measure, a small but significant Locus of Control × Value interaction emerged, accounting for only 3% of the total variance in adherence.

What can one conclude about this theoretical direction in the study of exercise motivation? To begin with, one would not expect generalized locus of control to predict exercise behavior. It is inconsistent with the definition of the construct, except for subjects who have never had experience with exercise—in which case it may predict initial involvement. Second, social learning theory proposes that reinforcements exist in a hierarchy. Hence, an individual may value exercise, yet due to family or occupation commitments fail to comply with an exercise prescription. Not a single study has given recognition to this idiosyncracy of reinforcement value. Third, as Long and Haney (1986) point out, subjects in their investigations have been volunteers who typically exhibit a fair degree of homogeneity on exercise locus of control. This greatly hinders statistical power. The percent of variance that they characterize as low may be more significant than it first appears. Fourth, it is now apparent that the expectancy construct (i.e., control) is more complex than Rotter and his colleagues' (1972) theoretical position acknowledged. Recall that Bandura (1977a) has made an important distinction between outcome expectancies and self-efficacy. Thus, although I may believe that exercise prevents heart disease for some people (an outcome expectancy), I may have little faith in its ability to deter the problems that I face with cardiovascular disease (self-efficacy). And fifth, a new approach to the measurement of reinforcement value is needed. We need to know what individual subjects expect to gain from exercise without limiting their responses. Moreover, it is time that we studied the underlying nature of anticipated rewards (i.e., their relative importance to the individual). In essence, the rigor provided by sound psychometric protocols must provide tools that explore, rather than ignore, the phenomenology of our subjects.

Theory of Reasoned Action

In 1975, Fishbein and Ajzen formally introduced the theory of reasoned action as an approach to the study of volitional behavior (see Figure 2). Similar to Rotter (1954), these authors developed their theoretical structure from an Expectancy × Value perspective. They incorporated a social component into their theory termed subjective norm and argued that the mediating link between attitudes and behavior was intention.

To date there have been three distinct directions of research in the area of exercise motivation. These include: (1) Attempts to verify that the theory is applicable to the study of exercise behavior, (2) an examination of how motivational strategies such as exercise testing and counseling influence variables in the model, and (3) efforts to contrast the theory of reasoned action against Triandis's attitudinal model and Bandura's social cognitive theory.

Validity of the Model in Exercise Settings

Riddle (1980) provided the first evidence that Fishbein and Ajzen's model might have utility in the study of exercise motivation. Using a survey approach, she identified and obtained questionnaire data from 149 joggers and 147 nonexercisers. Two weeks after the questionnaires had been completed, subjects were telephoned and asked if they had jogged regularly since completing the survey. The correlation between intention and behavior was .82, suggesting that these variables shared 67% of common variance. Additionally, attitude toward the behavior and the subjective norm component combined to explain 55% of the variance in intentions.

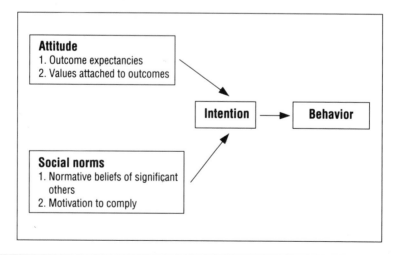

Figure 2.   Fishbein and Ajzen's theory of reasoned action. Adapted from Fishbein and Ajzen, 1975.

Sonstroem (1982) reported on pilot data from the University of Rhode Island involving a faculty fitness program. Despite the fact that all of the subjects had strong intentions to complete the program at the onset of the study, there was still a positive, albeit low, correlation ($r = .31$) between intentions and 12-week attendance records. Moreover, those with high attendance manifested different belief structures than those with low attendance. That is, high attenders "negated in a more pronounced fashion the ideas that exercise (1) requires too much discipline, (2) takes too much time, (3) tires the individual unduly, and (4) is unpleasant; they supported to a greater extent the idea that exercise (5) makes them feel good mentally" (p. 12).

Since Riddle's (1980) early investigation, reports on the common variance between intentions and exercise behavior have been substantially lower, ranging from a low of 9% (Wurtele & Maddux, 1987) to a high of 32% (Valois et al., 1988). (Other data relevant to this relationship are as follows: Godin and Shephard, 1986a = 12%; Godin and Shephard, 1986b = 17%; Godin, Colantonio, Davis, Shephard, and Simard, 1986 = 23%; whereas Godin, Valois, et al., 1987, found that intentions and behavior had 31% shared variance.) When examining the relationship between attitudes or the subjective norm and intentions, attitudes typically emerge as the best predictor (e.g., Dzewaltowski, 1989b; Godin, Cox, & Shephard, 1983; Godin & Shephard, 1986a; Riddle, 1980; Valois et al., 1988). Moreover, there are several studies where the subjective norm fails to exhibit a significant relationship to intentions (e.g., Dzewaltowski, 1989; Godin, Valois, et al., 1987; Valois et al., 1988) and the percent of combined common variance of attitudes and the subjective norm component with intentions has been lower than expected (Godin & Shephard, 1986a = 31%; Valois et al., 1988 = 9%; Pender & Pender, 1986 = 5.5%; Dzewaltowski, 1989 = 5%). When examining the relationship of Beliefs × Evaluation to attitudes, and Normative Beliefs × Motivation to Comply to the subjective norm, results are generally consistent with the model's predictions; for example, Dzewaltowski (1989) reported correlations of .58 and .67, respectively.

What has been interesting is the cognitive profile that seems to be emerging from research with this model. Like Sonstroem (1982), Godin, Shephard, and Colantonio (1986) found that sedentary individuals with good intentions perceived exercise to be physically demanding and had difficulty managing the time demands of exercise. Dzewaltowski (1989) recently reported that subjects who expressed high self-efficacy in the face of barriers such as fatigue and the time demands of exercise were more likely to adhere to planned exercise behavior.

Influence of Testing and Counseling on Variables in the Model

Two studies by Godin and his colleagues have examined the influence of various interventions on behavioral intentions. In 1983, Godin, Cox, and

Shephard studied a group of 172 self-selected adults who sought evaluation of their physical fitness. In half of the group, questionnaire items relevant to Fishbein's model were administered prior to testing and counseling, whereas in the remaining subjects the questionnaire assessment was performed following the manipulation. The counseling consisted of a detailed explanation of subjects' results together with a recommendation for a personalized exercise prescription. To the disappointment of the investigators, subjects who completed the questionnaire following performance of the test and receipt of counseling had exercise intentions that did not differ from the control group. However, two extraneous variables, current physical activity and level of fitness, were found to influence significantly intentions to exercise. In fact, subjects' level of physical activity predicted intentions over and above variables in the Fishbein model.

In a second investigation, Godin, Desharnais, Jobin, and Cook (1987) examined the impact of physical fitness test results and/or knowledge of health-age on behavioral intentions to exercise. Four conditions—either with or without knowledge of test results—were examined: (1) fitness testing, (2) knowledge of health-age, (3) fitness testing and health-age combined, and (4) a no treatment control group. Subjects' intentions were assessed immediately following the treatment as well as 3 months posttreatment. The findings demonstrated that knowledge of results was critical to the effects of the treatment. Both the physical fitness condition and the combined fitness/health-age group who received knowledge of their results had significantly higher intentions to exercise than the control group. However, these effects were not present at the 3-month mark and the manipulation of intentions did not influence leisure exercise behavior. The authors suggested that the fitness testing was similar to a pep talk and that a more detailed motivational strategy is required to enhance long-term exercise behavior.

Fishbein and Ajzen Versus Triandis and Bandura

Recent investigations have contrasted Fishbein's theory of reasoned action with Triandis's (1977) model of interpersonal behavior (Valois et al., 1988) and Bandura's (1986) theory of social cognition (Dzewaltowski, 1989). It is instructive to review the results of these studies in attempting to further evaluate Fishbein and Ajzen's theory of reasoned action.

Triandis.   Triandis's model, like the work of Fishbein and Ajzen, has relied heavily on an Expectancy × Value principle. It differs from Fishbein in several important respects (see Figure 3). First, whereas Fishbein emphasizes conscious volitional control over behavior through intentions, Triandis proposes that the probability of an act is a function of three major factors: intentions, habit strength, and facilitating conditions. Second, recall that the social component in the Fishbein model consists of Normative Beliefs × Motive to Comply. In Triandis's model, the social component has to do with the perceived

---

Probability of an Act = (Habit + Intention) x Facilitating Conditions

Intention = C (Outcome Expectancy x Value) + S (Social Forces) + A (Affect)

Social forces
1. Norms and roles
2. Self-concept

Figure 3. A model of interpersonal behavior. Adapted from Triandis, 1977.

"appropriateness" of the behavior; that is, is exercise viewed as appropriate for one's reference group, and is it consistent with role expectations and one's self-concept? And third, in Triandis's model the Perceived Consequences × Value of these consequences is termed a cognitive component as opposed to an attitude. More important, there is a separate affective component such that intentions are determined by four factors: social, cognitive, affective, and personal normative beliefs (as described by Valois et al., 1988, this last factor evaluates perceived moral obligation to perform the behavior in question).

The research by Valois et al. (1988), which contrasted Fishbein and Ajzen's theory with Triandis's model, employed 166 university employees. Initially, the individuals completed questionnaires designed to tap the components of each theoretical position. Three weeks later subjects were contacted and asked how many times during this period they had exercised for 20 minutes or more. To assist in recall, each of the three weeks were evaluated independently. Results indicated that attitudes and the subjective norm component from Fishbein and Ajzen's theory predicted 9% of the variance in intentions; however, attitude was the only significant component. In Triandis's model the four factors (affect, cognition, social, and personal normative beliefs) predicted 25% of the variance in intention, a finding that was due to the social, affective, and personal normative dimensions. Intention to exercise, from Fishbein and Ajzen's theory, explained 32% of the variance in behavior, a result that was nearly identical to the Triandis's model (33%). However, in the Triandis model, it was Habit × Facilitating Factor that predicted behavior rather than the Intention × Facilitating Factor.

It is instructive to underscore the fact that it was affect and not cognition that shared variance with intentions in Triandis's model. Valois et al. (1988) point to this pattern in the data and suggest that the emotional dimension of an attitude should be a prime target in health promotion. In addition, it is interesting that the social component of Fishbein and Ajzen's theory was unrelated to intentions, whereas it had a significant beta weight in the Triandis model. This suggests that normative beliefs and role expectations may be potent determinants of exercise intentions.

Despite the appeal that Triandis's (1977) model may have, there is serious question regarding its appropriateness in the domain of exercise. That is to say, the framework was developed in an attempt to understand interpersonal behavior. The operational definition of certain constructs reflects this orientation, and their meanings are neither relevant nor easily translated to exercise. For example, Valois et al. (1988) employed the following question to assess the personal normative belief component: "Personally, I have a moral obligation to participate in one or more physical activities regularly during my free time within the next three weeks" (p. 467).

Bandura. Another approach that has commanded enormous attention over the past 10 years has been Bandura's (1977a, 1986) work on social cognition. Whereas the original focus of his approach was exclusively on self-efficacy theory (1977a), Bandura's (1986) most recent theoretical articulation of social learning presents an expanded range of constructs that potentially strengthens its predictive power. Dzewaltowski (1989), who has contrasted Fishbein and Ajzen's theory of reasoned action with Bandura's (1986) paradigm, employed three important constructs from social cognitive theory self-efficacy, outcome expectancy, and self-evaluated dissatisfaction. An outcome expectation represents the probability that a given outcome will follow a specific behavior, whereas self-efficacy represents one's perceived confidence in performing the behavior. The third construct, self-evaluated dissatisfaction, refers to the disappointment experienced when an individual fails to attain a specific goal or standard. Motivation is predicted to be highest in situations in which subjects have high self-efficacy and are dissatisfied with performance. In support of this latter position, Bandura and Cervone (1983, 1986) found that persistence on an exercise ergometer task was maximized when feedback indicated that subjects were falling short of goals that they felt were obtainable (high self-efficacy).

To contrast the efficacy of Fishbein and Ajzen's theory with that of Bandura, Dzewaltowski (1989) studied the activity habits of 328 undergraduate students enrolled in physical education classes. Subjects completed the appropriate questionnaires, and then their exercise behavior was monitored for an eight-week period. Generally speaking, Fishbein and Ajzen's theory fit the data quite well; however, it accounted for only 5% of the variance in the total number of days subjects exercised. In contrast, after forcing the constructs from Fishbein and Ajzen's model into a regression analysis, Bandura's social cognitive theory explained an additional 10.8% of the variance in exercise behavior. Whereas self-efficacy and dissatisfaction were significant predictors in the model, the Expectancy Outcome × Self-efficacy variable was not. Furthermore, dissatisfaction was found to be related to behavior in a manner that ran counter to theoretical predictions; that is, those who were satisfied with their performance exhibited better compliance.

When self-efficacy was entered first into a regression model, behavioral intention failed to account for an additional variance in exercise behavior. This pattern in the results is interesting in light of Ajzen's (1985) theory of planned behavior. In this theory, Ajzen has modified the theory of reasoned action to include perceived control as a determinant of behavior independent of behavioral intentions. Perceived control represents the absence of environmental barriers; in short, a person's *will* is the only limiting factor in whether he or she chooses or does not choose to perform a specific behavior. Although Dzewaltowski (1989) noted that perceived control and self-efficacy are not identical constructs, it is difficult to distinguish between the two in this particular investigation. That is to say, most of the items in the self-efficacy assessment tool addressed environmental barriers. It tapped the general problems of coping with difficult situations; adhering to exercise in the face of work schedules, fatigue, injuries, family responsibilities, and other time demands. Operationalized in this manner, self-efficacy shares significant variance with Ajzen's (1985) concept of perceived control and echoes the cognitive profile of the noncomplier as characterized by other investigators (Godin, Shephard, & Colantonio, 1986; Sonstroem, 1982). Moreover, these data reinforce the logic inherent in relapse prevention training. Specifically, research has shown that exercise adherence can be enhanced by problem-solving potential barriers before they occur and by teaching clients how to cope effectively with setbacks (Belisle, Roskies, & Levesque, 1987; King & Frederikson, 1984; King, Taylor, Haskell, & DeBusk, 1988).

The major limitations of social cognitive theory and the accompanying research are as follows:

1. Studies have failed to assess the reinforcement value that subjects have for a given behavior. Obviously, self-confidence is important to the performance of an act; however, all the confidence in the world will mean very little if an individual doesn't value the outcomes produced.
2. There is an exclusive focus on process-oriented constructs. This creates the same dilemma as the theory of reasoned action—the study of individual differences is discouraged.
3. There are no constructs that specifically address the impact that significant others have on behavior. This presents a dilemma in view of the fact that building social relations is the most commonly espoused method for enhancing regular physical activity (Wankel, 1984).
4. As a general observation, social cognitive theory represents an amalgamation of several lines of research in social cognition rather than a tightly designed systematic theory (see also Roberts, this volume).

Dzewaltowski (1989) extracted three constructs for his investigation of exercise behavior; however, there are numerous other possibilities (Bandura, 1986). Hopefully this state of affairs is not a stable attribute, but rather is a transitional phase in the ongoing refinement of social cognitive theory (see also Ames, this volume; Nicholls, this volume).

Cognitive/Behavioral Modification

There have been a group of studies in exercise motivation that fall under the general rubric of cognitive/behavior modification. These investigations can be grouped under one of two major headings: reinforcement/stimulus control, or cognitive/self-control (Martin & Dubbert, 1982b).

Reinforcement and Stimulus Control

It is not surprising that reinforcement and stimulus control procedures, two important principles of behaviorism, have been utilized to increase the frequency of exercise behavior. With respect to reinforcements, there have been several different forms of intervention, including: contracting (Epstein, Wing, Thompson, & Griffin, 1980; Kau & Fischer, 1974; Oldridge, & Jones, 1983; Taggart, Taggart, & Siedentop, 1986; Wysocki, Hall, Iwata, & Riordan, 1979), the use of lottery procedures (Epstein et al., 1980; Martin et al., 1984), social rewards (Kau & Fischer, 1974; Martin et al., 1984; Wankel & Kreisel, 1983; Wankel & Yardley, 1982), and tokens (Libb & Clements, 1969).

An excellent practical-oriented review of this literature has been provided by Martin and Dubbert (1984). The general impression that emerges from perusal of their work is that reinforcements constitute a valuable means of enhancing exercise motivation, a conclusion that is based on the results of both quasi-experimental and experimental research. Whereas tokens have been found to be effective reinforcements of exercise behavior in institutionalized geriatric patients (Libb & Clements, 1969), social rewards in the form of feedback and praise have been found to be potent motivators in several different populations (King et al., 1988; Martin et al., 1984; Wankel & Kreisel, 1983). There is evidence that flexible goals are superior to fixed goals (Martin et al., 1984), and shaping (i.e., gradually increasing the demands of exercise) has been an important ingredient in much of the intervention research conducted by Martin and his colleagues (see Martin & Dubbert, 1984). On the basis of research conducted by Epstein, Wing, Thompson, and Griffin (1980) it would seem that the efficacy of behavior-oriented interventions can be enhanced by defining behavior-reward contingencies in specific terms and having clients sign an agreement verifying their understanding and acceptance of stated objectives. This procedure has received support in the context of a rehabilitative exercise program for post-MI patients as well (Oldridge & Jones, 1983).

Stimulus control procedures have not received an extensive amount of attention. In fact, there is only a single study that clearly falls in this category. In a clever design, Brownell, Stunkard, and Albaum (1980) positioned adjacent to an escalator a happy heart cartoon in which a heart appeared to prefer using the stairs. This simple manipulation was successful in increasing stair use relative to the escalator.

Although the operant model represented in reinforcement and stimulus control is initially very appealing, it has severe limitations. This orientation assumes a strict realist philosophical orientation. Thus no consideration is given to individual differences in perception. The result is that while behaviorism is extremely strong on process-oriented constructs, which are appealing from the perspective of intervention, it ignores the active role of social cognition as a determinant of behavior. Despite its limitations, however, behaviorism does serve as a good example of how an organized system of constructs can lead to a logical progression of inquiry. In addition, the centrality of reinforcement to human behavior cannot be ignored. In some shape or form, the concept of incentives seems essential to any theory that purports to predict behavior.

Cognitive Self-Control

As noted by Martin and Dubbert (1984), in contemporary psychology there are few therapists who question the influence of cognition on behavior. Thus, many of those who favor the principles of operant conditioning now employ interventions that combine cognitive theory with behaviorism. In the realm of exercise, we have seen the use of goal-setting (Martin et al., 1984; Weinberg, this volume), decision-making strategies (Faulkner & Stewart, 1978; Heinzelmann & Bagley, 1970; Hoyt & Janis, 1975; Wankel, 1984), self-monitoring (King et al., 1988; Oldridge & Jones, 1983; Wankel, Yardley, & Graham, 1985; Weber & Wertheim, 1989), perceived control over the choice of activity (Thompson & Wankel, 1980), and the use of cognitive restructuring during exercise itself (Martin et al., 1984).

Goal-Setting.   Collectively, the results of these investigations have been very informative (see also Weinberg, this volume). For example, the work of Martin et al. (1984) in the area of goal-setting suggests that flexible goals yield better compliance than those that are fixed. When subjects receive social rewards, there is no apparent advantage to using goals that are defined in terms of distance versus time; however, in the absence of social rewards, time goals lead to slightly better compliance than distance goals. These investigators also have found that distal goals (evaluated every six weeks) are more effective than proximal goals (weekly). Apparently, goals that are more distant offer clients greater flexibility in daily and weekly performance, providing greater control over rate of progression. With weekly goals clients are forced into a set rate of progression and the opportunity for failure feedback is frequent.

Decision-Making.   Research in the area of decision-making has taken three distinct directions. The first has been to evaluate the utility of group discussions in promoting adoption of exercise. Faulkner and Stewart (1978) contrasted the motivational effects of four separate interventions on recruitment of subjects for employee fitness programs. These interventions included: fitness testing, a poster/brochure awareness campaign, an educational seminar group, and the combined impact of fitness testing and small group discussions. They found that the best approach for promoting initial involvement was to combine fitness testing with group discussions. In a related study, Heinzelmann and Bagley (1970) reported that it was more effective to use small groups and a decision-making approach than a large lecture format in getting adults to initiate exercise programs.

The second decision-making intervention has been the use of decision balance-sheet procedures. The initial investigation in this area was conducted by Hoyt and Janis (1975). Their objective was to determine whether or not a telephone decision balance procedure yielded better attendance than an irrelevant decision balance procedure (i.e., smoking behavior) or a no treatment control. Women who were part of a university fitness program served as subjects, and the treatment was administered during the third week of a seven-week block of exercise. The data were quite impressive. Those in the exercise decision balance condition attended nearly twice as many sessions as those in either the sham or no treatment control groups.

As a follow-up to this study, Wankel and Thompson (1977) examined whether a decision-balance procedure could be used to reestablish the exercise behavior of health club members who had been delinquent in their attendance. The design consisted of four different groups: a normal telephone follow-up, a positive-only decision-balance procedure, a positive-negative decision-balance approach, and a no treatment control. The results of this research supported the merits of a telephone decision-balance procedure for intervening with clients who, for one reason or another, have terminated their involvement in structured exercise. Interestingly, there was no difference between the positive-only and positive-negative procedures. An emotional inoculation perspective would argue that exposing subjects to the negative consequences of exercise inoculates them against such effects when they occur. Failure to demonstrate superiority of the positive-negative condition over the positive balance-sheet only procedure supports the view that self-persuasion rather than emotional inoculation is the mechanism underlying the effectiveness of decision-making.

Finally, although King and her colleagues (1988) did not employ a structured decision balance-sheet procedure, their data do suggest that systematic telephone contacts produce better aerobic training effects. They followed 51 male subjects in home-based activity programs. Half of the subjects received biweekly telephone contacts (five minutes in duration) for six months, while the remainder received no such support. The content of the telephone conversations consisted of relapse prevention instruction and adherence tips. At the six-month mark, those who received the telephone manipulation manifested a higher increase in peak oxygen uptake. The authors concluded that continued phone contact by the staff can be useful in ensuring the success of moderate-intensity home-based exercise training programs.

Self-Monitoring.   A central component of any intervention involving self-regulation is a process known as self-monitoring. In health psychology, this procedure is typically employed as a method for identifying the frequency, antecedents, and consequences of behavior. In addition, self-monitoring is used to maintain clients' awareness of established targets and progress. It is this latter function that has been the focus of several studies in exercise.

Oldridge and Jones (1983) as well as Wankel, Yardley, and Graham (1985) were among the first investigators to implement self-monitoring as part of an intervention package designed to enhance exercise compliance. Although data from their research suggested that self-monitoring may improve rate of attendance, both investigations used multimodal packages. Thus it is unclear from these studies whether there are independent motivation effects due to self-monitoring. In an attempt to resolve this confound, Weber and Wertheim (1989) recently compared the effects of a self-monitoring only condition against a self-monitoring/increased staff attention manipulation and a no treatment control. The subjects were women aged 17 to 56 who belonged to a privately owned health club. The experimental treatment lasted 12 weeks, and at every 2-week interval clients posted a new self-monitoring sheet to plot the frequency of gym visits. Results indicated that attendance in the self-monitoring group was superior to the control condition. Attendance for the more elaborate self-monitoring/special attention manipulation did not differ statistically from either the self-monitoring only or control group. Parenthetically, it is worth noting that the self-monitoring posters included a cartoon illustrating that a visit to the gym was enjoyable. It is plausible, therefore, that stimulus control rather than self-monitoring was responsible for the observed effect.

In a very ambitious study, King and her associates (1988) examined the positive impact of self-monitoring on exercise maintenance. Subjects in this study were men and women involved in the second 6-month phase of a 12-month home-based exercise program. Individuals in this trial were randomly assigned to either a self-monitoring or control group. Those subjects who monitored, on a weekly basis, the frequency, intensity, and duration of their exercise as well as perceived enjoyment reported engaging in more exercise sessions per month than did controls. However, both groups experienced significant improvement in aerobic capacity from pre- to posttesting.

Perceived Choice of Activity and Cognitive Strategies during Exercise. Two final studies involving cognitive theories in the area of exercise motivation are an investigation by Thompson and Wankel (1980) concerning perceived choice over mode of exercise, and a study by Martin and his associates (1984) involving the use of cognitive restructuring during activity itself. In the Thompson and Wankel (1980) design, individuals from a private health club were randomly assigned to one of two conditions: a group in which subjects purportedly had control over the type of activity they would perform, or a no choice control condition. An important feature of this study was that both groups' programs actually consisted of activities that they had selected during an initial meeting; the no choice control group was simply told that a decision had been made to use a standardized program format for activity choice rather than individual preferences. During the fifth and sixth weeks of a 6-week exercise treatment period, the choice group had higher average attendance than no choice controls. Interestingly, those in the choice condition also voiced stronger intention to engage in future exercise than the no choice control group.

In the investigation of cognitive restructuring, Martin and his colleagues (1984) studied the impact of two cognitive strategies, association versus dissociation, on the attendance of males and females to a 12-week exercise program. They reported that dissociation yielded significantly better compliance rates than association (76.6% versus 58.7%). Close inspection of the cognitive strategies, however, suggests that their operational definitions of association and dissociation were inconsistent with contemporary theory (Rejeski, 1985). Normally, association is used to refer to a focus on physical sensations; the attempt is to tune subjects into physiological input so that less cognitive capacity is available for negative affective processing of sensory cues. In contrast, dissociation refers to attentional strategies designed to cover-up or distract subjects from the fatigue-producing effects of exercise. In the Martin et al. study, subjects who associated did focus on physiologic cues, but they were encouraged to "be their own coach," to set high personal standards, and to reemphasize in their own minds that they could do better than they had in the past. In contrast, those in the dissociation condition were told to attend to the environment and pleasant stimuli, to set realistic goals, and to replace self-defeating thoughts with positive coping statements. Thus, at best, their results imply that positive realistic cognitive restructuring is superior to cognitive sets in which performance is the focal point and continued improvement is the mark of success.

Concluding Comments on Cognitive Theory

A major drawback to the use of mini-cognitive theories in exercise motivation is that this research frequently proceeds with no acknowledgement of broader-based theories of behavior. As an example, goal-setting is an extremely valuable tool in intervention; however, to me it has greater heuristic value and clinical significance when studied in conjunction with social learning theory. Anyone with clinical experience in exercise therapy will tell you that incentives and individual differences in efficacy expectations are important in understanding both the utility and direction of goal-setting strategies. The point here is that defining systematic relationships between constructs is imperative if research is to yield unambiguous and meaningful practical guidelines.

Another danger of independent mini-theories is that operation of terms often creates misrepresentations of data within broader conceptual frameworks. This problem is evident in the work of Martin et al. (1984) on cognitive strategies. We should not allow these criticisms to mask the important contributions of mini-cognitive theories to our understanding of exercise motivation. What I am suggesting is that we recognize the strengths and weaknesses of the past, consolidate our knowledge into a more coherent structure, and proceed in the future with greater precision and parsimony.

Conclusion

The absence of a theoretical perspective has been a serious charge registered against research in exercise motivation. Despite some legitimacy to this criticism, I would submit that it fails to characterize several more critical problems. Specifically, theories have often been inappropriately applied, and several manifest questionable structural integrity. To rephrase an earlier position, the use of theory requires some wisdom on the part of investigators; indeed, the choice of theory is as pertinent to the growth of science as the internal validity of experimental designs. Additional problems stem from the failure of researchers to be precise in the operation of psychological constructs. Too often, inconsistencies in research findings can be attributed to error variance originating from a measurement technology that lacks construct validity, and conclusions reached about the status of a theory are misleading. This state of affairs makes it extremely risky to conduct literature reviews without close inspection of definitions and methods of assessing dependent variables. Also, external validity is as important to the verification of theory as tightly controlled experiments. Yet in journal reviews, the sine qua non of good hypothesis testing has been internal validity. The failure of psychological constructs to predict exercise behavior in volunteer populations does not constitute evidence for rejection of a particular construct or theoretical perspective.

On the bright side, there has been amazing consistency in demonstrating that exercise behavior is negatively affected by environmental and social barriers. This finding has cut across several theoretical models (i.e., the health belief model, Slenker et al., 1984; social cognitive theory, Dzewaltowski, 1989; the theory of reasoned action, Sonstroem, 1982), and descriptive research as well (Andrew & Parker, 1979). While these data suggest that perceived control or self-efficacy is a key process-oriented construct in intervention, future research should examine the mediational role of incentives on this relationship. Based on Rotter's (1954) social learning theory of personality, clients' hierarchy of needs ought to influence the presence of perceived barriers; that is, the more clients value exercise, the less they should be inclined to allow social and environmental barriers to interfere with planned exercise training. In other words, to a significant extent the barriers are self-constructions.

A second promising area of study is the role of social support in exercise behavior. Once again, the potential value of social networks has been identified in both descriptive (Heinzelmann & Bagley, 1970) and experimental (Wankel, 1984) research. However, it is important to emphasize that the term social support has meant many things to different investigators. For those who espouse Fishbein and Ajzen's (1975) theory of reasoned action, social support refers to the beliefs of significant others concerning clients' exercise behavior and clients' motives to comply with these beliefs, whereas in Triandis's (1977) model, the focus is on social psychological motives stemming from social norms and role expectations. For Heinzelmann and Bagley (1970), it meant the spouse's attitudes. In Wankel's (1984) research, social support has been operationalized as the combined effect of stimulus control procedures and instructor praise for desired behavior. And, in a clinical trial of home-based exercise programming by King et al. (1988), social support involved regular telephone contact designed to provide support and guidance. What we have learned from the collective efforts of this research is that social-based interventions have much to offer in the area of exercise motivation; yet, this is a relatively underdeveloped area of study. Neither Fishbein and Ajzen's (1975) nor Triandis's (1977) models seem to capture the full impact of how social influence may affect exercise behavior. As an organizational schematic, researchers may benefit from examining Cohen's (1988) work on social support and the etiology of disease. In this review paper, it is argued that the buffering effect of social support may serve any one of four functions. It may

1. provide information that leads to a benign appraisal of a stressor or enhances one's coping ability;
2. increase perceived control or self-esteem;
3. function as a social pressure that increases level of motivation for preventive health behavior; and
4. offer tangible resources that enhance appraisal processes and coping behavior.

Clearly social support is not a unidimensional construct.

In closing this chapter, there are several final observations I would like to offer the reader. First, there is some suggestion in the literature that activity history is an important individual difference variable in our quest to understand exercise behavior (Morgan et al., 1984; Valois et al., 1988). If this should hold to be true in future research, it would be instructive to know whether this is a function of habit strength (Valois et al., 1988), differences in objective/subjective responses to an exercise stimulus (Rejeski, 1985), or the fact that activity history provides an indirect index of the value subjects ascribe to exercise. Such insight would be useful from the standpoint of intervention.

Second, there is no doubt that biological variables influence exercise behavior (Rejeski, 1985). For example, Dishman and Gettman (1980) found that, in conjunction with self-motivation, percent body fat was a significant predictor of adherence in structured exercise programs. Also, physical symptoms associated with cardiovascular disorders can be powerful reminders of one's health status and can serve as a motivating factor for a prevenitive health behavior such as exercise. Currently, however, existing frameworks lack necessary theoretical rigor (e.g., Dishman & Gettman, 1980). It is time to expand beyond such functional relationships, and to consider biologically rooted content-oriented constructs within the realm of a more sophisticated theoretical model—one which is developed around the principles discussed earlier in this chapter.

Third, it is surprising that, with the exception of clinical reports (Rejeski & Kenney, 1988), there has been only a single descriptive study on a developmental perspective of exercise behavior (Heitman, 1982). It is highly likely that the values and beliefs held by clients concerning vigorous physical activity are subject to significant modification as a function of age. It would seem to make good sense that these differences are considered in the realm of intervention research.

Fourth, from research on the theory of reasoned action it is evident that cognitive variables are more powerful predictors of exercise behavior when measured in close proximity to one another. There are two possible explanations for this trend. On the one hand, cognitions may change across time. After exercising for six weeks and not seeing a tremendous change in weight, an originally optimistic individual may no longer view exercise to be a viable mechanism for weight control. However, it is also possible that measuring cognitions in a research study serves as a pep talk for change that quickly dissipates (Godin, Desharnais, Jobin, & Cook, 1987). Without repeated "booster shots" to remind individuals why they are exercising, motivation may decline. It is no doubt adaptive for human beings to forget, ignore, or suppress certain beliefs and values they hold. Thus, from a theoretical perspective, the time interval between a cognitive manipulation and the target behavior is crucial to producing the anticipated effect. Practically speaking, this point suggests that a key component surrounding the efficacy of cognitive manipulations is frequency of occurance.

Finally, we shouldn't be particularly disappointed with the low to moderate level of explained variance in exercise behavior that has been recovered by way of several different theoretical models. The theory-based critique provided by this chapter should have made it quite clear that we are only on the frontier of identifying the type of constructs and theoretical system requisite to understanding exercise motivation. Moreover, human behavior is best described as a motion picture, yet we use methods analogous to still photography to capture relevant variables for prediction. Work done over the past 20 years or so has provided an auspicious beginning for intervention research dealing with exercise. We ought to pay close attention to the lessons garnered in this brief history and recognize that progress in the future will depend upon a greater dedication to examining the quality of theory, increasing precision in operation of theoretical constructs, and recognizing the sensitive balance that exists between external and internal validity in the verification of experimental hypotheses.

Part II
Enhancing
Motivation

Achievement Goals, Motivational Climate, and Motivational Processes

Carole Ames

The study of achievement motivation concerns goal-directed behavior, including the causes, direction, and consequences of this activity. It concerns how individuals approach, engage in, and respond to achievement activities as well as the reasons why they engage in certain achievement behaviors. Considerable research (e.g., Dweck, 1986; Dweck & Leggett, 1988; Elliott & Dweck, 1988) has focused on defining adaptive patterns of motivation and differentiating these from maladaptive patterns. Adaptive motivation patterns involve a range of cognitive, metacognitive, and affective processes that facilitate the initiation and maintenance of achievement activity and that contribute to long-term involvement in learning and a personal investment in learning activities (see Brophy, 1983; Dweck, 1986). These adaptive patterns are evidenced by challenge-seeking (e.g., Dweck, 1986), high levels of cognitive engagement (Corno & Mandinach, 1983), and task persistence in the face of difficulty (Diener & Dweck, 1978).

A study of adaptive motivational patterns involves a focus on both the affective as well as the cognitive aspects of achievement activity (Brophy, 1986; McCombs, 1984, 1988; Weiner, 1986). The cognitive and metacognitive aspects involve the reasons for engagement, perceived causes of success and failure, self-perceptions of competence, and willingness to employ strategies that regulate attention, effort, information processing, and task engagement (e.g., Ames & Archer, 1988; McKeachie, Pintrich, & Lin, 1985). These cognitive components of motivation can enhance the quality of task engagement itself. The affective components involve feelings of satisfaction associated with effortful behaviors and the process of learning, including positive attitudes toward the activity, content, and broader aspects of the learning situation. Both components exert considerable influence on the direction of achievement behavior, the quality of involvement in achievement endeavors, and the commitment to learning (Brophy, 1983).

The research I will be describing in this chapter has been conducted in the classroom. Because children can develop and exhibit maladaptive or adaptive motivation patterns in any achievement context, the substance of this chapter is also relevant to sport and exercise contexts. There are some factors unique to exercise and sport contexts which influence the cognitive and affective dynamics of motivated behaviors (Roberts, this volume), and I will attempt to define parallels between our research and sport and exercise. Nevertheless, I encourage the reader to make connections to other settings whether they be exercise, sport, or even home and family.

A Mastery Goal Orientation

Recent research suggests that an adaptive motivational pattern is more likely to evolve when individuals adopt a *mastery goal orientation* (e.g., Ames & Archer, 1988; Dweck, 1986; Dweck & Leggett, 1988; see also Nicholls, this volume; Roberts, this volume). When individuals are mastery-oriented, they are focused on developing new skills, improving their own level of competence or skill, or attaining a sense of mastery based on an internalized set of standards. One's sense of efficacy is based on a belief that effort will lead to personal progress and mastery. A mastery goal orientation, then, is viewed as promoting a motivational pattern that places high value on effort and the process of learning. Effort is often viewed as a double-edged sword because one's self-concept of ability is threatened if high effort does not achieve success (Covington, 1984). With a mastery orientation, however, effort is viewed as the means for achieving mastery, personal bests, and a sense of personal satisfaction.

This goal construct, which I have labeled mastery, has also been described by others (see Roberts, this volume) and alternatively labeled as learning goal (Dweck, 1986; Dweck & Leggett, 1988; Elliott & Dweck, 1988), task involvement (Maehr & Nicholls, 1980; Nicholls, 1989, this volume), or as accomplishment (Maehr & Braskamp, 1986). Brophy's (1983) description of the "motivation to learn" where one's goal is to master skills or content is also compatible with this construct. An individual can also adopt performance, ego-involved, or extrinsic goals (see Ames & Ames, 1984b; Ames & Archer, 1988; Dweck, 1986; Nicholls, Patashnick, & Nolen, 1985), but these goals stimulate different patterns of cognition and affect, and shape achievement activity in different ways.

An individual's goal preference becomes evident when he or she is faced with a choice or has to make a decision (Dweck, 1986; Dweck & Leggett, 1988). These *decision or choice points* occur frequently. Parents make their goal preferences evident when they talk to their child about schoolwork and ask questions about activities, and when they seek information from teachers or coaches, and encourage certain types of activities (see Ames & Archer, 1987). When a child returns from a weekly soccer game and a parent asks, "Did you win?", the child receives a rather clear message about what was most important.

In sport contexts, coaches' goals are evident by how they design practice sessions, how they group children, how they give recognition, how they evaluate performance, and by what they see as desirable characteristics. Does a coach congratulate players on scores or good effort? How does the coach react when the team loses? Does he or she focus on what the players did well, on what improvements they made; or does the coach schedule extra workouts or make the team "take a lap." Teachers' preferences emerge when they use specific instructional practices that relate to how they design tasks, group children for learning, and evaluate those children. A teacher, parent, or coach can encourage a particular goal orientation by making certain cues, rewards, and expectations salient. The adult shapes or structures the home, classroom, or sport setting and, in so doing, establishes a motivational climate that conveys certain goals to children.

Research related to achievement goals has progressed along two relatively separate tracks. One has focused on individual differences in preferred goal orientation. Research in this tradition has examined the correlates of different goal orientations and has established impressive evidence that different goals are associated with different patterns of cognition and affect (see, for example, Dweck, 1986; Dweck & Leggett, 1988; Elliott & Dweck, 1988; Nicholls, 1984a, 1989). Another task has focused on situational influences and has studied how the structure and demands of a learning environment can evoke different goal orientations, and, as a result, different motivational patterns (e.g., Ames & Ames, 1984b; Ames & Archer, 1988). The differences between these two trends, however, are more artificial than real (see also Duda, this volume; Roberts, this volume). In any situation, the value of a particular goal is influenced by the salience of specific cues to an individual. And, in most situations, these cues and demands are not the same for all participants; individuals are not only treated differently, they often differ in how they interpret quite similar cues. How individuals give meaning to their experiences and what this individual meaning is depends on their prior experiences as well as specific expectations (Maehr, 1984).

In our own research, we (e.g., Ames & Ames, 1984a; Ames & Archer, 1988) have been studying how the structure of achievement situations influences the adoption of a mastery goal orientation and resulting motivation patterns. However, there is now abundant evidence to suggest that the concept of a general motivational climate or structure is not sensitive to differences in how individuals are actually treated and how they interpret their experiences (Ryan & Grolnick, 1986). Teammates and classmates receive different types of instruction, assignments, and feedback. Because individuals differ in how they give meaning to their experiences, it is perhaps better to refer to the *psychological climate* (Maehr, 1984; Maehr & Braskamp, 1986), which places emphasis on the role of individual experience, meaning, and interpretation. Achievement goal theory provides us with a conceptual framework for studying individuals in their environment, whether that environment involves the home, classroom, gymnasium, or playing field.

Mastery-related cues are conveyed by many aspects of a learning environment—from how tasks are defined, to how children are grouped, recognized, and evaluated. From a motivational perspective, the subjective meaning (Maehr, 1983) of the environment is the critical factor in predicting cognitive and affective components of motivational processes. The premise of our program of research has been that the nature of children's experiences and how they interpret these experiences can influence the degree to which a mastery orientation is perceived as salient, and, consequently, the likelihood that a child will develop adaptive motivational patterns. Although much of our recent research has been conducted in classroom settings, characteristics of classrooms are shared by other contexts where the authority structure is adult-defined, and the reward structure is adult-imposed.

Classroom and organized sport activities, for example, involve children in achievement-related ventures where the outcomes are seen as important and valued, and formal evaluation is externally imposed. Individual performance is public, and children are often stratified or grouped by ability—and self-worth is often linked to normative comparisons. In these settings, achievement behavior can be evaluated either in terms of improvement and progress toward individual goals, or in relation to normative standards. Children, therefore, can either focus on developing their abilities and learning new skills, or they can focus on demonstrating or protecting their ability. Extrinsic rewards, recognition, and adult coercion can become the reason for engaging in the activity; or, personal satisfaction can come from participation, a sense of social belonging, or a belief that one's effort brings improvement. In these ways, sport and academic settings share many similar structural features.

In this chapter, I will refer to and describe our research conducted in classroom settings, but the implications of our research extend beyond the classroom to other environments where children learn, perform, and receive evaluation. This chapter will describe how our program of research has addressed each of the following questions:

1. How can we define the theoretical construct of a mastery goal in relation to the parameters of a particular learning environment? How do the principles underlying a mastery orientation translate into instructional practices and children's experiences?
2. Are students who see their classroom experiences as mastery-oriented more likely to engage in adaptive motivational patterns?
3. As students progress through school, can certain patterns of motivation become stabilized? Can certain kinds of experiences over time begin to have cumulative effects on student motivation?
4. Can children's motivation be enhanced by increasing the salience of a mastery orientation in the learning environment? How can we design such a field intervention?

Achievement Goals: High School Students

Our first question asked whether there is a link between the student's motivation and the character or structure of the student's classroom experiences. The broader question is whether the goal structure of an achievement setting impacts the motivation patterns of the individual learners or performers. Of special interest here are those environments where individuals participate in learning and skill development activities and are then evaluated in these activities. To what extent can we explain differences and variations in student motivation by assessing how students interpret or experience their learning environment? This latter issue was the focus of a previously published study (Ames & Archer, 1988) in which we examined the relationship between specific motivational processes and high school students' perceptions of classroom goal orientation. This study involved 136 students who were enrolled in a high school for academically advanced students.

For this study, we developed a measure of mastery orientation—that is, students' perceptions of the mastery orientation of their classroom. We first identified the theoretical dimensions of a mastery goal and then translated these dimensions to actual classroom parameters (see Table 1). These dimensions, however, are relevant to a wide range of environments that extend beyond the classroom. For other contexts or environments, the dimensions remain the same, although the parameters and actual scale items may vary according to the type of activity. The scale we developed for this study and have since adapted for use with younger children included 15 items; and across several administrations to varied groups, we have obtained consistent coefficient alphas in the range of .80 to .90.

Table 1   Dimensions of a Mastery Goal

Theoretical dimensions	Mastery goal
How is success defined?	Individual progress, improvement
What is valued?	Effort
How is child evaluated?	Progress, effort
How are mistakes viewed?	Part of learning
Why engage in activity?	Develop new skills
Why does child feel satisfied?	Successful effort, challenge, personal best
What are children focused on?	Learning of skills
What is leader focused on?	Development, learning

Note. Adapted from Ames and Archer (1988).

In addition to the perceived mastery orientation of the classroom, we also assessed students' use of effective learning strategies, preference for tasks that offer challenge, attributional beliefs, and attitude toward class. Learning strategies have motivational components when they involve the monitoring and regulation of one's attention, effort, and task behaviors. These strategies also include effective ways of dealing with difficulty and overcoming obstacles. Strategies of this type are generic in that they are important to a wide range of achievement activities. Moreover, they are effort-driven in that a willingness to employ such strategies requires both a belief in the efficacy of one's effort for achieving success or mastery and a willingness to put forth the necessary effort. Other research has focused on how children develop and acquire specific strategies, but from a motivational perspective we are interested in whether they exhibit a willingness to use the strategies. A willingness to apply effective strategies is essential for maintaining achievement-directed behavior over time.

The findings of the Ames and Archer study (1988) established a strong relationship between mastery goal orientation and motivation in a field setting. Students who saw their experiences as mastery-oriented were more likely to use effective strategies, to prefer challenging tasks, to like their class more, and to believe that effort and success covary. These findings suggested that achievement goal theory provides a meaningful framework for conceptualizing students' achievement experiences. Moreover, a mastery goal orientation appeared to be a salient feature of the classroom structure, and cognitive and affective motivational processes varied according to how students perceived and interpreted this structure.

Particularly striking to us was that these relationships were evident in this group of academically advanced students. We might expect that most students belonging to this "elite" group would exhibit adaptive motivation patterns. Certainly knowledge and use of effective strategies and techniques, a preference for challenge, and positive affect are the very characteristics we tend to associate with the rise to eliteness. Our findings, however, suggest that the motivation of individuals, even in elite groups, is responsive to how the environment or climate is defined.

Extrapolating from the classroom to sport settings, the environment in which children learn and practice skills and compete is important. Even the motivation patterns of better sport participants may vary considerably over time depending on the goal orientation they adopt. And, certainly, the coach or teacher can enable these participants to adopt a mastery orientation if they establish a structure that conveys a mastery orientation. For example, in the context of swimming, a coach can focus swimmers on their individual improvement, personal bests, and skill development and, in so doing, establish the basis for a mastery orientation. Such a structure emphasizes personal challenge in small, achieveable steps; it stresses learning new techniques; and it fosters an attitude of enjoyment (see Chambliss, 1989). Even among elite swimmers, maintenance of adaptive motivational processes can serve to enhance further their skill development and performance.

These findings led us to ask what the long-term consequences of participation or involvement in mastery or nonmastery types of environments are. For example, what happens to students as they move on to new classes with different teachers? Is there evidence of cumulative effects of certain kinds of experiences? To study these questions, we tracked these same high school students one year later when they were in different classrooms with different teachers (Ames & Archer, 1990).

We first examined changes in students' motivation patterns as they moved to classes that were stronger or weaker in mastery orientation. Students' use of effective strategies, preference for challenge, positive attitudes toward learning, and attributions to effort were all found to covary with changes in mastery motivational climate. As shown in Table 2, when students saw an increase

Table 2   Changes in Perceived Goals Correlated With Changes in Motivation (Year 2 Minus Year 1)

Motivation variable	Mastery goal
Strategy use	.59***
Task preference	.26**
Positive attitude	.69***
Attribution/effort	.37***
Self-concept of ability	.22*

Note. From Ames and Archer (1990).
* = $p < .05$. ** = $p < .01$. *** = $p < .001$.

in the mastery orientation of their classroom (Year 2 minus Year 1), there was a corresponding increase in each of the motivation variables (Year 2 minus Year 1).

We then divided the students into three groups according to the number of years they spent in a classroom they saw as mastery oriented. We asked whether the motivation of students who had had mastery-oriented experiences for two consecutive years differed from those students who had had such experiences for only one year, and whether these latter students differed from those who had not experienced a mastery climate for either year. We found that students' use of effective strategies and positive attitudes toward the subject matter area were enhanced by the number of years they had mastery-oriented experiences (see Figure 1). By the end of the second year, the discrepancy between those students who had had mastery experiences for two consecutive years and those who had had none became quite marked. In sports, children also move to new settings as they move from one age group to another or from a lower level to the next higher level of a sport; as they do so, children often encounter a different climate, coach, and philosophy. Children's motivation and commitment in the sports area may show similar trends over time according to how the sport activity is structured.

These first two studies show that student motivation occurs within a context, and that this context or, more importantly, students' perception and interpretation of it, is an important factor in understanding the cognitive and affective components of student motivation. From these findings, we can also see how and why students differ in the motivational patterns they exhibit. The "why" depends on how students give meaning to their classroom learning experiences, and achievement goal theory is a way of defining these "meanings." Both of these studies involved high school students, and our next question concerned whether we might find similar relationships and patterns emerging among younger children.

Achievement Goals: Elementary School Students

On the one hand, we might expect the structure of the elementary school classrooms in general to appear more mastery oriented, or at least more supportive, than high school classrooms. At least, we have visions that in the early years of elementary school, children are actively engaged in learning and are involved in a variety of different learning activities. We envision that teachers are more likely to attend to individual progress and improvement, to use little or no normative grading, and to use all kinds of strategies to give children feelings of confidence and worth. However, there is also much literature that suggests that there is considerable variation in how elementary school classrooms are structured for learning—and that we should be concerned about the quality of student engagement at this level. For in many classrooms,

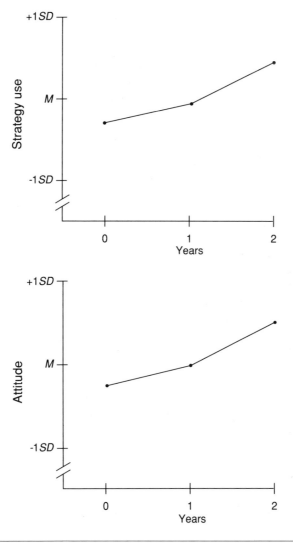

Figure 1. Students' use of effective strategies and positive attitudes toward subject matter are enhanced by the number of years in mastery-oriented experiences.

teachers rely heavily on extrinsic incentives, ability grouping is the venue for instruction, students have few opportunities for making choices or decisions, and seatwork with uniform tasks occupies much class time (Brophy, 1983). Many students are more concerned about completing assignments than about understanding the content or the purpose of the activity.

Similarly, in sport situations we think of children's first experiences as play-like and fun, with little emphasis on the competitive aspects. However, there is much evidence to the contrary. Children's first experiences with soccer and baseball, for example, are often with organized, competitive team play. In these situations, children must play according to established rules, they have little control over which positions they play, and they are often more focused on winning the game than on skill development. The competitive aspects of organized sport activity are becoming more evident at earlier ages (Roberts, 1984); and, as a consequence, children with less developed skills are likely to find themselves on the sidelines or bench with few opportunities to participate and develop the necessary skills.

We draw on findings from three studies with elementary school-age children to suggest that the relationship between mastery goals and adaptive motivation patterns exists for younger populations. In her thesis research, Powell (1990) surveyed 120 fourth grade children in their math class. She found that the degree to which students viewed their math learning experiences as mastery oriented was significantly related to whether they reported using effective strategies for learning math as well as to their interest in learning math (see Table 3). Maehr and Ames (1989) found similar patterns of relationship in a survey administered to 150 students in junior high school science classes (see Table 3). Students who saw their science class as mastery oriented were more likely to use effective strategies and to show a preference for challenging tasks (i.e., tasks that offer opportunities to learn new things but also risk failure).

Finally, we (Ames & Maehr, 1989) examined these relationships for a group of "at-risk" children. In both sport and academic settings, there are some children who have few skills, are often physically awkward or cognitively unprepared for learning, lack self-confidence, and are fearful about making a commitment. These children are typically labeled at-risk because they are likely to drop out or become nonparticipants, even when they remain in the situation.

With a sample of 73 classes (Grades 2-6), we asked teachers to nominate four to five students whom they considered at-risk according to certain criteria (e.g., poor performance, poor motivation, lacking appropriate strategies for

Table 3   Relationships Between Mastery Climate and Motivation Related Variables Across Different Populations

Variable	Powell (1990) Grade 4 ($n = 120$)	Maehr & Ames (1989) Junior high ($n = 150$)	Ames & Maehr (1989) Grades 2-6 At-risk ($n = 192$)	Ames & Maehr (1989) Grades 2-6 Non-at-risk ($n = 336$)
Learning strategies	.42***	.46***	.58***	.63***
Intrinsic motivation	.54***		.60***	.56***
Attitude/class			.49***	.44***
Task challenge		.35***		

*** = p < .001

doing well in school, poor self-concept). Within each classroom, we then randomly selected five additional children as representing a non-at-risk group. To establish that these groups were significantly different from each other, we compared the at-risk group with the non-at-risk group across classrooms and found significant differences on a wide range of motivational variables favoring the non-at-risk group. After establishing that these two classifications were "motivationally different," we then examined the relationship between perceived mastery orientation of the classroom and other motivation variables for each group (see Table 3). What is particularly striking is that the pattern and strength of relationship were consistent for these different classifications of students.

To date, our findings suggest that a mastery goal orientation is related to a pattern of cognition and affect that is likely to enhance children's involvement in learning as well as the quality of their involvement in learning. We have studied different kinds of students ranging from the elite to the at-risk. We have looked into high school and elementary school classrooms, and we have surveyed a wide range of subject matter areas. The utilization of effective strategies as well as the expression of positive attitudes has been a consistent focus of this research. The use of effective strategies or techniques and the development of positive attitudes are central to achieving excellence in academics as well as sports (see comments by Chambliss, 1989). Taken together, this research shows that achievement goals provide a meaningful framework for understanding how students react to their classroom experiences. Moreover, a mastery orientation goal appears to evoke a pattern of motivational processes that are associated with adaptive or desirable achievement behaviors. This research, however, has been correlational, and the question that emerges is whether the mastery orientation of those environments where children learn and perform can be increased, and if so doing results in more adaptive motivation patterns particularly among those students who are at-risk.

Research in Progress

Based on the theoretical and empirical literature on achievement goals and student motivation, we (e.g., Ames & Ames, 1984a; Ames & Archer, 1988) are now conducting a series of experimental interventions that are designed to increase the frequency and quality of children's mastery-oriented experiences in classroom settings. The interventions are directed toward giving the teacher new choices and changing the teacher's decisions and instructional practices so that a mastery orientation characterizes the classroom environment. The interventions are being carried out in elementary school classroom settings, but the principles and framework are applicable to other achievement settings where individuals are involved in learning activities, skill development, and performance evaluation.

With the intervention, we are focused especially on at-risk children—those who lack skills and self-confidence and who are likely to participate at low levels or drop out. Our criteria and methods for identifying the at-risk student are the same as those described for the previous Ames and Maehr study (1989) in which this group was first examined. For the present study, at-risk students were once again teacher-nominated according to our specific criteria and numbered about four to five students for each class.

In designing such an intervention, we outlined the principles that underlie a mastery orientation (see Table 1), then searched the literature for strategies that a teacher or leader can and should use to foster a mastery orientation. Actually, as noted by Brophy and Merrick (1987), the motivation literature is rich with general and specific strategies that are conceptually consistent with a mastery orientation and that can be translated into actual classroom practices. At the same time, we grouped these mastery principles and strategies into six areas of the learning environment. These areas are identified by the acronym TARGET, which was initially coined and described by Joyce Epstein (1988, 1989). Epstein used TARGET to refer to the *task, authority, recognition, grouping, evaluation*, and *time* dimensions or structures of a learning environment, and they are briefly defined in Table 4. The reader is referred to Epstein's work (1988) for a more elaborated description of each TARGET area. Along with the basic principles underlying a mastery achievement goal orientation, the strategies and techniques that translate these principles into actual classroom practices formed the content of the intervention (see Table 4). By bringing together a wide range of strategies and mapping these strategies onto all aspects of the learning environment, we have attempted to achieve a comprehensible plan for impacting children's motivation over the long term.

The design of this research benefitted greatly from the work of Brophy and his colleagues (Brophy & Merrick, 1987) who have conducted intervention studies with the goal of changing teacher behaviors. Their methodology and description of "field-setting problems" proved especially helpful in planning our procedures for implementation and monitoring. Similar to Brophy and Merrick, our method included three main steps. The first involved identifying those strategies that are consistent with a mastery goal orientation and organizing these strategies into Epstein's six TARGET areas. Second, we operationalized each strategy in terms of a wide range of specific instructional practices to facilitate teachers' actual implementation of the strategies. And, third, we set up a record-keeping system to monitor teacher's actual implementation of the practices and strategies.

Approximately 77 elementary school teachers (Grades 2-6) participated in the first year of the project. Although this was a field study, we were able to assign teachers randomly to intervention and control groups, controlling for grade level and school representation. The project is ongoing and preliminary results are described in more detail elsewhere (Ames, 1990a). The goal is aimed at increasing the likelihood that children, especially those

Table 4   Description of TARGET Areas and Motivational Strategies

TARGET area descriptions	Strategies
Task Class activities, assignments and homework; design of tasks	Design activities for variety, individual challenge, and active involvement Help children set realistic, short-term goals
Authority Student participation in the instructional process	Involve children in decision-making and leadership roles Help students develop self-management and self-monitoring skills
Recognition Reasons for recognition; distribution of rewards; opportunities for rewards	Recognize individual progress and improvement Assure equal opportunities for rewards Focus on each child's self-worth
Grouping Manner and frequency of students working together	Use flexible and heterogeneous grouping arrangements Provide for multiple grouping arrangements
Evaluation Standards for performance; monitoring of performance; evaluative feedback	Use criteria of individual progress, improvement, and mastery Involve children in self-evaluation Make evaluation private and meaningful
Time Schedule flexibility; pace of learning; management of classwork	Provide opportunities and time for improvement Help children establish work and practice schedules

Note. TARGET area descriptions and strategies were adapted from Epstein (1988, 1989).

who are motivationally and academically at-risk, will develop adaptive motivation patterns.

In the first year of the project, teachers implemented strategies in each TARGET area over the course of the spring semester. Teachers were given materials that described the concepts and principles associated with a mastery goal orientation, the six TARGET areas, the strategies within each area, and a wide range of actual instructional practices that operationalized each strategy. Treatment implementation was monitored by teachers keeping weekly records of which strategy and TARGET area they implemented. Teachers were encouraged to use as many strategies as they could, but were instructed to use strategies from one of the TARGET areas each week. Finally, we asked the teachers to focus especially on the at-risk students in their classroom, although they were encouraged to use the ideas with the entire class.

The effects of the intervention in the first year have been assessed by comparing the at-risk students in the treatment and control classrooms on several measures, including learning strategies, intrinsic motivation, self-concept of ability, attitudes, and perceived competence. These measures were administered in the fall and at the end of the spring semester. Previous research suggested to us that the self-perceptions and motivation of students may be expected to decline over the course of the year (e.g., Brophy & Merrick, 1987; Good & Brophy, 1986). Thus, we expected to find a similar pattern for students in the control classrooms, and these expectations were confirmed. We found significant declines in motivation for the at-risk students in the control classes. When we looked at the students in the treatment classrooms, however, this downward trend was not evident. Although we did not find significant increases in several of the motivational variables over the course of the semester, we did not find any declines.

Our findings suggest that a first step may involve arresting a downward trend in motivation that tends to occur over the course of the school year and across school years. At the time of the spring assessment, we found scores on measures of learning strategies, intrinsic motivation, and attitudes significantly more positive for students in the treatment classrooms than in the control classrooms. Moreover, students' responses on the mastery climate questionnaire provided evidence that the intervention had the effect of increasing the salience of a mastery orientation in the treatment classrooms.

The findings from the first year of the project are encouraging. The expected declines in self-perceptions and motivation over the course of the year were not found in the intervention classrooms; by the end of the semester, there was evidence that the motivational climate in the intervention classrooms was significantly impacted by changes in teachers' strategies. The project is now in its second year, and teachers are implementing the intervention for the entire academic year.

Although our research has been conducted in classrooms, the intervention model itself is easily extended to sport and exercise settings. Organized sport settings for children are often stratified by ability (children have to try out for the next league or level of the sport). Normative and social comparison is unavoidable (i.e., key and valued positions are given to the better players, playing time correlates with performance on the field), individual performance is public and unambiguous, and recognition is given to the few who score the most or achieve the highest level. In these settings, at-risk children— those who are less physically mature, less coordinated, or novice players— are often faced with an environment that contributes to feelings of helplessness.

In these environments, however, tasks or activities can be structured to help children develop new skills and techniques and to help them establish reasonable short-term goals. Even less able children can be given leadership roles and positions of importance. Children can be recognized for their individual progress and improvement. Moreover, individual progress and constructive feedback can be made private and meaningful to each child.

A mastery-oriented climate in swimming, for example, would involve focusing children on their individual progress so that they can begin setting goals and monitoring their progress toward their goals. It might also involve providing for variety and challenge in daily training to keep children interested in participation. Varied grouping arrangements may be important so that "C" and "B" level swimmers have opportunities to see how the "A" level swimmers swim and train. Recognition for effort, improvement, and personal bests is important to build children's sense of efficacy.

In team sports, children need to have practice playing a variety of positions and to not be locked into a position for the sole purpose of ensuring a team win or preventing a loss. Some children will need more playing time to develop the necessary skills. Often, those children who need the most practice are the ones who receive the least playing time or who get to play only one position. Children need much recognition and appreciation of their participation and involvement. Children also need to be evaluated for their improvement and effort, and evaluation and constructive feedback should be individual and private. These are examples of some of the ways the TARGET areas can be structured so that a mastery climate is enhanced.

Conclusion

To date, most motivational interventions have been short term and have focused on individual students. Once deficiencies or maladaptive processes are identified, motivation training takes on the role of individual remediation. The goal is to make the student or child more motivationally equipped to deal with a variety of different learning situations. When we look at classrooms, school, and sport situations, however, more attention needs to be given to the context of participation—to the motivational climate that is created.

Because achievement behaviors occur within a context, the structure and climate must support, enhance, and facilitate those achievement-directed behaviors that we desire over the long term. We must be careful not to focus on immediate achievement, scores, or performance. Instead, we must attend to children's participation, involvement, interest, and goals. We want children to be active participants, to focus on their skill development, to opt for those activities and challenges where they can best develop these skills, and to have positive feelings toward both the activity and their involvement in the activity.

The classroom and other learning environments have an important role in shaping and socializing students' motivational patterns. Moreover, it is the individual student's experiences in these environments and, more importantly, their perception and interpretation of these experiences that are critical. Our evidence suggests that if we want children to employ effortful strategies, seek challenging tasks, and respond positively to learning situations, we need to move toward enhancing the mastery orientation of the learning environment— whether that environment involves the classroom, home, or playing field.

Achievement goals provide the reason and impetus for different patterns of motivation. When the environment conveys a mastery goal orientation, children are more likely to exhibit adaptive motivational processes. An approach to restructuring the environment requires identifying those principles and strategies that will make a mastery orientation salient to the individual participants. With this approach, "motivation training" involves a comprehensive restructuring that focuses on ways to envelop children's experiences within mastery goal principles. It involves changing the strategies and practices of the teacher, parent, or leader. Emphasis is placed on the choices and decisions that are made by the adult leaders because these choices convey the goal priority of the adult: the valued activities, outcomes, and individual characteristics.

In my research I have defined an adaptive motivation pattern in terms of how students approach, engage in, and respond to learning activities. There is theoretical and empirical support to show that adaptive patterns are associated with a mastery goal orientation and that children's experiences can be described in relation to mastery goal concepts (e.g., Dweck, 1986; Dweck & Elliott, 1983). Achievement goal theory, then, is a conceptual framework for studying individuals in their environments whether that environment involves the classroom, home, or playing field.

In sport, success is typically defined by success in competition, and, in this sense, success is unambiguous. Adhering to this belief and placing major emphasis on this outcome offers many children few opportunities to define their experiences as mastery oriented. As in the classroom, many children cease to participate, or participate at such a low level that they stand little chance of developing the necessary skills and a sense of "I belong here," (see Chambliss, 1989) or "I am a valued player." Unlike school, children can actually drop out of sports at any time. Nevertheless, organized sports for children are contexts where children are to learn and develop skills, and these contexts can be defined and structured so that a mastery orientation is salient and is adopted by children, even when the interpersonal (as in swimming) and interteam (as in soccer) competitive elements remain intact.

Goal-Setting and Motor Performance: A Review and Critique

Robert Weinberg

Much of human behavior seems to persist over time despite the fact that external rewards are often minimal or nonexistent. When external inducements are sparse, individuals are assumed to be self-motivated to sustain their actions and complete their tasks. One important source of self-motivation is goal-setting. The use of goal-setting as a motivational technique for enhancing productivity and performance has become extremely popular in industrial, academic, and sport settings. Although there has been an abundant amount of empirical research conducted in organizational settings on goal-setting, it is only recently that sport psychologists have begun to study systematically the relationship between goals and sport performance. The purpose of the present paper is to summarize the findings investigating the relationship between goal-setting and performance. First, I will review the goal-setting studies conducted in industrial and organizational settings together with the variables mediating the goal-performance relationship. Second, goal-setting studies conducted in sport and exercise settings will be discussed. Third, methodological, theoretical, and interpretive limitations in the goal-setting literature will be addressed. Finally, future directions for research in goal-setting within sport and exercise settings will be suggested.

The Concept of Goal-Setting

By definition, a goal is what an individual is trying to accomplish; it is the object or aim of an action. For example, in most goal-setting studies, the term *goal* refers to attaining a specific standard of proficiency on a task, usually within a specified time limit. The basic assumption of goal-setting research is that goals are immediate regulators of human action. Although goals can certainly influence behavior, no one-to-one correspondence between goals and action can be assumed because people make errors, or lack the ability to obtain their objectives, or subconsciously subvert their conscious goals (Locke, Shaw, Saari, & Latham, 1981). The exact degree of association between goals and actions is an empirical question that has been dealt with extensively in the recent literature on goal-setting which will be reviewed later in the paper.

Much of the early research on goal-setting was initiated by two major sources, one academic and one organizational. The academic source extends back to the early 1960s and focuses on the associated concepts of intention, task set, and level of aspiration (see Ryan, 1970, for a review). The organizational line of research can be traced back to the work of Taylor (1911/1967). A key element of this original work was the concept of *task*, which was defined as a specific assignment (or goal) given to a worker each day. This initial task concept helped lead to the application of goal-setting in the form of management-by-objectives programs, now widely employed in industrial settings (Odiorne, 1978). These two schools of thought have converged in the work of Locke (1966, 1978, 1980, 1982), Latham and his colleagues (Latham & Lee, 1986; Latham & Locke, 1975; Latham & Yukl, 1975, 1976), and others who have investigated the effect of goal-setting on task performance.

According to Locke's theory of goal-setting, which he set forth in his seminal article (1966), hard goals result in a higher level of performance and effort than easy goals, and specific hard goals result in a higher level of performance than do no goals or a generalized goal of "do your best." Along these lines, Locke (1966, 1968) initiated a program of detailed empirical research and theoretical analysis that laid a solid foundation for what has become one of the most active areas of research in the applied behavioral sciences. In fact, much of the research on goal-setting and task performance has set out to test the propositions concerning the effect of goal difficulty and goal specificity on task performance. We will now briefly review the industrial/organizational literature concerning the relationship between goals and task performance.

Goal-Setting and Task Performance

Research on goal-setting as a motivational strategy has been proliferating so rapidly in recent years that reviews by Latham and Yukl (1975) and Steers and Porter (1974) became outdated, necessitating a more updated review (Locke et al., 1981). Even more recently, using the statistical technique of meta-analysis, which enables the reviewer to aggregate research findings across studies by using both inferential and descriptive statistics, researchers have continued to update the ever expanding literature on goal-setting and human performance (e.g., Mento, Steel, & Karren, 1987; Tubbs, 1986). In further support of the utility of goal-setting, Miner (1984) found that out of 32 theories within the organizational sciences domain, goal-setting was only one of four that were both valid and useful. Finally, in his text on work motivation, Pinder (1984) stated that ''goal setting theory has demonstrated more scientific validity to date than any other theory or approach to work motivation'' (p. 169).

The most tested aspect of Locke's theory revolves around the relationship of goal difficulty/specificity and performance. As previously stated, Locke (1966, 1968) has argued that specific, difficult, challenging goals lead to higher levels of task performance than either do-your-best, easy goals, or no goals. In Locke and colleagues' (1981) review of the goal-setting literature, 99 of 110 studies were found to support this hypothesis. These results were found in a variety of laboratory studies using tasks such as brainstorming (Bavelas & Lee, 1978), chess (Campbell & Ilgen, 1976), card sorting (London & Oldham, 1976), anagrams (Rothkopf & Kaplan, 1972), perceptual speed (Mento, Cartledge, & Locke, 1980), and reaction time (Locke, Cartledge, & Knerr, 1970). In addition, these laboratory findings have been replicated in several experiments designed to solve practical organizational problems. For example, Latham and Locke (1975) using logging crews, Yukl and Latham (1978) with typists, Latham and Baldes (1975) with truck drivers, Ivancevich (1977) with maintenance technicians, and Blumenfeld and Leidy (1969) using salesmen have all demonstrated the positive effects of goal-setting, indicating the robust nature of setting specific, challenging goals on performance.

More recent reviews of literature using meta-analytic techniques (Mento et al., 1987; Tubbs, 1986) have also investigated the goal difficulty/specificity propositions put forth by Locke. The conclusions from both of these meta-analyses strongly support the goal difficulty/specificity relationship noted above with specific difficult goals having stronger mean effect sizes than easy goals, no goals, or do-your-best goals. Mento et al. (1987) go as far as to argue that "if there is ever to be a viable candidate from the organizational sciences for elevation to the lofty status of a scientific law of nature, then the relationships between goal difficulty/specificity and task performance are most worthy of serious consideration" (p. 74).

Goal-Setting in Sport and Exercise

Such consistent findings from the industrial and organizational literature have led many coaches, players, and physical educators to employ goal-setting techniques to improve physical performance. However, until very recently, little empirical research has investigated the effects of goal-setting on performance enhancement in sport and exercise settings. Rather, most of the articles on goal-setting in sport are designed to provide practical ideas that can assist in maximizing the personal growth and development of sport participants rather than empirically testing the goal setting-performance relationship (e.g., Botterill, 1978, 1979, 1980; Gould, 1984; McClements & Botterill, 1979).

Prior to 1985, there was a dearth of studies investigating the goal setting-performance relationship in sport. And the few studies that were conducted produced equivocal findings. For example, Barnett and Stanicek (1979) found that subjects in a goal-setting group improved their archery performance significantly over the course of a 10-week class compared to subjects in a no goal-setting group. Similarly, Botterill (1977) found that subjects who set specific hard goals performed significantly better than subjects who were told to do their best. However, other variables such as who set the goal (subject or experimenter; group or individual) confounded the issue of whether specific, hard goals were better than do-your-best goals in Botterill's study. In contrast to these findings, which tend to support the idea that specific hard goals can enhance performance, studies by Barnett (1977) and Hollingsworth (1975) found no significant differences between goal-setting and no goal-setting groups performing a novel minor skill.

An important turning point to the beginning of a more systematic and concerted effort to study the relationship between goals and performance in sport and exercise settings came with the publication of Locke and Latham's (1985) article on the application of goal-setting to sports. Locke and Latham argue that tasks performed in organizational settings and in the laboratory have much in common with sport activities in that both involve mental and physical actions directed toward some goal. This being the case, goal-setting should work equally well in the realm of sports as it does in organizational settings. In fact, Locke and Latham suggest that goal-setting could work even better in sports than in organizations because the measurement of an individual's performance (a precondition for the positive effects of goal-setting) is typically easier in sports than in organizational settings. Based on the organizational literature, they suggest 10 specific hypotheses (1985, p. 209) concerning how goals can work in sport settings:

1. Specific goals will regulate action more precisely than general goals.
2. For quantitative (specific) goals, the higher the goal the better the performance, assuming sufficient ability and commitment.
3. Specific, difficult goals will lead to better performance than goals of "do your best" or no goals.
4. Using short-term goals plus long-term goals will lead to better performance than using long-term goals alone.
5. Goals will affect performance by directing activity, mobilizing effort, increasing persistence, and motivating the search for appropriate task strategies.
6. Goal-setting will be most effective when there is feedback showing progress in relation to the goal.
7. With goals that are difficult, the higher the degree of commitment the better the performance.
8. Commitment can be affected by asking the individual to accept the goal, showing support, allowing participation in the setting of the goals, in training, in selection, and in incentives and rewards.
9. Goal attainment will be facilitated by a suitable plan of action or strategy, especially when the task is complex or long term.
10. Competition will improve performance to the degree that it leads to the setting of higher goals and/or increases in goal commitment.

In addition to providing specific hypotheses for empirically testing the effects of goal-setting in sports. Locke and Latham (1985) also gave several practical examples of how goals could be applied in sport settings. These included goals for practice, goals during competition, goals to increase self-confidence, as well as long-term and short-term goals. Since the publication of this article, sport psychologists have started to study systematically the effectiveness of various goal-setting procedures in both laboratory and applied settings by testing some of Locke and Latham's (1985) hypotheses. A review of this literature reveals that sport psychology researchers have predominantly focused on the areas of goal specificity, goal proximity, and goal difficulty. Although several of the recent studies in sport and exercise settings have investigated these areas simultaneously, for simplicity each area is reviewed separately. Finally, some recent research which has examined the effectiveness of goal-setting training programs in enhancing performance will be reviewed.

Goal Specificity

Probably the hypothesis that specific, hard goals enhance performance significantly more than no goals or do-your-best goals has generated the most research in sport and exercise settings. In Locke and associates' (1981) review, it was noted that this specific hypothesis received support from 25 field studies and 27 laboratory studies with only two studies finding no differences between goal-setting groups. In addition, meta-analytic studies (Mento et al., 1987; Tubbs, 1986) demonstrated strong effect sizes for goal specificity. Thus, the robust nature of this effect is undeniable from the organizational literature.

Weinberg, Bruya, and Jackson (1985) were among the first to test Locke and Latham's (1985) goal specificity hypothesis in a physical activity setting. In this field experiment, subjects (college students in conditioning classes) were matched on baseline measures of the 3-minute sit-up test and randomly assigned to one of four goal-setting conditions. In three of these conditions, subjects had a specific, difficult goal, whereas the fourth group was just told to "do your best." Results indicated no differences in sit-up performance throughout the 5-week experimental period between the three specific goal-groups and the do-your-best group. This finding is contrary to the literature in organizational psychology. Thus several studies have followed up in studying goal specificity in sport and exercise settings.

For example, Weinberg, Bruya, Jackson, and Garland (1987) and Garland, Weinberg, Bruya, and Jackson (1988) also investigated the goal specificity hypothesis in an exercise setting. The 3-minute sit-up was again used as the major dependent variable over the course of the 5-week field experiment. Results were in agreement with findings of Weinberg et al. (1985) indicating no differences in performance between subjects given specific, difficult goals versus do-your-best goals. Consistent with these findings, Hall, Weinberg, and Jackson (1983) using circuit training, and Stitcher, Weinberg, and Jackson (1983) employing weight lifting, both found no significant differences between specific goal groups and do-your-best groups over the course of the experimental period.

In contrast to these findings, several studies conducted in sport and exercise settings have found significant differences between specific goal groups and do-your-best groups. That is, subjects with specific, hard goals performed significantly better than subjects with do-your-best goals. For example, Weinberg, Bruya, Longino, and Jackson (1988) used elementary-aged children in physical education classes to study goal specificity. Subjects were matched and randomly assigned to a specific goal group or a do-your-best control group. Improvement in a 2-minute sit-up test over the course of the 10-week experimental period was the major dependent variable. Results indicated that all three specific goal groups performed significantly better than the do-your-best group, especially toward the end of the 10-week period. In the only other study using children to study goal specificity effects on performance, Erbaugh and Barnett (1986) found that children in the specific goal condition performed a jumping task better than children in a control condition. In a final study using the 3-minute sit-up with conditioning classes, Hall and Byrne (1988) found partial support for the goal specificity hypothesis. That is, only the specific goal groups that set both short-term and long-term goals displayed significantly better sit-up performance than the do-your-best group; the long-term goal group displayed no differences.

Hall, Weinberg, and Jackson (1987) conducted one of the only laboratory studies investigating goal specificity and performance using a grip strength endurance task. Subjects were pretested by being asked to maintain a grip that was one third of their maximum for as long as they could. Based on the length of time they could maintain their grip, specific hard goals were established. Two groups received specific hard challenging goals (improve by 40 seconds; improve by 70 seconds), while a third group was simply told to ''do your best.'' Results indicated that both specific, hard goal groups improved significantly on the posttest whereas the do-your-best group showed no improvement.

In summary, results in the sport psychology literature concerning the effects of goal specificity and performance have been equivocal, with only some of the studies supporting Locke and Latham's (1985) hypothesis that specific hard goals would produce higher levels of performance than no goals or do-your-best goals. These studies have been conducted in both field and laboratory settings, used children and adults as subjects, and focused on exercise and sport environments. These inconsistent findings are partly due to the different methodologies employed in goal-setting studies along with moderator variables which mediate the goal setting-performance relationship. These methodological and procedural issues will be addressed later in the chapter.

Goal Proximity

Another area of goal-setting that has received recent attention in the sport psychology literature is goal proximity. Locke and Latham (1985) have hypothesized that using short-term goals plus long-term goals will lead to better performance than using long-term goals alone. They feel that long-term goals are often too abstract and too far into the future to have motivational significance in the present. Other psychologists (Bandura, 1982; Carver & Scheier, 1982) have also argued that short-term goals should produce the most substantial and long-lasting self-regulated behavioral change. For example, Bandura (1982) states that short-term (proximal) goals are particularly important in improving performance because they provide immediate incentives and feedback about an individual's progress, whereas long-term (distal) goals are too far removed in time to summon much effort or direct one's present actions. In essence, focusing on the distant future makes it easy to slacken efforts in the present. On the other hand, the attainment of subgoals provides indicators of mastery that in turn enhance one's self-confidence and feelings of competence. The notion that short-term goals are important in improving performance is also held by many coaches and sport psychologists (Bell, 1983; Carron, 1984; Gould, 1984; O'Block & Evans, 1984).

Despite the agreement concerning the importance of short-term goals as an adjunct to long-term goal attainment, little empirical research has been conducted and the extant literature is inconclusive. For instance, Bandura and Simon (1977) found that subjects in a weight loss program who set weekly goals for weight loss were only effective when daily subgoals were also set. Similarly, Bandura and Schunk (1981), using children solving arithmetic problems, found the short-term goals allowed children to progress more rapidly in self-directed learning than did long-term goals. However, in a recent position paper, Kirschenbaum (1985) argues that the results of these studies are inconclusive due to the confounding amounts of performance feedback for the various treatment conditions. After carefully reviewing the literature, Kirschenbaum (1985) concludes that short-term goals should be flexible rather than rigid as is usually the case in experimenter-set goals. For example, having to exercise every day for 30 minutes would not be a flexible goal, whereas exercising 30 minutes a day for four days a week would allow for some flexibility. If short-term goals are not flexible, then a sense of failure could be felt if uncontrollable events such as injury and illness prevent attainment of one's long-term goal.

Research in sport psychology has only recently begun to address the issue of the effectiveness of short-term and long-term goals to enhance performance in both exercise and sport settings. In Weinberg, Bruya, and Jackson's (1985) study, subjects were matched on their baseline 3-minute sit-up test and randomly assigned to either a short-term, long-term, or short-term plus long-term goal condition. Long-term goal subjects were told that their goal was to improve their baseline assessment by 20% over the course of the 5-weeks. No mention of weekly or any other short-term goals was made. Each week, short-term goal subjects were given a goal that was 4% higher than their previous week's sit-up performance. No mention of long-term goals was made. Finally, the short-term plus long-term goal group received a combination of the instructions. Results indicated that although all groups did improve over the course of the 5-weeks, there were no significant differences between any of the goal-setting groups. Weinberg et al. (1988) replicated their study using elementary school children and a 2-minute sit-up test. Results again indicated no differences between the three goal proximity groups, although they all improved significantly more than the do-your-best group.

Hall and Byrne (1988) investigated the effect of goal proximity on sit-up performance although they used Kirschenbaum's (1985) suggestions and also varied the flexibility that subjects had in setting their short-term goals. Subjects were randomly assigned to one of the following conditions: (a) long-term goals, (b) long-term plus experimenter-set short-term goals, (c) long-term plus subject-set short-term goals, and (d) do-your-best goals. In the experimenter-set goal condition, subjects were assigned specific goals by the experimenter, and thus they had no flexibility in altering their weekly goals. In contrast, subjects in the subject-set goal condition were asked to set weekly goals for themselves that they felt were realistic based upon their previous performance and how much they had practiced since the last trial. Results indicated no significant performance differences between subjects holding either self-set subgoals, experimenter-set subgoals, or long-term goals, although both experimenter-set and self-set groups were significantly better than the do-your-best control group. Thus, none of these three studies found any significant performance differences between long-term and short-term goal groups, regardless of whether the goals were flexible or not.

Goal Difficulty

One of the recommendations from Locke and Latham's (1985) article is that performers be encouraged to strive for goals that are difficult but realistic. It is argued that unrealistic goals should be avoided because if goals are so difficult that this results in continuing failure, motivation will drop and subsequent performance will deteriorate. This goal attainability assumption has clearly had an impact on sport psychology literature, in which researchers have strongly recommended to both physical educators and coaches that performance goals be realistic (Botterill, 1978, 1979, 1980; Gould, 1984; Harris & Harris, 1984; McClements & Botterill, 1979).

Garland (1983) has questioned the basis of the goal attainability assumption. He notes that in many laboratory experiments on goal-setting, monotonically positive relationships have been observed between goal difficulty and performance, even when hard goals assigned to individuals have been beyond their reach. In some of these experiments, subjects assigned a hard goal experienced repeated failure over a considerable number of task trials, yet no evidence of a decline in either motivation or performance was found among these subjects (Garland, 1983). If repeated failure produces a decrease in motivation, then one would expect some type of inverted U relationship between goal difficulty and performance; but this does not appear to be the case. In one study (Locke, 1982), 14 levels of goal difficulty were manipulated, with the top nine levels all beyond the reach of the subject population. Results indicated that performance decrements did not occur among subjects assigned goals that were unattainable; rather subjects with unrealistically difficult goals performed equally well as those given more realistic performance standards.

The goal attainability assumption was tested by Weinberg, Bruya, Jackson, and Garland (1987) using a physical activity setting. In their first experiment, subjects were matched and randomly assigned to either an easy, moderately difficult, or very difficult goal group. Goal difficulty was determined by previous testing using the 3-minute sit-up. For example, subjects in the "very difficult" goal group were assigned a goal of improving by 45 sit-ups over the course of the 5-week study. Of the over 200 previously tested subjects, not one of them had improved by 45 sit-ups, thus making it unrealistic for most subjects. Results indicated no significant performance differences among the three specific goal conditions, although they all improved over the course of the study. It is interesting to note that although no significant performance differences were found among groups, 3 of the 10 subjects in the "very difficult" goal group actually improved by more than 45 sit-ups. This finding is impressive considering 200 prior subjects could not reach this level of improvement. Conversely, some of the other subjects in this group showed hardly any improvement in performance over the 5-week study. This underscores the notion that individual differences are probably an important consideration when testing the effectiveness of a goal-setting program.

In Weinberg and co-workers' (1987) second experiment, goal attainability was made even more difficult by placing subjects in a "very hard" goal group (improve by 40 sit-ups) or a "highly improbable" goal group (improve by 60 sit-ups). In addition, a do-your-best control group was added. Results again indicated no significant performance differences between any of the groups. Thus, even though none of the subjects in the improve-by-60 group actually reached their goal, there appeared to be no detriment in performance as they performed as well as the improved-by-40 group. These two studies support Garland's notion that increasing goal difficulty will not produce performance decrements. In fact, there is some evidence that it can enhance performance, especially for certain individuals.

Goal-Setting Training Programs

Goal-setting researchers have recently begun to investigate the effectiveness of goal-setting training programs in enhancing performance. For example, Burton (1989b) conducted a field study investigating the effectiveness of a goal-setting training program over the course of a season for a university swim team. This study is noteworthy because it is one of the only studies that has investigated sport participants throughout the course of a competitive season. The effectiveness of a goal-setting training program was evaluated by comparing swimmers who participated in the 5-month program with swimmers from another university who did not participate in any type of psychological training program. The lack of an appropriate true control group limited the internal validity of the study although the field nature of the study enhanced its external validity. Swimmers in the goal-setting program were taught to set specific rather than general goals, short-term rather than long-term goals, and mastery instead of outcome goals. Results indicated that swimmers who were good at setting specific, realistic, short-term goals performed the best and demonstrated cognitions consistent with a mastery-involved focus; this suggests that goal-setting can mediate task involvement (see Roberts, this volume). In another recent study, Stitcher (1989) tested the effectiveness of a goal-setting program on a university lacrosse team. Players were matched and randomly assigned to either a goal-setting group or do-your-best control group. In conjunction with the coach, Stitcher gave players in the goal-setting group specific, difficult goals for different aspects of offensive and defensive performance. These goals were periodically reevaluated throughout the course of the lacrosse season. Although results revealed no statistically significant differences between the groups, inspection of mean differences indicated the superiority of the goal-setting group from a practical point of view.

Miller and McAuley (1987) designed a study to examine the effects of a goal-setting training program on basketball free-throw performance, perceptions of success, and self-efficacy. Subjects were matched by free-throw shooting ability and then randomly assigned to either a goal-training or no goal-training group for a period of five weeks. Subjects in the goal-training group were instructed on how to establish performance objectives using principles derived from previous research (Locke & Latham, 1985). Results indicated that although the goal-training group reported significantly higher perceptions of success and self-efficacy, no significant differences were found between the groups on free-throw accuracy. Thus, similar to the research on goal difficulty and goal proximity in sport and exercise settings, results attesting to the effectiveness of goal-setting training programs remain equivocal. Many of the inconsistencies can be traced back to differences in procedures, including methodological and design limitations along with potential mediating variables. These issues will be specifically addressed in the next section.

Methodological and Design Considerations

Goal-setting research in exercise and sport environments is still in its embryonic stage. Other than a few isolated studies in the late 1970s and early 1980s, there has been no systematic attempt by sport psychologists to study the effectiveness of goal-setting techniques. Most researchers have initially set out to test Locke's (1966, 1968) original propositions and more recently, Locke and Latham's (1985) hypotheses concerning the application of goal-setting findings in organization and industrial settings. In attempting to make the jump from industrial to sport and exercise settings, however, several methodological considerations and limitations have become evident.

Spontaneous Goal-Setting in Control Groups

One of the recurring problems in sport psychology goal-setting research is the spontaneous setting of goals by subjects in control do-your-best conditions. This makes it difficult to state any firm conclusions concerning the effectiveness of specific goal groups when compared to a control group. For example, in the 1985 Weinberg et al. study, manipulation checks indicated that in both experiments, 83% of the subjects in the do-your-best condition set their own goals despite the fact that they were not given any specific goals by the experimenter. These goals were both short-term and long-term in nature and thus, in reality, the specific-goal groups and the do-your-best control groups were similar in that all were striving to reach some specific goal.

This problem is typical for studies attempting to determine the efficacy of goal-setting for enhancing performance in sport and exercise settings. Hall and Byrne (1988) attempted to deal with this problem by reducing the amount of competition between subjects. They argued that competition and social comparison leads subjects who are given do-your-best instructions to begin setting goals. In essence, some subjects' performance levels become others' goals. This can be seen in the organizational literature where studies by Latham and Baldes (1975) and Komaki, Barwick, and Scott (1978) found that when subjects in specific goal groups were given feedback, spontaneous competition occurred. Despite Hall and Byrne's attempt to limit competition, 55% of subjects in the control group spontaneously set specific goals. In a partial replication of Hall and Byrne's study, Weinberg, Bruya, and Jackson (1990) still found that 34% of subjects in a do-your-best control group set goals on their own. Thus, there is a definite tendency for subjects not given specific goals to set goals.

There are two methodological refinements that sport psychology researchers can use to help alleviate this problem. First would be to reduce or eliminate the feedback that is given to control subjects. When control subjects are provided feedback concerning their performance, this information could be (and usually is) used to set goals for the next trial. In studies that used the 3-minute sit-up as the task, control subjects would not be given any feedback concerning how many sit-ups they had accomplished. This would have to be accompanied by a specific goal treatment group that also received no feedback concerning their performance to avoid the confound of feedback effects. However, even this approach might fail since subjects could count how many sit-ups they were doing and set goals based on that number. Therefore, the second refinement to cope with this counting problem would be to tell subjects that each trial would be between 2 minutes 45 seconds, and 3 minutes 15 seconds long, although in reality, each trial would be exactly 3 minutes long. In this way, a given number of sit-ups could not be considered a standard upon which to set a goal because the subject would not know how long the previous trial was or how long the next trial would be. These methods will probably not totally eliminate spontaneous goal-setting, but certainly they will make it much more difficult for subjects in control conditions to set specific goals on their own. In any case, researchers need to be sensitive to this issue and to structure their methodology and feedback to account for the propensity of control subjects to set their own goals. In this way, more definitive conclusions can be put forth concerning the effectiveness (or lack of effectiveness) of specific goal-setting treatment conditions and programs in enhancing performance in sport and exercise environments.

Task Characteristics

One variable that might mediate the effectiveness of goal-setting in sport and exercise environments is the nature of the task. A recent meta-analysis (Wood,

Mento, & Locke, 1987) from the organizational literature has found that the attentional, effort, and persistence benefits of goals have a more direct effect on simple tasks, whereas more complex tasks require effective strategy development to occur first before the motivational effects of goals can benefit performance. In essence, specific goals should enhance performance on simple tasks significantly more than on complex tasks. Burton (1989a) used seven different basketball tasks varying in task complexity and had subjects set specific goals over the course of the 8-week study. A do-your-best control group was also employed. Results indicated that specific-goal subjects performed better than do-your-best subjects on two of the seven basketball skills. Task complexity seemingly mediated this relationship because greater performance improvement tended to be demonstrated for some simple and moderately complex skills, but never for high complexity skills. More research is necessary that systematically varies the complexity of motor tasks in an attempt to determine its impact on the effectiveness of goal-setting programs.

As previously noted, many studies testing the effects of goal-setting on performance used the 3-minute sit-up task (e.g., Hall & Byrne, 1988; Weinberg et al., 1985, 1987, 1988). The nature of this specific task may have attenuated any potential effects due to goal-setting interventions. Specifically, the 3-minute sit-up task provides salient, physiological feedback concerning an individual's level of performance, effort, and fatigue. This is in contrast to most tasks in the academic and organizational literature which require effort and provide feedback in terms of productivity (e.g., truck loading, logging, sales ship loading, key punching) but do not elicit fatigue or pain cues to the extent a 3-minute sit-up test does. In essence, the salient pain cues inform the subjects that they are trying extremely hard and are approaching their maximum performance. For example, most subjects will fatigue before 3-minutes elapse, rest a while, do a few more sit-ups, and continue this cycle until total fatigue sets in. Perhaps learning to cope with pain and fatigue while doing "just a few more" sit-ups might override any thoughts about what goal they are striving for. In fact, Locke et al. (1981) note that when more effort leads to immediate results, goals will only work if they lead subjects to work harder. Thus, a specific goal may not result in more motivation to work hard because subjects feel they are already exerting maximum effort.

Motivation and Commitment

Two important mediating psychological variables in studying goal-setting in sport and exercise settings are motivation and commitment. In terms of motivation, Locke et al. (1981) note that goal-setting operates primarily as a motivational mechanism to influence one's degree of effort and persistence in striving toward a goal. If subjects are highly motivated to start with, then the impact of setting specific goals would be lessened. In fact, I and my colleagues (Weinberg et al., 1987, 1988) have noted that this might have been a problem in our studies because subjects were taken from conditioning classes. These classes were voluntarily chosen by subjects, and perhaps they were already motivated to improve their physical fitness, of which sit-ups is one component. If this were the case, then the addition of a specific goal would not necessarily cause these subjects to try harder and persist longer in their sit-ups. This, in turn, might have contributed to the findings of no differences between specific goal groups and do-your-best control groups. Future studies need initially to control for selecting subjects with high levels of motivation if the motivational effects of goal-setting are to be determined.

Goal commitment is another important factor that will affect the effectiveness of goal-setting procedures. Goal commitment is closely related to goal acceptance although they are distinguishable concepts. Locke et al. (1981) state that goal commitment implies a determination to try to reach a goal, although the exact source of the goal is not specified (e.g., the goal may be assigned or self-set). On the other hand, goal acceptance implies that one has agreed to commit to a specific type of goal. As most studies have used assigned goals, the two concepts are often used interchangeably.

In most studies in the organizational as well as sport psychology goal-setting literature, goal commitment and acceptance have been assessed in a pre-experimental questionnaire which would typically consist of a direct, face-valid question such as, "How committed are you to attaining your goal?" Although subjects generally report that they are committed to their goals, other evidence sometimes suggests otherwise. For example, in several sport psychology studies (Garland, Weinberg, Bruya, & Jackson, 1988; Weinberg et al., 1985, 1987), subjects reported setting either different or additional goals than the ones they were assigned despite the fact that virtually all subjects stated that they accepted and were highly committed to their assigned goal. Furthermore, Garland et al. (1988) found that subjects' personal goals were a much better predictor of performance than their assigned goals. This is consistent with some research in the organizational literature (Mento et al., 1980) that also found that personal goals were more closely related to performance than assigned goals. In essence, researchers need to measure subjects' own self-set goals in addition to any goal assigned to the subject to get a clearer and more accurate picture of how goals are related to performance. This will be discussed in the next section in relation to Garland's (1985) cognitive mediation theory.

Another problem with measuring goal acceptance and commitment may reflect the difficulty of assessing higher-order cognitive processes via self-report assessment procedures (Nisbett & Wilson, 1977). Specifically, Nisbett and Wilson provided evidence that many times

> when people attempt to report on their cognitive processes, that is, on the processes mediating the effects of a stimulus on a response, they do not do so on the basis of any true introspection. Instead, their reports are based on a priori causal theories or judgments about the extent to which a particular stimulus is a plausible cause of a given response. (p. 231)

Locke et al. (1981) offer a potential solution to this problem. They argue that designs should encourage a wide range of goal commitment, such as those with a choice of various possible goals, with commitment to each goal being measured after goal choice is made. This should reduce the introspective burden and increase the variance of the answers on the commitment scale.

Competition

As noted, one of the methodological limitations of goal-setting research in sport and exercise settings is the setting of specific goals by subjects in do-your-best control groups. The question becomes, "Why do subjects instructed to do their best on a task engage in spontaneous goal setting?" Hall and Byrne (1988) suggest that spontaneous goal-setting might be due to the interpretation of the performance context by individuals in control groups. Specifically, if the situation is perceived to be one where social comparison is salient, then subjects may start to compete against each other despite being assigned to individual goals. This suggestion would seem likely because most sport and exercise situations tend to emphasize social comparison, and hence competition. Along these lines, Locke and Latham (1985) suggest that competition tends to encourage subjects who are given do-your-best instructions to begin setting goals, as well as subjects assigned specific goals to raise them even higher. In essence, the performance of others is used to help set one's own goals.

Hall and Byrne (1988) conducted the first sport psychology goal-setting study that was specifically designed to control for competition effects in a field setting by minimizing both between-group and within-group interactions. In previous studies (e.g., Weinberg et al., 1985, 1987), subjects were randomly assigned to goal-setting conditions within each class. This meant that subjects in do-your-best conditions were performing sit-ups in the same class as other subjects who had specific goals. This would naturally increase the likelihood that subjects given do-your-best instructions would be exposed to, and influenced by, subjects who were working toward specific goals. To reduce this possibility, Hall and Byrne (1988) randomly assigned classes, rather than subjects, to one of four goal-setting conditions. Thus, subjects in the do-your-best condition were all in the same class and not exposed to other subjects who were assigned to specific goal groups in other classes. Hall and Byrne note that although randomly assigning classes rather than subjects to experimental conditions is a potential design weakness in that the unit of analysis could conceivably be viewed as a class rather than the subjects within class, the design was selected to eliminate problems inherent in previous studies concerning competition among subjects.

Results indicated only partial support for the effectiveness of goal-setting as not all specific goal groups improved significantly more than the do-your-best group. Hall and Byrne explain these findings by arguing that their attempt to control for competition among subjects was not entirely successful. That is, questionnaire findings indicated that over 55% of the control group were setting goals on their own, and 56% of all subjects stated that they had engaged in competition at some point during the experimental period. Thus, despite stringent efforts to control for competition, the true effects of goal-setting on task performance appear to be influenced by other motivating factors inherent in the exercise and sport situation. A more recent study by Weinberg, Bruya, and Jackson (1990) replicated the Hall and Byrne study and was able to reduce competition among subjects further; but still approximately 30% of all control subjects engaged in competition, as well as set their own goals. Clearly, more research is necessary, investigating the effects of competition on the goal setting-performance relationship in both sport and exercise settings.

Future Direction for Research

In the previous section, I pointed out several methodological problems that have plagued goal-setting research in sport and exercise. Based on some of these shortcomings, as well as the many variables impacting on the effectiveness of goal-setting, there are a number of directions that sport psychology researchers could take to help clarify and extend the existing literature. Directions for future research will be discussed in the hope that a firm foundation can be established concerning the effectiveness of goal-setting in sport and exercise environments.

Goal-Setting and Sport Performance

One of the major practical applications for the use of goal-setting techniques is with individual and team players over the course of a season. As noted previously, several sport psychologists have written about how to set up goal-setting training programs for sport participants so that motivation can be maintained over the course of a season. In addition, anecdotal reports and testimonials from coaches and players indicate that goal-setting is used fairly regularly in the sport domain, and that for many of them it is an effective motivational technique. Unfortunately, there is a dearth of studies that have tested the effectiveness of a goal-setting training program over the course of a season. To date, only studies by Burton (1989b) using collegiate swimmers, and Stitcher (1989) using collegiate lacrosse players have investigated the effects of goal-setting on sport performance over the course of a season lasting at least several months.

Although both of these studies had some limitations due to the nature of field investigations, their strengths lie in their high external validity. Sport psychologists (Martens, 1987; Smith, 1988) have recently argued for the use of idiographic techniques and qualitative assessments in addition to the more traditional nomothetic techniques. Unfortunately, outcome studies testing the effectiveness of psychological interventions over time are inherently difficult to carry out. Despite these difficulties, studies of this nature need to be conducted in the area of goal-setting and sport performance before we can attest to the effectiveness of goal-setting for enhancing the performance of participants. It is not enough to say that because goal-setting enhances performance and productivity in industrial and organizational settings, it will also be effective in sport settings. The challenge to goal-setting researchers in sport is to conduct field studies and experiments that maximize external validity but at the same time do not entirely compromise internal validity.

Goal Orientation

An important variable mediating the potential effects of goal-setting in sport and exercise settings is the goal orientation of the individual. Recently, researchers studying the area of motivation have argued for the relevance of considering differences in goal perspective as we attempt to understand variations in the thoughts, feelings, and actions of individuals in specific situations (e.g., Ames, 1984a, 1984b; Maehr, 1984; Maehr & Braskamp, 1986; Maehr & Nicholls, 1980). Based upon a theoretical orientation relevant to sport and exercise (Maehr & Nicholls, 1980), sport researchers began to investigate goal orientations in sport (e.g., Duda, 1981; Ewing, 1981). These goal orientations differ to the extent to which individuals perceive success and failure in sport settings. The two goal orientations found to be most relevant to sport and exercise are ego involvement and task involvement (Duda, 1989a, this volume; Roberts, 1982, 1984b, this volume). Individuals with an ability (ego) orientation define success and failure in terms of winning and losing. Their goal is "to maximize the subjective probability of attributing high ability to oneself" (Maehr & Nicholls, 1980, p. 237). Individuals with a task orientation define success and failure in terms of personal mastery and self-improvement. Their goal is "to produce an adequate product or to solve a problem for its own sake rather than to demonstrate (superior) ability" (Maehr & Nicholls, 1980, p. 239).

Based on the work of Maehr and Nicholls (1980), a number of studies have recently been conducted investigating the relationship between goal perspective and behavior in sport and exercise settings. For example, studies have shown that multiple goals exist in sport and exercise settings and that variations in goal perspective may be related to person factors such as age, gender, and culture. In addition, it also appears that the specific goals of task and ego involvement are related to certain behaviors such as intensity of participation, persistence of participation, and adherence to exercise programs (see Duda, 1989a, for a review; Roberts, this volume).

These findings point out the importance of assessing goal orientation when conducting goal-setting research in sport and exercise settings. Recognizing the existence of multiple achievement goals has important implications for goal-setting research. That is, specific, difficult mastery-oriented goals typically used in sport psychology research are not pertinent for all individuals. For example, a subject may receive specific mastery goal-setting instructions but still focus on competitive goals. Thus, it would seem likely that a mastery goal-setting condition would only be motivating to the extent that an individual perceives the situation as personally meaningful (i.e., possesses a strong mastery orientation).

A recent study by Giannini, Weinberg, and Jackson (1988) examined the relationship between goal orientation and specific goal-setting instructions on performance of a basketball shooting task and a basketball one-on-one offensive task. Subjects were matched based on pretest performance and placed into one of five conditions: competitive goal, cooperative goal, mastery goal, do-your-best with feedback, and do-your-best without feedback. Subjects also responded to questionnaires assessing the strength of mastery, competitive, and social goal orientations, which were assumed to reflect personal achievement goals held before goal-setting instructions were offered. Results indicated that subjects' goal orientations were not related to performance in the competitive and cooperative goal conditions, but, as predicted, mastery-oriented subjects did perform best under mastery-goal instructions. More studies are necessary examining the relationship between goal orientation, goal-setting instructions, and performance. The question that future researchers should consider is not if goal-setting is effective or not; rather, it is what are the most appropriate goals for people with different personality and motivational styles.

In addition to setting the most appropriate goals for different individuals, it would seem important to create the proper motivational climate that would facilitate effective learning and performance (see Ames, this volume). Along these lines, Ames (1984a, 1984b) has demonstrated that school children react differently in terms of motivational processes, based on their perceptions of the salient mastery and performance goals in their classroom. Students were asked to respond to a questionnaire on their perceptions of the classroom goal orientation, of their use of effective learning strategies, and on their task choices, attitudes, and causal attributions. Results indicated that students who perceived an emphasis on mastery (task) goals in the classroom reported using more effective strategies, preferred challenging tasks, had a more positive attitude toward the class, and had a stronger belief that success follows from one's effort. Students who perceived ego (ability) goals as salient tended to focus on their ability, to evaluate their ability negatively, and to attribute failure to lack of ability. Thus, these results suggest that classroom goal orientation may facilitate the maintenance of adaptive motivation patterns when mastery (task) goals are salient and adopted by students. These findings need to be tested in sport and exercise environments to help us determine the optimal motivational climate for our participants. If, in fact, a climate that emphasizes mastery goals as opposed to ego goals leads to more positive attitudes and enhanced motivation, then coaches, teachers, and exercise leaders would need to structure their programs accordingly. Research efforts in this area, however, are necessary before more firm conclusions can be put forth.

As with many other areas of research, most goal-setting studies have concentrated on high school- and college-aged subjects, because this population is typically more readily available. However, there is a need to extend this to other age groups, particularly young children and older adults, if we are to broaden our base of knowledge in this area. For example, only two studies have investigated the relationship between goal and performance in young children. Erbaugh and Barnett (1986) studied the effects of goal-setting and modeling on a jumping task using primary grade children. Results indicated that children in the goal-setting and modeling-plus-goal-setting conditions learned more than children in either the control or modeling conditions. Weinberg, Bruya, Longino, and Jackson (1988) investigated the effects of goal proximity and goal specificity on endurance performance of fourth, fifth, and sixth graders. Results revealed significant gender and grade effects, with boys and sixth graders exhibiting the best performance. In addition, the specific goal groups (i.e., short-term and long-term) all performed significantly better than the do-your-best group over the last three weeks of the experimental period.

Although these studies as well as studies from the organizational literature (e.g., Masters, Furman, & Barden, 1977; Rosswork, 1977) indicate that goal-setting can be beneficial for young children, obviously more empirical research is necessary to determine the situational and personal variables mediating the goal setting-performance relationship in sport for this age group. For example, research by Ewing, Roberts, and Pemberton (1983) reveals that goal perspective may be related to development stage. They found that 9- to 11-year-old sport participants were more likely to be task involved whereas 12- to 14-year-olds were primarily ego involved. If sport psychologists are to develop effective goal-setting training programs for youth sport, then it is imperative that data be collected with this age group in ecologically valid environments so that both personal development and performance enhancement are fostered.

In addition to young children, older adults also need to be studied more extensively in terms of their goal-setting behavior. As our population has become older, it has become increasingly apparent that regular physical activity can help older adults lead more healthful and enjoyable lives. Unfortunately, despite the fact that there are many benefits to regular physical activity, and that there is a trend for older adults to be more interested and concerned with health and fitness issues, research has indicated that physical activity levels diminish with age (McPherson, 1983; Rudman, 1986). Thus, there appears a need to develop and design exercise programs for the elderly which are sensitive to their needs (see McAuley, this volume).

A logical starting point would be to assess what goals are important for older adults in terms of their participation in exercise programs. Here again, goal perspective would appear important as one would want to tailor the exercise program to meet the goals of the elderly population. Some initial research has been undertaken investigating goal orientation and exercise in elderly populations (Duda & Tappe, 1989a, 1989b), but more research is necessary to pinpoint the situational and personal variables impacting on this relationship. In addition, the actual process of how older adults set goals along with the relationship between goal-setting and behavioral measures such as intensity, persistence, and adherence to exercise needs further investigation so that participation of older adults in exercise programs is maximized.

Cognitive Mediation Theory

Most of the goal-setting research in both organization and sport settings has been targeted at testing Locke's (1966, 1968) postulations concerning the relationship between goals and task performance. This line of research has certainly been fruitful, resulting in a large body of empirical literature. However, more recently, Garland (1985) has proposed a new approach to the study of goal-setting through his conception of cognitive mediation theory.

In this theory, Garland asserts that an individual's task goal, defined as "an image of a future level of performance that the individual wishes to achieve" (1985, p. 347), influences performance through two cognitive constructs: performance expectancy and performance valence. Performance expectancy is defined as a composite of an individual's subjective probabilities for reaching each of a number of different performance levels over a range of performances that might be considered. In essence, it is suggested that individuals develop expectancies for reaching many different performance levels, not just that level represented by some task goal. For example, two basketball players with different task goals of 50% and 60% for field goal percentage would be asked to state their subjective probabilities for shooting at least 40%, 50%, 60%, and 70%. For each player, an index of performance expectancy could be computed by averaging across these subjective probabilities. This index of expectancy would no longer be confounded with task goal level and could be used to measure expectancy for all basketball players' field goal percentages. It should be noted that Garland's concept of performance expectancy is virtually identical to Bandura's (1977b) concept of self-efficacy (for a discussion of self-efficacy in sport and exercise, see Feltz, this volume; McCauley, this volume). In fact, Garland equates these two concepts.

Performance valence is defined as a composite of those satisfactions an individual anticipates will be gained by producing each of a number of different performance levels over a range of performances that might be considered. Using the basketball example, we could ask how satisfied each player would be with having a field goal percentage of 40%, 50%, 60%, and 70%. An index of performance valence could be computed by averaging across these four anticipated satisfactions.

Cognitive mediation theory predicts that an individual's task goal exerts a positive influence on performance expectancy and a negative influence on performance valence. In addition, performance expectancy is proposed to exert a positive influence on performance, while performance valence is proposed to exert a negative influence on performance. In a recent investigation, Garland et al. (1988) found support for the positive relationship between performance expectancy and performance. In addition, by using a path analysis, the study found support for the linkages between task goals, performance expectancies, and performance. Cognitive mediation theory provides researchers in sport psychology another approach with which to study the relationship between goals and performance. This approach can be compared and contrasted to that of Locke, and Bandura's self-efficacy theory can also be incorporated as it relates to the concept of goal-setting (Bandura & Cervone, 1983; Locke, Frederick, Lee, & Bobko, 1984).

Summary

The purpose of this paper was to provide an overview of research in the area of goal-setting and task performance. A brief review of the vast literature on goal-setting in industrial and organizational settings was provided followed by a review of the relatively sparse goal-setting literature in sport and exercise. In many cases, the goal-setting literature in sport and exercise has produced equivocal findings. These discrepancies were noted and a number of methodological and procedural issues were raised concerning the use of goal-setting in sport and exercise environments. Variables such as task complexity, type of setting, goal difficulty, spontaneous goal-setting, and competition were discussed as potential mediators of the goal-setting performance relationship. Future directions for research were offered including the need for more studies using sport participants over the course of a season, including goal orientation and other individual difference variables, and reflecting an awareness of developmental differences across the life cycle. Researchers need to help obtain the answers to how goal-setting operates in sport and exercise environments so that we can begin to develop programs and interventions that will maximize performance and personal growth of individuals participating in sport and exercise.

The Construct
of Sport Enjoyment

Tara K. Scanlan
Jeffery P. Simons

This chapter focuses on the new motivational construct of sport enjoyment. In so doing, it brings positive affect to light in this volume on motivation, and adds a little "heart" to the otherwise highly cognitive treatment of the topic. The rationale for the development of the sport enjoyment construct is nicely conveyed by Harter's (1981a, p. 4) statement of nearly a decade ago that "we should resurrect 'joy' as a legitimate construct and restore affect and emotion to its rightful place, as central to an understanding of behavior."

Our discussion begins with an overview of a motivational model we are developing to study individuals' commitment to sport. To more comprehensively explore the motivation behind continued participation, the model examines enjoyment along with other variables predicted to influence sport commitment. The model is briefly presented in this chapter (a) to show the centrality of affect in our conceptualizations of motivational factors influencing continued participation and (b) to provide the broader motivational context into which the enjoyment research fits. The remainder of this chapter presents the theoretical work to date on the development of the sport enjoyment construct, details the empirical findings and their implications, and delineates future research directions.

An Overview of the Sport Commitment Model

The concept of *commitment* has been used by social psychologists to describe a set of factors that can explain why people stay in relationships or continue involvement in activities (e.g., Brickman, 1987; Kelley, 1983; Rusbult & Farrell, 1983). Adapting concepts from interdependence theory (Kelley & Thibaut, 1978), Rusbult (1980a) has developed a particularly useful model specifying these factors and their impact on commitment. Her investment model proposes that commitment is a function of one's satisfaction with a relationship, the perceived attractiveness of the best available alternative to the relationship, and one's level of investment in the relationship. Rusbult's (1980a) model has proven effective in predicting commitment to romantic relationships (Rusbult, 1983) and to friendship relationships (Rusbult, 1980b), and has been successfully adapted to predict commitment to work (Farrell & Rusbult, 1981; Rusbult & Farrell, 1983).

Our formulation of the *sport commitment model*[1] is presented in Figure 1. The model is grounded in prior theoretical concepts, but has been significantly modified and extended to examine the specific nature of commitment

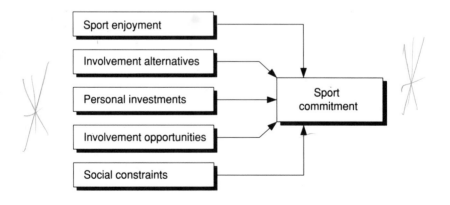

Figure 1. The sport commitment model. *Note.* From "Social Psychological Aspects of the Competitive Sport Experience for Male Youth Sport Participants: 4. Predictors of Enjoyment" by T.K. Scanlan and R. Lewthwaite, 1986, *Journal of Sport Psychology*, **8**(1), p. 33. Copyright 1986 by Human Kinetics. Reprinted by permission.

in sport. The model proposes that commitment to sport participation is a function of an individual's sport enjoyment, the attractiveness of involvement alternatives, personal investments in participation, the involvement opportunities afforded by continued participation, and social constraints to continue participating (Scanlan, Simons, Schmidt, Carpenter, & Keeler, 1991). Each of the model's components is considered at the level of individual perceptions. Importantly, this new model takes into account both cognitive and affective factors in an individual's commitment to continue involvement in sport.

Sport commitment is a "psychological construct representing the desire and resolve to continue sport participation" (Scanlan et al., 1991). It can be examined globally (i.e., commitment to sport in general) or specifically (i.e., commitment to a particular program or team). *Sport enjoyment* is "a positive affective response to the sport experience that reflects generalized feelings such as pleasure, liking, and fun" (Scanlan et al., 1991). Greater enjoyment is proposed to promote greater commitment. *Involvement alternatives* represent "the attractiveness of the most preferred alternative(s) to continued participation in the current endeavor" (Scanlan et al., 1991). For example, young sport participants might consider playing a musical instrument, going to a shopping mall with friends, or even doing nothing at all instead of being involved in their sport. The more attractive the alternative, the lower the commitment to participate. *Personal investments* are "resources that are put into the activity which cannot be recovered if participation is discontinued" (Scanlan et al., 1991), and include expenditures of time, effort, and money. According to the model, increasing investments creates greater commitment. *Involvement opportunities* are "valued opportunities that are present only through continued involvement" (Scanlan et al., 1991). These may include such things as the chance for sport mastery, the chance to be with friends, or the chance to obtain extrinsic rewards. *Social constraints* are "social expectations or norms which create feelings of obligation to remain in the activity" (Scanlan et al., 1991), such as feeling one has to play to please parents. Because high feelings of obligation are expected to undermine the sense of self-determination, the model predicts that sport commitment will be higher when social constraints are low.

Scales have been developed to measure each component of the model, and work has already begun to test its efficacy for understanding continued involvement in youth sport settings. Initial results are encouraging (Scanlan, Carpenter, Simons, & Keeler, 1990; Scanlan, Carpenter, Simons, Keeler, & Schmidt, 1990; Scanlan et al., 1991; Simons, Scanlan, Carpenter, & Schmidt, 1990). For the present discussion, however, the model is presented simply to illustrate the broader framework under which our investigations of sport enjoyment are proceeding.

As a whole, the sport commitment model has three important features. First, sport commitment strictly addresses psychological attachment to an activity. It focuses directly on the psychological desire and resolve to continue participation, and does not involve estimations of the actual probability. Second, sport commitment is a product of both cognitive and affective factors. For example, it is easy to see the strong cognitive component involved in weighing the relative desirability of an alternative activity and the strong affective component contributed by sport enjoyment. Thus, the importance of affect to motivated behavior is recognized along with cognition. The third important feature of the sport commitment model is its ability to illuminate widely differing psychological states of participants who might report equal levels of commitment. For example, one might be highly committed because of the intense enjoyment that she or he derives from performing the requisite skills, whereas another might be equally committed due to her or his great investment of time and energy, despite low levels of enjoyment.

The contention that the nature of the sport experience may be grossly different for those who report equivalent levels of commitment highlights a significant issue. While our study of commitment is concerned with predicting the desire and resolve to persist at an activity, considerations of the quality of experience and the developmental and leisure aspects of sport involvement are also of specific interest. In reference to participation motivation in school settings, Nicholls (1990) suggests that all students might be better served by attention to how they might "find value in the work they do or to find work to do that they can value" (p. 39). Similarly, in sport we are concerned not just with commitment, but more directly with the meaning behind the commitment that individuals hold for the activities in which they participate. Our current thinking is that those aspects of the sport experience which produce enjoyment are not only important to continued involvement, but are also key to positive meanings for participants in physical activities.

Sport Enjoyment

We now turn our discussion to the principle variable of interest in this chapter, sport enjoyment. In this section, the construct is defined, its motivational consequences are presented, and the major objectives and methodological approach guiding our research efforts are shared.

The Sport Enjoyment Construct

When we originally became interested in studying sport enjoyment, there was so little theoretical and empirical work on the topic that we needed to start at the most fundamental level of construct definition. Hence, in the first article launching our research in this area, we established a working definition of sport enjoyment and clarified its relationship to intrinsic motivation (Scanlan & Lewthwaite, 1986). Only slight changes have been made in the operational definition of sport enjoyment, currently identified as a positive affective response to the sport experience that reflects generalized feelings such as pleasure, liking, and fun. This construct is more differentiated than global positive affect, but more general than a specific emotion such as excitement. For investigations in youth sport, fun and enjoyment are often used synonymously because "fun" is the term that children commonly use for "enjoyment." Data presented by Wankel and Sefton (1989) provide empirical support for the notion that fun represents a general positive emotional state to young people and our recent findings consistently show that items reflecting the operational definition of enjoyment reliably cluster together (Cronbach's alpha reliabilities range from .88 to .94).

We also felt it necessary to clearly distinguish enjoyment from intrinsic motivation, because they are not synonymous constructs (see Scanlan & Lewthwaite, 1986, for greater elaboration on this issue). While enjoyment is often used to indicate intrinsic motivation (e.g., Csikszentmihalyi, 1975; Deci & Ryan, 1980), we theorize enjoyment to be a broader and more inclusive construct. Enjoyment can be derived from extrinsic sources (e.g., social achievement, social recognition, and interpersonal relationships), as well as intrinsic sources (e.g., autonomous achievement and sensory/movement experiences). It also can be the product of both achievement (e.g., goal attainment) and nonachievement (e.g., affiliation) outcomes. Therefore, as Deci and Ryan (1980, p. 52) discuss, something can be enjoyable without being intrinsically motivating.

Motivational Consequences

While sport enjoyment has only recently received concentrated research attention, the participation motivation literature has already produced consistent evidence of its important motivational consequences. Studies of children and adolescents in youth sport and school programs have repeatedly shown that the desire for enjoyment or fun is a major reason given for participating in a program, while lack of enjoyment is a particularly important determinant of dropping out (e.g., Gill, Gross, & Huddleston, 1983; Sapp & Haubenstricker, 1978; see also reviews by Gould & Horn, 1984, and Weiss & Petlichkoff, 1989).

Our recent findings with youth sport wrestlers (Scanlan & Lewthwaite, 1986) and elite figure skaters (Scanlan, Stein, & Ravizza, 1989) further reinforce the important motivational consequences of sport enjoyment. For example, a correlation of .70 was found between wrestlers' seasonal enjoyment and their desire for future participation in the sport. Similarly, the skaters reported that enjoyment enhanced their desire to continue skating, their desire to exert effort, and their perceptions of their actual effort output. Given that these participants spent an average of 6 years training 5 1/2 hours per day, 6 days per week, 50 weeks per year, the continued participation and effort variables reflect extremely long-term, intense commitment.

Research Objective and Approach

Our primary interest in studying enjoyment is that we consider it to be a cornerstone of motivation in sport. Knowledge of what makes the sport experience enjoyable to the participant is the key to understanding and enhancing motivation. Therefore, a major objective of our research is to achieve a comprehensive, in-depth understanding of the sources of sport enjoyment. This includes examination of generic as well as unique sources. Generic sources are those that generalize across various types of sports and participants, while unique enjoyment predictors are specific to various sport classifications (e.g., individual versus team sports) and participant samples. Examples of important participant differences of interest include: gender, developmental level, competitive experience, talent level, and ethnicity.

To achieve this objective, we are employing a multi-method research approach, including quantitative and qualitative methodologies, comprised of nomothetic and idiographic strategies. Nomothetically, we are carrying out field studies with large, diverse samples of participants so that generalizable findings can be obtained. Idiographically, we have conducted extensive interviews which provide the depth, richness, and complexity to truly understand the phenomenon, and do so from the point of view of the participants.

Sources of Sport Enjoyment

In the following sections research into the sources of sport enjoyment is reviewed with reference first to work undertaken by other investigators and then to work emerging specifically from our laboratory.

Research By Other Investigators

There has been little research addressing the sources of enjoyment in sport settings. Although there are consistencies in the enjoyment sources illuminated by this literature, it should be noted that there are numerous differences in the construct under investigation. Participants have been asked to rate questions pertaining to enjoyment (Brustad, 1988; Csikszentmihalyi, 1975; Wankel & Kreisel, 1985a, 1985b), liking (Brustad, 1988), fun (Harris, 1984; Wankel & Sefton, 1989), and mood (Chalip, Csikszentmihalyi, Kleiber, & Larson, 1984). Furthermore, the level of analysis has varied from questions about the sport in general (Csikszentmihalyi, 1975; Harris, 1984; Wankel & Kreisel, 1985a, 1985b), to the specific team and current season (Brustad, 1988), to specific instances of involvement in sport (Chalip et al., 1984; Wankel & Sefton, 1989). Although these variations make it difficult to directly compare results across studies, some consistencies in enjoyment sources have emerged.

In the general achievement motivation literature, concepts of enjoyment have been discussed primarily with reference to intrinsic motivation (e.g., Csikszentmihalyi, 1975; Deci & Ryan, 1985). Building upon the ideas of such theorists as White (1959) and deCharms (1968), Deci (1975) posited that feelings of enjoyment are experienced when involvement in an activity creates a sense of competence and self-determination. According to Deci and Ryan (1985), enjoyment is a reward experienced from the performance of intrinsically motivated behavior. Furthermore, ratings of enjoyment are often used to operationally define levels of intrinsic motivation. Therefore, within this framework, intrinsically motivated activities and the corresponding perceptions of competence and control are the implicit sources of enjoyment. Similarly, Csikszentmihalyi (1975) explains that instances of intrinsic motivation characteristically produce feelings of enjoyment, and he also uses the report of enjoyment to indicate the presence of intrinsically motivated actions. Applying the general perspective of Deci and Ryan (1985) and Csikszentmihalyi (1975), we would predict that intrinsically motivating aspects of sport would be enjoyable. However, the specific sources of enjoyment in the sport context remain undefined.

To better specify enjoyment sources, Csikszentmihalyi (1975) constructed a list of eight relatively independent reasons for enjoying sport activities based on interviews with college soccer and hockey players. He then presented the list to 40 male high school basketball players and asked them to rank the reasons for enjoying basketball. From most important to least important, the order was

- competition/measuring self against others,
- development of personal skills,
- friendships/companionship,
- activity itself,
- enjoyment of the experience/use of skills,
- measuring self against own ideals,
- prestige/reward/glamour, and
- emotional release.

While the eight reasons may all be sources of enjoyment in sport, it is interesting to note that the primary reason these players gave for enjoying basketball was identified by Csikszentmihalyi (1975, p. 14) as "definitely more extrinsic." Even though Csikszentmihalyi (1975) emphasized the link between intrinsic motivation and enjoyment, the two "almost purely intrinsic" (p. 14) sources were ranked only fourth and fifth by the players. These data support the idea that sources of enjoyment in sport span a broader spectrum than is subsumed under the concept of intrinsic motivation.

Chalip, Csikszentmihalyi, Kleiber, and Larson (1984) employed Csikszentmihalyi's (1975) flow model to examine the subjective experiences encountered by male and female high school students in three sport settings. Enjoyment was operationally defined according to the flow model as "a balance between the challenges of an activity and the skills of the participant" (Chalip et al., 1984,

p. 109). Generally, greater perceived challenge was associated with greater situational enjoyment of participation across organized sport, informal sport, and physical education class settings. The authors concluded that "physical activity can provide a context in which the adolescent may learn to experience challenges as potentially pleasurable" (Chalip et al., 1984, p. 114). In addition, informal sport settings appeared to provide a better balance between challenges and abilities, and therefore increased enjoyment. Overall, these results support the connections between the elements of intrinsic motivation and enjoyment described by Deci and Ryan (1985) and Csikszentmihalyi (1975).

Harris (1984) employed ethnographic techniques to explore psychological concepts salient to 10- to 12-year-old boys in organized baseball leagues. Among these were concepts related to fun in their sport program. Although her results revealed fun to be less salient than other aspects of participation, she did find that more fun was experienced when players reported higher activity levels and greater control of the action. Harris also reported that the players appeared to desire more challenge and more chances to display competence. Like the results of Chalip et al. (1984), these findings generally support theoretical links between the elements of intrinsic motivation and enjoyment of activities.

Wankel and Kreisel (1985a) developed 10 items reflecting sources of enjoyment based on earlier research, achievement motivation theory, and interviews with 50 youth sport participants. A Thurstone paired-comparison inventory was constructed from the 10 items and administered to 822 boys, 7- to 14-years-old, playing in baseball, soccer, or hockey programs. The boys' responses were used to rank the sources by perceived importance to enjoyment of the particular sport. The investigators grouped the items into three conceptual classifications, presented here in order of their ranking across the whole sample. Intrinsic or Process factors were highest ranked and consisted of "comparing skills," "excitement of the game," "personal accomplishments," "improving skills," and "doing skills." Ranked next in importance, the Social factors classification was made up of "being on the team" and "being with friends." Ranked lowest in importance, Extrinsic or Product factors consisted of "winning," "getting rewards," and "pleasing others." In a follow-up study by Wankel and Kreisel (1985b), the same sample of boys answered open-ended questions about sources of sport enjoyment. Although some of the rankings of individual items differed from the first study, the responses were largely found to fit within the concepts defined by the 10-item questionnaire.

In his investigation of positive and negative affective experiences in youth sport, Brustad (1988) examined sources of season-long enjoyment, employing concepts from Harter's (1981a) competence motivation theory and some items adapted from the enjoyment research of Scanlan and Lewthwaite (1986). Boys ($n = 107$) and girls ($n = 100$), aged 9- to 13-years, from a youth basketball league rated their seasonal enjoyment on a two-item scale that assessed (a) how much they enjoyed playing basketball during their season and (b) how much they liked playing basketball for their team. The motivational orientation to prefer high degrees of challenge rather than easy skills was associated with higher basketball enjoyment for both boys and girls. This finding supports predictions within Harter's (1981) theory. In addition, boys and girls who perceived less parental pressure reported greater seasonal enjoyment. Together, these two significant predictors accounted for 23% of the enjoyment variance. Interestingly, perceived competence was not a significant predictor of season-long enjoyment, a finding which fails to support theories of intrinsic motivation (e.g., Deci & Ryan, 1985).

In contrast to examining the sources of overall seasonal enjoyment, Wankel and Sefton (1989) investigated sources of post-game ratings of fun at 12 games during one season. Girls ($n = 55$) on ringette teams and boys ($n = 67$) on hockey teams, aged 7 to 15 years, completed questionnaires assessing positive affect, activation, intrinsic motivation, and state anxiety to determine the best predictors of responses to the question, "How much fun did you have in the game today?" (p. 359). Positive affect, as measured by the Semantic Differential Mood State Scale (Chalip et al., 1984), was the strongest predictor of fun. However, Wankel and Sefton (1989, p. 359) conceded that "the affective mood state measures might be considered alternate indicators of fun," so additional analyses were performed without this variable. Once positive affect was removed, "how well one played" was the most important predictor of fun. This item reflects perceived competence, and is consistent with concepts of intrinsic motivation (e.g., Deci & Ryan, 1985) and most prior research (Chalip et al., 1984; Harris, 1984; Wankel & Kreisel, 1985a, 1985b). In accordance with Csikszentmihalyi's (1975) flow model and the research of Chalip et al. (1984), "challenge" was also found to be important to fun. Lastly, there was some evidence that game outcome also affected reports of fun, with winners reporting more fun in the game than losers.

Despite the difficulties in directly comparing results of these studies, some consistencies begin to emerge. Items related to perceptions of competence (Chalip et al., 1984; Csikszentmihalyi, 1975; Harris, 1984; Wankel & Kreisel, 1985a, 1985b; Wankel & Sefton, 1989) and challenge (Brustad, 1988; Chalip et al., 1984; Csikszentmihalyi, 1975; Harris, 1984; Wankel & Sefton, 1989) repeatedly arise as sources of sport enjoyment in this literature. Likewise, elements of the activity itself (Csikszentmihalyi, 1975; Harris, 1984; Wankel & Kreisel, 1985a, 1985b), social interactions (Brustad, 1988; Csikszentmihalyi, 1975; Wankel & Kreisel, 1985a, 1985b), and extrinsic rewards (Csikszentmihalyi, 1975; Wankel & Kreisel, 1985a, 1985b) have been identified as enjoyment sources in several studies. By no means are these thought to be exhaustive of the potential sources of enjoyment in sport. However, they do suggest the wide range of sources that may be revealed in the sport setting.

Research From Our Laboratory

Efforts in our laboratory have been directed toward defining the sport enjoyment construct, developing items to reflect the diverse sources of sport enjoyment, and examining the relative influence of these sources across intrapersonal variables and sport contexts. In the first study to investigate sources of sport enjoyment, Scanlan and Lewthwaite (1986) examined predictors of seasonal enjoyment for 76 male wrestlers aged 9 to 14 years. In addition to intrapersonal factors, this study was the first to explore the role of parents and coaches on youth experiences in sport. Enjoyment was operationalized by a two-item scale measuring (a) how much fun the wrestlers had during their season and (b) how much they liked to wrestle. Two categories of predictors were examined. The first category included age and perceived ability. The second category, significant adult influences, included items relating to parent and coach actions, reactions, and interactions. Adult influence items were subjected to factor analysis, and the eight factors which emerged were used as predictors of enjoyment along with age and perceived ability. Five variables were found to significantly predict seasonal enjoyment, accounting for 38% of the variance. Table 1 contains the significant predictors, and in the case of adult factors, the items corresponding to the factor. In order, Adult Satisfaction with Performance, Negative Maternal Interactions, Age, and Perceived Ability were significant, and Positive Adult Involvement approached significance. Note that *lower* levels of Negative Maternal Interactions and *younger* Age were related to greater enjoyment. The significant contribution of perceived ability supports its theorized link to enjoyment (e.g., Deci, 1975). However, the importance of significant adult influences, which had not previously been investigated, underscores the need to search for sources of sport enjoyment from among the wide variety of factors which can affect the youth sport experience.

As a launching point for further research, Scanlan and Lewthwaite (1986) presented a two-dimensional framework to provide a broader view of potential sources of sport enjoyment. The purpose was to expand the search beyond those sources which are intrinsic and achievement related. As illustrated in Figure 2, sport enjoyment is thought to be influenced by both achievement and nonachievement factors, which can be either intrinsic or extrinsic in origin. Achievement-Intrinsic factors (Quadrant I) are those relating to perceptions of competence and control that are self-reinforced, like feelings of mastery in performing a skill. Achievement-Extrinsic sources (Quadrant II) are related to feelings of competence and control that are dependent on feedback from other people, such as through positive social recognition. Nonachievement-Intrinsic factors (Quadrant III) are those which are tied to the experience of the activity, like movement sensations or the thrill of competition. Nonachievement-Extrinsic sources (Quadrant IV) are related to the nonperformance aspects of sport, such as social interactions with peers and significant others. The framework was not designed to be predictive, but rather to serve as a heuristic for the study of enjoyment sources.

Table 1 Significant Predictors of Seasonal Enjoyment in Youth Wrestlers

Predictor variable/items	Beta	F	p
Adult satisfaction with season's performance	.31	9.27	.003
How pleased do you think your mom (dad, coach) is with the way you wrestled this season?[a]			
Negative maternal interactions	−.28	9.02	.004
My mom makes me uptight and nervous about my wrestling.[b]			
My mom gets upset with me when I don't wrestle well.[c]			
Age	.24	5.60	.02
Perceived ability	.22	5.33	.02
Positive adult involvement and interactions	.16	2.87	.09
I wrestle because my parents and I have fun going to the tournaments together.[d]			
I wrestle because my dad or mom helps me with my wrestling and I like this.[d]			
I wrestle because I like my coach.[d]			
My coach tries to make me feel good when I don't wrestle well.[c]			

Note. Model $F(5,70) = 9.87$, $p < .001$, adjusted $R^2 = .38$. From "Social Psychological Aspects of the Competitive Sport Experience for Male Youth Sport Participants: 4. Predictors of Enjoyment" by T.K. Scanlan and R. Lewthwaite, 1986, *Journal of Sport Psychology*, **8**(1), p. 33. Copyright 1986 by Human Kinetics. Adapted by permission.
[a]1 = very pleased to 5 = not pleased at all.
[b]1 = how I feel to 3 = not how I feel.
[c]1 = usually to 3 = hardly ever.
[d]1 = a very important reason for why I wrestle to 5 = not an important reason at all for why I wrestle.

In the next investigation into sources of enjoyment, Scanlan, Stein, and Ravizza (1989) moved the focus from participants in youth sport programs to especially talented individuals who had shown intense, long-term commitment to their sport and who had achieved high levels of success. In addition, qualitative methods were employed to more completely reveal the wide range of enjoyment sources present in the multifaceted sport experience of participants. An inductive analysis of quotes from extensive interviews of 26 former elite figure skaters produced rich and detailed retrospective data on their enjoyment sources. For the present discussion, only the most basic explanation of the procedure and the two highest order themes derived from the data will be presented. Scanlan et al. (1989) provide complete details of the analysis and empirical results.

The inductive analysis involved clustering verbatim quotes from taped interviews into themes based upon similarity of meanings. The themes at the first level were then clustered into the next higher order according to underlying

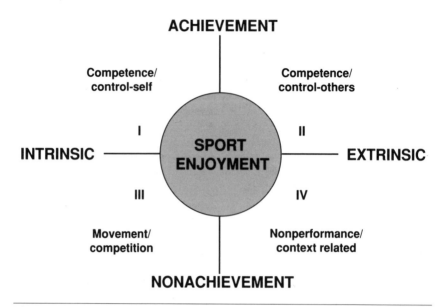

ACHIEVEMENT

Competence/
control-self

Competence/
control-others

I

II

INTRINSIC — SPORT ENJOYMENT — EXTRINSIC

III

IV

Movement/
competition

Nonperformance/
context related

NONACHIEVEMENT

Figure 2. A framework for investigating the diverse sources of sport enjoyment. *Note.* From "An In-Depth Study of Former Elite Figure Skaters: 2. Sources of Enjoyment" by T.K. Scanlan, G.L. Stein, and K. Ravizza, 1989, *Journal of Sport and Exercise Psychology*, **11**(1), pp. 70-71. Copyright 1989 by Human Kinetics. Reprinted by permission.

commonalities. The process is designed to continue until no higher order themes can be defined by further clusters of lower order themes. At each step, acceptance of items into themes requires consensus of independent raters. In the Scanlan et al. (1989) study, up to four theme levels were derived from the original quotes. Figure 3 presents an example of the progression of theme levels from a single quote. Although not detailed in Figure 3, recognize that concepts are combined with others of the same level to define the next higher order theme (see Scanlan et al., 1989, for complete details).

The inductive analysis produced five distinct highest order themes for the sources of enjoyment reported by elite figure skaters. The five themes are presented here with reference to the lower order themes which define them. Table 2 provides a quick reference for the themes at these two levels. Importantly, sources emerged from this process which did not previously exist in the literature. Moreover, the inductive approach provided depth of understanding for both the new sources and those which had been previously identified. By giving the skaters the opportunity to elaborate on perceived sources of enjoyment, we obtained greater insight into their meaning to the skaters themselves. Overall, the inductive analysis contributed breadth, depth, and personal meaning to the literature on enjoyment sources.

The *social and life opportunities* theme is defined by three lower order themes. "Friendship opportunities through skating" are the opportunities to

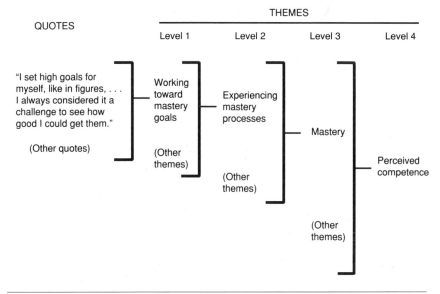

Figure 3. Example of the progression of themes under the inductive process employed by Scanlan, Stein, and Ravizza (1989). Note that additional information is included at each level as indicated by the statements in parentheses.

make friends or share friendships in and around the context of competitive skating. "Opportunities afforded by going to competitions and touring" reflected the personally enriching experiences gained by touring, traveling, and experiencing new places, cultures, or special treats. Finally, the "family/coach relationships" theme was based on positive interactions with significant adults, or the opportunity to bring them pleasure or pride.

Four lower order themes made up the *perceived competence* theme. The first two, "mastery" and "competitive achievement," are common to research and theory in achievement motivation. Mastery reflected the development of competence (autonomous achievement), and competitive achievement was based on evaluations of social achievement, such as winning or being better than others. A category newly identified by this research, "performance achievement" also reflected social achievement, but with a different evaluative focus. Performance achievement was related to the performance aspects of the sport, such as showmanship and interaction with the audience. The experience of interchange between performer and audience was a significant source of enjoyment for a number of the skaters. Lastly, "demonstration of athletic ability" contributed to the perceived competence theme as an experience of being better than nonskating peers at a sport.

Social recognition of competence was defined by two lower themes. "Achievement recognition" reflected the public recognition, adulation, or fame from the skating community, nonskating peers, and the public in general. This category was most closely aligned with competitive achievements, such

Table 2   Highest Order Themes Representing Sources of Enjoyment Identified by Former Elite Figure Skaters

---

  I. Social and life opportunities
     Definition: "Forming relationships with peer and adult significant others and/or having broadening experiences outside the routine of sport life." (p. 75)
     A. Friendship opportunities through skating
     B. Opportunities afforded by going to competitions and touring
     C. Family/coach relationships

 II. Perceived competence
     Definition: "Personal perceptions of competence derived from one's autonomous and/or social achievement in sport." (p. 76)
     A. Mastery
     B. Competitive achievement
     C. Performance achievement
     D. Demonstration of athletic ability

III. Social recognition of competence
     Definition: "Receiving recognition, even acclaim, for having skating competence through others' acknowledgment of one's performances and achievements." (p. 77)
     A. Achievement recognition
     B. Performance recognition

IV. Act of skating
    Definition: "Sensations, perceptions, and/or self-expressiveness associated with the act of skating itself." (p. 78)
    A. Movement and sensations of skating
    B. Self-expression/creativity
    C. Athleticism of skating
    D. Flow/peak experiences

 V. Special cases
    Definition: "Two separate themes which do not share a common conceptual basis with one another or any of the other themes." (p. 79)
    A. Sense of specialness
    B. Coping through skating

Note. Adapted from Scanlan, Stein, and Ravizza (1989).

as being ranked and winning. "Performance recognition" was most associated with performance achievement, and was defined as recognition or adulation that came directly from the audience due to a display of talent or showmanship. This category was also new to the literature, and is indicative of the entertainment aspects of a sport like figure skating.

The *act of skating* theme was based on four lower order themes. The "movement and sensations of skating" theme was defined by experiences of kinesthetic and tactile sensations, a sense of physical exhilaration, and special feelings derived from the movement itself, such as jumping, gliding, going fast, and flowing with the music. "Self-expression/creativity" reflected the sense of communicating personal creativity through the performance. "Athleticism of skating" was defined by the feelings of fitness and strength, and the satisfaction experienced in the process of hard physical training. Memorable peak experiences that appeared effortless and near perfection made up the theme of "flow/peak experiences."

The *special cases* theme was a miscellaneous grouping of two important themes which were unrelated to the other themes or to each other. The first independent theme, "sense of specialness," was based on personal perceptions of being exceptionally talented and having abilities beyond the ordinary. "Coping through skating" reflected the use of the sport itself as a way of coping with life problems and gaining a sense of personal control.

In addition to the identification of specific sources of enjoyment, the data from these former elite skaters demonstrate (a) the value of combining the open-ended interview method and inductive analysis in discovering new constructs such as performance achievement and performance recognition, and (b) the depth of understanding that can be achieved when participants are allowed to thoroughly discuss their experiences in their own terms. Moreover, exploring sources of enjoyment with a sample so different than has been previously assessed helps to illuminate potential factors that might otherwise be missed.

We are currently pursuing this line of research using a nomothetic approach. A comprehensive questionnaire has been developed by using the conceptual dimensions of the sport enjoyment framework (Scanlan & Lewthwaite, 1986) as a guide. The enjoyment sources generated by the past literature, including the new qualitative database, have served as specific resources in item development. The responses of large samples of young sport participants are being examined to determine definable factors ordering the sources of enjoyment. In addition, work is in progress to examine common and unique sources of enjoyment across groups differing by sport type and intrapersonal variables.

Applications for Enhancing Motivation *re promoting*

The data from the elite skaters are consistent with the findings from youth sport and interscholastic sport in showing that (a) sport enjoyment is an important affect related to motivation, and (b) its sources are diverse. These results support the contentions of the previously described enjoyment framework (Scanlan & Lewthwaite, 1986) by revealing a multifaceted set of sources ranging across intrinsic/extrinsic and achievement/nonachievement dimensions. Clearly, sport is an arena rich in potentially rewarding experiences, both for elite performers as well as the wide range of youth sport participants and interscholastic sport participants.

These findings lead to two major conclusions that would help adults, particularly parents and coaches, enhance motivation in youth sport. First, it is important to understand the significance of positive affect, and certainly enjoyment, to an individual's motivation in sport. In the operation of sport programs, the motivating power of joy should not be overlooked. Second, it is important to understand the nature of the sources of enjoyment and, in this regard, the following points need to be considered.

1. There are a variety of sources that can make sport enjoyable, many of which are common across sport contexts. While any particular source may be more significant to one individual than to another, there are certainly ample opportunities to experience this positive emotion in sport. The key is to make certain that a variety of sources are available to assure that enjoyment can be experienced.

2. Achievement and its recognition are enjoyable. While this statement might appear obvious, it is a point frequently missed. The enjoyment construct often suffers from a preconceived notion of frivolity, or what we now refer to as the "pizza parlor phenomenon." That is, enjoyment is something that is experienced after the job is done, like when teammates socialize over pizza. This conception fails to recognize that there can be fun (a) in the striving for achievement experienced while doing the task, as well as (b) in the sense of accomplishment felt, or recognition received, after its successful completion.

3. Non-achievement-related sources of enjoyment demonstrate the potential richness of the sport experience and the broad meaning it can have for the participants. Moreover, these nonachievement sources also can contribute to the motivation needed to achieve. For example, interacting with friends on the team can be enjoyable, and might play an important function in keeping some participants involved in sport over the long haul—certainly a major factor in long-term achievement.

4. Finally, sources of enjoyment related directly to movement itself, such as movement sensations and athleticism, might be the key to attracting an individual to the sport setting, rather than to some other talent domain. Bloom's (1985) research has demonstrated similarities across diverse talent domains such as music, art, and sport. We might also expect that these talent fields share a number of common enjoyment sources. The logical exception, besides physical prowess, would be specific movement-derived sources. This uniquely enjoyable feature of sport and movement activities might be crucial to initial and continued involvement in these endeavors.

Conclusion

To achieve a more complete understanding of motivation and its enhancement, this chapter encourages researchers to incorporate positive emotion into their study of motivation. We advocate the inclusion of affect to any theoretical perspective guiding one's research, and in this respect, present our work merely as one example. In our particular case, we have incorporated enjoyment into a larger motivational framework designed to explain sport commitment.

We look forward to a future in which qualitative and quantitative methods are used more extensively in combination to study motivational issues. Qualitative methods can yield a rich, ecologically valid database that is not limited by the conceptual impositions and experiential deficits of the researchers. This database is an important outcome unto itself. In addition, it is this foundation that can be built upon to develop more comprehensive survey instruments, and to interpret the resulting data with greater understanding of their meaning to participants.

Acknowledgments

Preparation of this chapter and the research presented was supported by three sources of funding to the first author: The Amateur Athletic Foundation of Los Angeles, UCLA Academic Senate Grant 3188, and grant monies from the former UCLA Dean of Life Sciences (J.D. O'Conner).

We thank Marci Lobel for her feedback on an earlier draft of this manuscript.

Notes

[1] Greg Schmidt and Paul Carpenter have contributed significantly to the development of the sport commitment model as members of our research team.

References

Ajzen, I. (1985). From intentions to actions: A theory of planned behavior. In J. Kuhl & J. Beckman (Eds), *Action-control: From cognition to behavior* (pp. 11-39). Heidelberg: Springer.

Allison, M.T. (1982). Sportsmanship: Variation based on sex and degree of competitive experience. In A.O. Dunleavy, A.W. Miracle, & C.R. Rees (Eds.), *Studies in the Sociology of Sport*. Fort Worth, TX: Texas Christian University.

Ames, C. (1984a). Competitive, cooperative, and individualistic goal structures: A cognitive-motivational analysis. In R. Ames & C. Ames (Eds.), *Research on motivation in education: Vol. 1. Student motivation* (pp. 177-208). New York: Academic Press.

Ames, C. (1984b). Conceptions of motivation within competitive and non-competitive goal structures. In R. Schwarzer (Ed.), *Self-related cognitions in anxiety and motivation*. Hillsdale, NJ: Erlbaum.

Ames, C. (1987). The enhancement of student motivation. In D. Kleiber & M. Maehr (Eds.), *Advances in motivation and achievement* (pp. 123-148). Greenwich, CT: JAI Press.

Ames, C. (1990a). *Achievement goals and classroom structure: Developing a learning orientation in students*. Paper presented at the annual meeting of the American Educational Research Association, Boston, MA.

Ames, C. (1990b). Motivation differences of at-risk and non-at-risk elementary school children. Unpublished manuscript.

Ames, C., & Ames, R. (1981). Competitive versus individualistic goal structures: The salience of past performance information for causal attributions and affect. *Journal of Educational Psychology*, **73**, 411-418.

Ames, C., & Ames, R. (1984a). Systems of student and teacher motivation: Towards a qualitative definition. *Journal of Educational Psychology*, **76**, 535-556.

Ames, C., & Ames, R. (Eds.) (1984b). *Research on motivation in education: Vol. 1. Student motivation*. New York: Academic Press.

Ames, C., & Archer, J. (1987). Mothers' beliefs about the role of ability and effort in school learning. *Journal of Educational Psychology*, **18**, 409-414.

Ames, C., & Archer, J. (1988). Achievement goals in the classroom: Students' learning strategies and motivation processes. *Journal of Educational Psychology*, **80**, 260-267.

Ames, C., & Archer, J. (1990). *Longitudinal effects of mastery goal structure on students' learning strategies and motivation*. Manuscript submitted for publication.

Ames, C., & Maehr, M.L. (1989). *Home and school cooperation in social and motivational develotment*. Unpublished raw data. Project funded by U.S. Office of Education, Office of Special Education and Rehabilitative Services, Contract No. DE-HO23T80023.

Andrew, G.M., Oldridge, N.B., Parker, J.O., Cunningham, D.A., Rechnitzer, P.A., Jones, N.L., Buck, C., Kavanagh, T., Shephard, R.J., Sutton, J.R., & McDonald, W. (1981). Reasons for dropout from exercise programs in postcoronary patients. *Medicine and Science in Sports and Exercise*, **13**, 164-168.

Andrew, G.M., & Parker, J.O. (1979). Factors related to dropout of post-myocardialinfarction patients from exercise programs. *Medicine and Science in Sports and Exercise*, **11**, 376-378.

Asch, S. (1952). *Social psychology*. Englewood Cliffs, NJ: Prentice-Hall. (Reissued by Oxford University Press, 1988).

Atkins, C.J., Kaplan, R.M., Timms, R.M., Reinsch, S., & Lofback, K. (1984). Behavioral exercise programs in the management of chronic obstructive pulmonary disease. *Journal of Consulting and Clinical Psychology*, **52**, 591-603.

Atkinson, J.W. (1957). Motivational determinants of risk-taking behavior. *Psychological Review*, **64**, 359-372.

Atkinson, J.W. (Ed.) (1958). *Motives in fantasy action and society*. Princeton, NJ: Van Nostrand.

Atkinson, J.W. (1964). *An introduction to motivation*. Princeton, NJ: Van Nostrand.

Ausubel, D.P., Novak, J.D., & Hanesian, H. (1978). *Educational psychology: A cognitive view* (2nd Ed.). New York: Holt, Rinehart & Winston.

Balague, G., & Roberts, G.C. (1989, November). *A social cognitive scale to measure mastery and competitive achievement goals in sport*. Paper presented at the symposium entitled "Motivation in sport and exercise," University of Illinois at Urbana-Champaign.

Bandura, A. (1977a). Self-efficacy: Toward a unifying theory of behavioral change. *Psychological Review*, **84**, 191-215.

Bandura, A. (1977b). *Social learning theory*. Englewood Cliffs, NJ: Prentice-Hall.

Bandura, A. (1982). Self-efficacy mechanism in human agency. *American Psychologist*, **37**, 122-147.

Bandura, A. (1984). Recycling misconceptions of perceived self-efficacy. *Cognitive Therapy and Research*, **8**, 231-255.

Bandura, A. (1986). *Social foundations of thought and action: A social cognitive theory*. Englewood Cliffs, NJ: Prentice-Hall.

Bandura, A. (1989, September). *Perceived self-efficacy in the exercise of personal agency*. Coleman Griffith Memorial Lecture at the Annual Conference of the Association for the Advancement of Applied Sport Psychology, Seattle.

Bandura, A., & Adams, N.E. (1977). Analysis of self-efficacy theory of behavioral change. *Cognitive Therapy and Research*, **1**, 287-310.

Bandura, A., & Cervone, D. (1983). Self-evaluative and self-efficacy mechanisms governing the motivational effects of goal systems. *Journal of Personality and Social Psychology*, **45**, 1017-1028.

Bandura, A., & Cervone, D. (1986). Differential engagement of self-reactive influences in cognitive motivation. *Organizational Behaviors and Human Decision Processes*, **38**, 92-113.

Bandura, A., & Schunk, D.H. (1981). Cultivating competence, self-efficacy, and intrinsic interest through proximal self-motivation. *Journal of Personality and Social Psychology*, **41**, 586-598.

Bandura, A., & Simon, K.M. (1977). The role proximal intentions in self-regulation of refractory behavior. *Cognitive Therapy and Research*, **1**, 177-193.

Bandura, A., & Wood, R. (1989). Effect of perceived controllability and performance standards on self-regulation of complex decision making. *Journal of Personality and Social Psychology*, **56**, 805-814.

Barling, J., & Abel, M. (1983). Self-efficacy beliefs and tennis performance. *Cognitive Therapy and Research*, **7**, 265-272.

Barnes, B. (1977). *Interests and the growth of knowledge*. London: Routledge & Kegan Paul.

Barnett, M.L. (1977). *Effects of student-led small group and teacher-pupil conference methods of goal-setting on achievement in a gross motor task*. Unpublished doctoral dissertation, University of Michigan, Ann Arbor.

Barnett, M.L., & Stanicek, J.A. (1979). Effects of goal setting on achievement in archery. *Research Quarterly*, **50**, 328-332.

Baumeister, R.F. (1989). The optimal margin of illusion. *Journal of Social and Clinical Psychology*, **8**, 176-189.

Bavelas, J.B., & Lee, E.S. (1978). Systems analysis of dyadic interaction: Prediction from individual parameters. *Behavioral Science*, **23**, 177-186.

Beck, K.H., & Lund, A.K. (1981). The effects of health threat seriousness and personal efficacy upon intentions and behavior. *Journal of Applied Social Psychology*, **11**, 401-415.

Becker, M.H. (Ed.) (1974). The health belief model and personal health behavior. *Health Education Monograph*, **2**, 511.

Becker, M.H., Haefner, D.P., Kasi, S.V., Kirscht, J.P., Maiman, L.A., & Rosenstock, I.M. (1977). Selected psychosocial models and correlates of individual health-related behaviors. *Medical Care*, **15**, 27-47.

Belisle, M., Roskies, E., & Levesque, J.M. (1987). Improving adherence to physical activity. *Health Psychology*, **6**, 158-172.

Bell, K.F. (1983). *Championship thinking: The athlete's guide to winning performance in all sports.* Englewood Cliffs, NJ: Prentice-Hall.

Berger, B.G., Friedman, E., & Eaton, M. (1988). Comparison of jogging, the relaxation response, and group interaction for stress reduction. *Journal of Sport Exercise Psychology,* **10,** 431-447.

Bernier, M., & Avard, J. (1986). Self-efficacy, outcome and attrition in a weight reduction program. *Cognitive Therapy and Research,* **10,** 319-338.

Blair, S. (1985). Professionalization of attitudes toward play in children and adults. *Research Quarterly for Exercise and Sport,* **56,** 82-83.

Blair, S.N., Pate, R.R., Blair, A., Howe, H.G., Rosenberg, M., & Parker, G.M. (1980). Leisure time physical activity as an intervening variable in research. *Health Education,* **11,** 8-11.

Bloom, B.S. (1985). *Developing talent in young people.* New York: Ballantine Books.

Blumenfeld, W.S., & Leidy, T.R. (1969). Effectiveness of goal setting as a management device. Research note. *Psychological Reports,* **24,** 752.

Blumenthal, J.A., Williams, R.S., Wallace, A.G., Williams, R.B., & Needles, T.L. (1982). Physiological and psychological variables predict compliance to prescribed exercise therapy in patients recovering from myocardial infarction. *Psychosomatic Medicine,* **44,** 519-527.

Bonds, A.G. (1980). The relationship between self-concept and locus of control and patterns of eating, exercise, and social participation in older adults. *DAI,* **41,** 1397A.

Bonnano, J.A., & Lies, J.E. (1974). Effects of physical training on coronary risk factors. *American Journal of Cardiology,* **33,** 760-764.

Borg, G. (1962). *Physical performance and perceived exertion.* Lund, Sweden: Gleerup.

Botterill, C. (1977). *Goal setting and performance on an endurance task.* Paper presented at the Canadian Psychomotor Learning and Sport Psychology Conference, Banff, AB.

Botterill, C. (1978). The psychology of coaching. *Coaching Review,* **1,** 1-8.

Botterill, C. (1979). Goal setting with athletes. *Sport science periodical on research and technology in sport.* **BU-1,** 1-8.

Botterill, C. (1980). Psychology of coaching. In R.M. Suinn (Ed.), *Psychology in sports: Methods and applications.* Minneapolis: Burgess.

Boyd, M.P. (1990). *The effects of participation orientation and success-failure on post-competitive affect in young athletes.* Unpublished doctoral dissertation, University of Southern California, Los Angeles.

Brawley, L.R., & Roberts, G.C. (1984). Attributions in sport: Research foundations, characteristics, and limitations. In J.M. Silva & R.S. Weinberg (Eds.), *Psychological foundations of sport* (pp. 197-213). Champaign, IL: Human Kinetics.

Bredemeier, B.J. (1985). Moral reasoning and the perceived legitimacy of intentionally injurious sport acts. *Journal of Sport Psychology,* **7,** 110-124.

Brickman, P. (1987). *Commitment, conflict, and caring*. Englewood Cliffs, NJ: Prentice-Hall.

Brody, E.B., Hatfield, B.D., & Spalding, T.W. (1988). Generalization of self-efficacy to a continuum of stressors upon mastery of a high-risk sport skill. *Journal of Sport Psychology*, **10**, 32-44.

Brophy, J. (1983). Conceptualizing student motivation. *Educational Psychologist*, **18**, 200-214.

Brophy, J. (1986). *On motivating students*. (Occasional Paper No. 101.) East Lansing, MI: Institute for Research on Teaching.

Brophy, J., & Merrick, M. (1987). *Motivating students to learn: An experiment in junior high social studies classes* (Research Series No. 183). East Lansing: Michigan State University, Institute for Research on Teaching.

Brownell, K.D. (1982). Exercise and obesity. *Behavioral Medicine Update*, **4**, 7-11.

Brownell, K.D. (1989, June). When and how to diet. *Psychology Today* (pp. 41-46).

Brownell, K.D., Stunkard, A.J., & Albaum, J.M. (1980). Evaluation and modification of exercise patterns in the natural environment. *American Journal of Psychiatry*, **137**, 1540-1545.

Bruce, E.H., Frederick, R., Bruce, R.A., & Fisher, L.D. (1979). Comparison of active participants and dropouts in CAPRI cardiopulmonary rehabilitation programs. *American Journal of Cardiology*, **37**, 53-59.

Brustad, R.J. (1988). Affective outcomes in competitive youth sport: The influence of intrapersonal and socialization factors. *Journal of Sport and Exercise Psychology*, **10**, 307-321.

Bukowski, W.M., & Moore, D. (1980). Winners' and losers' attributions for success and failure in a series of athletic events. *Journal of Sport Psychology*, **2**, 195-210.

Burton, D. (1989a). Impact of goal specificity and task complexity on basketball skill development. *The Sport Psychologist*, **3**, 34-47.

Burton, D. (1989b). Winning isn't everything: Examining the impact of performance goals on collegiate swimmers' cognitions and performance. *The Sport Psychologist*, **3**, 105-132.

Burton, D., & Martens, R. (1986). Pinned by their own goals: An exploratory investigation into why kids drop out of wrestling. *Journal of Sport Psychology*, **8**, 183-197.

Butler, R. (1987). Task-involving and ego-involving properties of evaluation: The effects of different feedback conditions on motivational perceptions, interest and performance. *Journal of Educational Psychology*, **79**, 474-482.

Butler, R. (1988). Enhancing and undermining intrinsic motivation: The effects of task-involving and ego-involving evaluation on interest and performance. *British Journal of Educational Psychology*, **58**, 1-14.

Butler, R. (1989). Interest in the task and interest in peers' work in competitive and noncompetitive conditions: A developmental study. *Child Development*, **60**, 562-570.

Campbell, D.J., & Ilgen, D.R. (1976). Additive effects of task difficulty and goal setting on subsequent task performance. *Journal of Applied Psychology*, **61**, 319-324.

Carron, A.V. (1984). *Motivation: Implications for coaching and teaching.* London, ON: Sport Dynamics.

Carver, C.S., & Scheier, M.F. (1982). Control theory: A useful conceptual framework for personality, social, clinical, and health psychology. *Psychological Bulletin*, **92**, 111-135.

Chalip, L., Csikszentmihalyi, M., Kleiber, D., & Larson, R. (1984). Variations of experience in formal and informal sport. *Research Quarterly for Exercise and Sport*, **55**(2), 109-116.

Chambliss, D. (1989). The mundanity of excellence: An ethnographic report on stratification and Olympic swimmers. *Sociological Theory*, **7**, 70-86.

Chaumeton, N., & Duda, J. (1988). Is it how you play the game or whether you win or lose?: The effect of competitive level and situation on coaching behaviors. *Journal of Sport Behavior*, **11**, 157-174.

Chen, K., & Duda, J.L. (1990, May). *Personal investment in exercise/sport: A cross-cultural analysis.* Paper presented at the annual meeting of the North American Society for the Psychology of Sport and Physical Activity, University of Houston.

Coakley, J.J. (1986). Socialization and youth sports. In C.R. Rees & A.W. Miracle (Eds.), *Sport and social theory* (pp. 135-143). Champaign, IL: Human Kinetics.

Cobb, S. (1976). Social support as a moderator of life stress. *Psychosomatic Medicine*, **38**, 300-314.

Cohen, S. (1988). Psychosocial models of the role of social support in the etiology of physical disease. *Health Psychology*, **7**, 269-297.

Cohen, S., & Syme, S. (1985). *Social support and health.* New York: Academic Press.

Cole, M., & Scribner, S. (1974). *Culture and thought: A psychological introduction.* New York: Wiley.

Collins, J. (1982, March). *Self-efficacy and ability in achievement behavior.* Paper presented at the meeting of The American Educational Research Association, New York.

Cooper, K.G. (1968). *Aerobics.* New York: Bantam Books.

Coppel, S. (1982). *The relationship of perceived social support and self-efficacy to major and minor stressors.* Unpublished doctoral dissertation, University of Washington, Seattle.

Corbin, C.B., Laurie, D.R., Gruger, C., & Smiley, B. (1984). Vicarious success experience as a factor influencing self-confidence, attitudes, and physical activity of adult women. *Journal of Teaching in Physical Education*, **4**, 17-23.

Corno, L., & Mandinach, E. (1983). The role of cognitive engagement in classroom learning and motivation. *Educational Psychologist*, **18**, 88-108.

Covington, M.V. (1984). The motive for self-worth. In R. Ames & C. Ames (Eds.), *Research on motivation in education* (pp. 77-113). New York: Academic Press.

Covington, M.V., & Omelich, C.L. (1979). It's best to be able and virtuous too: Student and teacher evaluative response to successful effort. *Journal of Educational Psychology*, **71**, 688-700.

Crabtree, M.K. (1987). *Self-efficacy, social support, and social incentives as predictors of diabetic self-care.* Paper presented at the Society of Behavioral Medicine, Washington, DC.

Crandall, V.C. (1963). Achievement. In H.W. Stevenson (Ed.), *Child psychology* (pp. 416-459). Chicago: University of Chicago Press.

Crandall, V.C. (1969). Sex differences in expectancy of intellectual and academic reinforcement. In C.P. Smith (Ed.), *Achievement-related motives in children.* New York: Russell Sage.

Crews, D.J., & Landers, D.M. (1987). A meta-analytic review of aerobic fitness and reactivity to psychosocial stress. *Medicine and Science in Sports and Exercise*, **19**, S114-S120.

Crutchfield, R.S. (1962). Conformity and creative thinking. In H.E. Gruber, G. Terrell, & M. Wertheimer (Eds.), *Contemporary approaches to creative thinking.* New York: Prentice-Hall.

Csikszentmihalyi, M. (1975). *Beyond boredom and anxiety.* San Francisco: Josey-Bass.

Csikszentmihalyi, M., & Nakamura, J. (1989). The dynamics of intrinsic motivation: A study of adolescents. In R. Ames & C. Ames (Eds.), *Research on motivation in education: Vol. 3. Goals and cognitions* (pp. 45-72). New York: Academic Press.

Cutrona, C.E., & Troutman, B.R. (1986). Social support, infant temperament, and parenting self-efficacy: A mediational model of postpartum depression. *Child Development*, **57**, 1507-1518.

Cutrona, C.E., & Russell, D. (1987). The provisions of social relationships and adaptation to stress. In W.H. Jones & D. Perlman (Eds.), *Advances in personal relationships: Vol. 1.* (pp. 37-68). Greenwich, CT: JAI Press.

Davis, K.E., Jackson, K.L., Kronenfeld, J.J., & Blair, S.N. (1984). Intent to participation in worksite health promotion activities: A model of risk factors and psychosocial variables. *Health Education Quarterly*, **11**, 361-377.

deCharms, R. (1968). *Personal causation.* New York: Academic Press.

deCharms, R., & Dave, P.N. (1965). Hope of success, fear of failure, subjective probability, and risk-taking behavior. *Journal of Personality and Social Psychology*, **1**, 558-568.

Deci, E.L. (1975). *Intrinsic Motivation.* New York: Plenum Press.

Deci, E.L., & Ryan, R.M. (1980). The empirical exploration of intrinsic motivational processes. In L. Berkowitz (Ed.), *Advances in experimental social psychology: Vol. 13* (pp. 39-80). New York: Academic Press.

Deci, E.L., & Ryan, R.M. (1985). *Intrinsic motivation and self-determination in human behavior.* New York: Plenum Press.

Dennett, D.C. (1978). *Brainstorms: Philosophical essays on mind and psychology.* Montgomery, VT: Bradford.

Department of Health and Human Services, Office of Disease Prevention and Health Promotion. (1982). *Prevention '82.* (DHHS Publication No. PHS 82-50157). Washington, DC: U.S. Government Printing Office.

Desharnais, R., Bouillon, J., & Godin, G. (1986). Self-efficacy and outcome expectations as determinants of exercise adherence. *Psychological Reports,* **59**, 1155-1159.

Dewey, J. (1966). *Democracy and education.* New York: Free Press. (Original work published 1916.)

Diener, C., & Dweck, C.S. (1978). An analysis of learned helplessness: Continuous changes in performance, strategy, and achievement cognitions following failure. *Journal of Personality and Social Psychology,* **36**, 451-462.

Dishman, R.K. (1982). Compliance/adherence in health-related exercise. *Health Psychology,* **1**, 237-267.

Dishman, R.K. (1986). Exercise compliance: A new view for public health. *The Physician and Sports Medicine,* **14**, 127-145.

Dishman, R.K. (1988). *Exercise adherence: Its impact on public health.* Champaign, IL: Human Kinetics.

Dishman, R.K., & Gettman, L.R. (1980). Psychobiologic influences on exercise adherence. *Journal of Sport Psychology,* **2**, 295-310.

Dishman, R.K., & Ickes, W. (1981). Self-motivation and adherence to therapeutic exercise. *Journal of Behavioral Medicine,* **4**, 421-437.

Dishman, R.K., Ickes, W., & Morgan, W.P. (1980). Self-motivation and adherence to habitual physical activity. *Journal of Applied Social Psychology,* **10**, 115-132.

Dishman, R.K., Sallis, J.F., & Orenstein, D.R. (1985). The determinants of physical activity and exercise. *Public Health Reports,* **100**, 158-171.

Duda, J.L. (1981). *A cross-cultural analysis of achievement motivation in sport and the classroom.* Unpublished doctoral dissertation, University of Illinois, Urbana.

Duda, J.L. (1985). Goals and achievement or orientations of Anglo and Mexican-American adolescents in sport and the classroom. *International Journal of Intercultural Relations,* **9**, 131-155.

Duda, J.L. (1986a). A cross-cultural analysis of achievement motivation in sport and the classroom. In L. VanderVelden and J. Humphrey (Eds.), *Psychology and sociology in sport: Current selected research: Vol. 1.* New York: AMS Press.

Duda, J.L. (1986b). Perceptions of sport success and failure among white, black, and Hispanic adolescents. In J. Watkins, T. Reilly, & L. Burwitz (Eds.), *Sport Science* (pp. 214-222). London: E. & F.N. Spon.

Duda, J.L. (1987). Toward a developmental theory of children's motivation in sport. *Journal of Sport Psychology,* **9**, 130-145.

Duda, J.L. (1988). The relationship between goal perspectives and persistence and intensity among recreational sport participants. *Leisure Sciences*, **10**, 95-106.

Duda, J.L. (1989a). Goal perspectives and behavior in sport and exercise settings. In C. Ames & M. Maehr (Eds.), *Advances in Motivation and Achievement: Vol. 6.* (pp. 81-115). Greenwich, CT: JAI Press.

Duda, J.L. (1989b). Goal perspectives, participation and persistence in sport. *International Journal of Sport Psychology*, **20**, 42-56.

Duda, J.L. (1989c). The relationship between task and ego orientation and the perceived purpose of sport among male and female high school athletes. *Journal of Sport and Exercise Psychology*, **11**, 318-335.

Duda, J.L., & Chi, L. (1989, September). *The effect of task- and ego-involving conditions on perceived competence and causal attributions in basketball.* Paper presented at the meeting of the Association for the Advancement of Applied Sport Psychology, University of Washington, Seattle.

Duda, J.L., Chi, L., & Newton, M. (1990, May). *Psychometric characteristics of the TEOSQ.* Paper presented at the annual meeting of the North American Society for the Psychology of Sport and Physical Activity, University of Houston, TX.

Duda, J.L., & Huston, L. (1990). *The relationship of competitive level and goal orientation to perceptions of the legitimacy of aggressive acts among football players.* Unpublished manuscript.

Duda, J.L., Newton, M., & Chi, L. (1990, May). *The relationship of task and ego orientation and expectations to multidimensional state anxiety.* Paper presented at the annual meeting of the North American Society for the Psychology of Sport and Physical Activity, University of Houston, TX.

Duda, J.L. & Nicholls, J.G. (1989a). *Dimensions of achievement motivation in schoolwork and sport: Situational specificity or general traits.* Unpublished manuscript.

Duda, J.L. & Nicholls, J.G. (1989b). *The Task and Ego Orientation in Sport Questionnaire: Psychometric properties.* Unpublished manuscript.

Duda, J.L., Olson, L.K., & Templin, T.J. (1991, March). The relationship of task and ego orientation to sportsmanship attitudes and the perceived legitimacy of injurious acts. *Research Quarterly for Exercise and Sport*, **62**, 79.

Duda, J.L., Sedlock, D.A., Noble, B., Cohen, B., & Chi, L. (1990, March). *The influence of goal perspective on perceived exertion and affect ratings during submaximal exercise.* Paper presented at the annual meeting of the American Alliance for Health, Physical Education, Recreation and Dance, New Orleans, LA.

Duda, J.L., Smart, A., & Tappe, M. (1989). Personal investment in the rehabilitation of athletic injuries. *Journal of Sport and Exercise Psychology*, **11**, 367-381.

Duda, J.L., & Tappe, M.K. (1988). Predictors of personal investment in physical activity among middle-aged and older adults. *Perceptual and Motor Skills*, **66**, 543-549.

Duda, J.L., & Tappe, M.K. (1989a). Personal investment in exercise among adults: The examination of age- and gender-related differences in motivational orientation. In A. Ostrow (Ed.), *Aging and motor behavior* (pp. 239-256). Indianapolis: Benchmark Press.

Duda, J.L., & Tappe, M.K. (1989b). Personal investment in exercise among middle-aged and older adults. In A. Ostrow (Ed.), *Aging and motor behavior* (pp. 219-238). Indianapolis: Benchmark Press.

Duda, J.L., Tappe, M.K., & Savage, M. (1990, September). *Predictors of personal investment in exercise among young adults.* Paper presented at the annual meeting of the Association for the Advancement of Applied Sport Psychology, San Antonio, TX.

Dulce, J.J., Crocker, M.F., Moletterie, C., & Doleys, D.M. (1986). Exercise quotas, anticipatory concern and self-efficacy expectancies in chronic pain: A preliminary report. *Pain,* **24**, 365-372.

Duncan, T.E. (1989). *The influence of social support and efficacy cognitions in the exercise behavior of sedentary adults: An interactional model.* Unpublished doctoral dissertation, University of Oregon, Eugene.

Duncan, T.E., & McAuley, E. (1991). Social support and efficacy cognitions in exercise adherence: A latent growth curve analysis. Manuscript submitted for publication.

Dunning, E., & Sheard, K. (1979). *Barbarians, gentlemen and players: A sociological study of the development of Rugby football.* New York: New York University Press.

Dweck, C.S. (1975). The role of expectations and attributions in the alleviations of learned helplessness. *Journal of Personality and Social Psychology,* **31**, 674-675.

Dweck, C.S. (1986). Motivational processes affecting learning. *American Psychologist,* **41**, 1040-1048.

Dweck, C.S. & Bempechat, J. (1983). Children's theories of intelligence: Consequences for learning. In S. Paris, G. Olson, & H.W. Stevenson (Eds.), *Learning and motivation in the classroom* (pp. 239-256). Hillsdale, NJ: Erlbaum.

Dweck, C.S., & Elliott, E. (1983). Achievement motivation. In M. Hetherington (Ed.), *Handbook of child psychology, (4th Ed.), Vol. 4: Socialization, personality and social development* (pp. 643-691). New York: Wiley.

Dweck, C.S., & Leggett, E.L. (1988). A social-cognitive approach to motivation and personality. *Psychological Review,* **95**, 256-273.

Dzewaltowski, D.A. (1989). Toward a model of exercise motivation. *Journal of Sport and Exercise Psychology,* **11**, 251-269.

Dzewaltowski, D.A., Noble, J.M., & Shaw, J.M. (1990). Physical activity participation: Social cognitive versus the theories of reasoned action and planned behavior. *Journal of Sport and Exercise Psychology,* **12**, 388-405.

Eccles, J., Midgley, C., & Adler, T. (1984). Grade-related changes in the school environment: Effects on achievement motivation. In J. Nicholls (Ed.), *The development of achievement motivation* (pp. 283-332). Greenwich, CT: JAI Press.

Elliott, E.S., & Dweck, C.S. (1988). Goals: An approach to motivation and achievement. *Journal of Personality and Social Psychology*, **54**, 5-12.

Ellis, A. (1962). *Reason and emotion in psychotherapy.* New York: Lyle Stuart Press.

Epstein, J. (1988). Effective schools or effective students? Dealing with diversity. In R. Haskins & B. MacRae (Eds.), *Policies for America's public schools.* Norwood, NJ: Ablex.

Epstein, J. (1989). Family structures and student motivation: A developmental perspective. In C. Ames and R. Ames (Eds.), *Research on motivation in education: Vol. 3.* New York: Academic Press.

Epstein, L., & Cluss, P.A. (1984). A behavioral medicine perspective on adherence to long-term medical regimens. *Journal of Consulting and Clinical Psychology*, **50**, 950-971.

Epstein, L., & Perkins, L. (1988). Methodology in exercise adherence research. In R.K. Dishman (Ed.), *Exercise adherence: Its impact on public health.* Champaign, IL: Human Kinetics.

Epstein, L.H., Wing, R.R., Thompson, J.K., & Griffin, W. (1980). Attendance and fitness in aerobics exercise: The effects of contract and lottery procedures. *Behavior Modification*, **4**, 465-479.

Erbaugh, S.J., & Barnett, M.L. (1986). *Effects of modeling and goal setting on the jumping performance of primary-grade children.* Paper presented at the North American Society for the Psychology of Sport and Physical Activity, Scottsdale, AZ.

Ewart, C.K., Stewart, K.J., Gillilan, R.E., Kelemen, M.H. (1986). Self-efficacy mediates strength gains during circuit weight training in men with coronary artery disease. *Medicine and Science in Sports and Exercise*, **18**, 531-540.

Ewart, C.K., Stewart, K.J., Gillilan, R.E., Kelemen, M.H., Valenti, S.A., Manley, J.D., & Kaleman, M.D. (1986). Usefulness of self-efficacy in predicting overexertion during programmed exercise in coronary artery disease. *American Journal of Cardiology*, **57**, 557-561.

Ewart, C.K., Taylor, C.B., Reese, L.B., & DeBusk, R.F. (1983). Effects of early post myocardial infarction exercise testing on self-perception and subsequent activity. *American Journal of Cardiology*, **51**, 1076-1080.

Ewing, M.E. (1981). *Achievement motivation and sport behavior of males and females.* Unpublished doctoral dissertation, University of Illinois, Urbana.

Ewing, M., Roberts, G., & Pemberton, C. (1983, May). *A developmental look at children's goals for participating in sport.* Paper presented at the Annual Meeting of the North American Society for the Psychology of Sport and Physical Activity, Michigan State University, East Lansing, MI.

Farrell, D., & Rusbult, C.E. (1981). Exchange variables as predictors of job satisfaction, job commitment, and turnover: The impact of rewards, costs, alternatives, and investments. *Organizational Behavior and Human Performance*, **27**, 78-95.

Faulkner, R.A., & Stewart, G.W. (1978). Exercise programs: Recruitment/ retention of participants. *Recreation Canada*, **36**, 21-27.

Feltz, D.L. (1982). Path analysis of the causal elements in Bandura's theory of self-efficacy and an anxiety-based model of avoidance behavior. *Journal of Personality and Social Psychology*, **42**, 764-781.

Feltz, D.L. (1988a). Gender differences in the causal elements of self-efficacy on a high avoidance motor task. *Journal of Sport Psychology*, **10**, 151-166.

Feltz, D.L. (1988b). Self-confidence and sports performance. In K.B. Pandolf (Ed.), *Exercise and sport sciences reviews* (pp. 423-457). New York: MacMillan.

Feltz, D.L., Bandura, A., & Lirgg, C.D. (1989, August). Perceived collective efficacy in hockey. In D. Kendzierski (Chair), *Self-perceptions in sport and physical activity: Self-efficacy and self-image.* Symposium conducted at the meeting of the American Psychological Association, New Orleans.

Feltz, D.L., & Brown, E.W. (1984). Perceived competence in soccer skills among young soccer players. *Journal of Sport Psychology*, **6**, 385-394.

Feltz, D.L., Landers, D.M., & Raeder, U. (1979). Enhancing self-efficacy in high avoidance motor tasks: A comparison of modeling techniques. *Journal of Sport Psychology*, **1**, 112-122.

Feltz, D.L., & Mugno, D.A. (1983). A replication of the path analysis of the causal elements in Bandura's theory of self-efficacy and the influence of autonomic perception. *Journal of Sport Psychology*, **5**, 263-277.

Feltz, D.L., & Petlichkoff, L. (1983). Perceived competence among interscholastic sport participants and dropouts. *Canadian Journal of Applied Sport Sciences*, **8**, 231-235.

Feltz, D.L., & Riessinger, C.A. (1990). Effects of *in vivo* emotive imagery and performance feedback on self-efficacy and muscular endurance. *Journal of Sport and Exercise Psychology*, **12**, 132-143.

Fishbein, M., & Ajzen, I. (1974). Attitudes towards objects as predictors of single and multiple behavioral criteria. *Psychological Review*, **81**, 59-74.

Fishbein, M., & Ajzen, I. (1975). *Belief, attitude, intention and behavior: An introduction to theory and research.* Reading, MA: Addision-Wesley.

Fitzsimmons, P.A., Landers, D.M., Thomas, J.R., & van der Mars, H. In press. Does self-efficacy predict performance in experienced weightlifters? *Research Quarterly for Exercise and Sport.*

Garland, H. (1983). Influence and ability, assigned goals and normative information on personal goals and performance: A challenge to the goal attainability assumption. *Journal of Applied Psychology*, **68**, 20-30.

Garland, H. (1985). A cognitive mediation theory of task goals and human performance. *Motivation and Emotion*, **9**, 345-367.

Garland, H., Weinberg, R., Bruya, L., & Jackson, A. (1988). Self-efficacy and endurance performance: A longitudinal field test of cognitive mediation theory. *Applied Psychology: An International Review*, **34**, 381-394.

⅄ Gayton, W.F., Matthews, G.R., & Burchstead, G.N. (1986). An investigation of the validity of the physical self-efficacy scale in predicting marathon performance. *Perceptual and Motor Skills*, **63**, 752-754.

Giannini, J., Weinberg, R., & Jackson, A. (1988). The effects of mastery, competitive, and cooperative goals on the performance of simple and complex basketball skills. *Journal of Sport and Exercise Psychology*, **10**, 408-417.

Gill, D.L. (1986). Competitiveness among females and males in physical activity class. *Sex Roles*, **15**, 239-247.

Gill, D.L., & Deeter, T.E. (1988). Development of the Sport Orientation Questionnaire. *Research Quarterly for Exercise and Sport*, **59**, 191-202.

Gill, D.L., Gross, J.B., & Huddleston, S. (1983). Participation motivation in youth sport. *International Journal of Sport Psychology*, **14**, 1-14.

Gillilan, R.E., Chopra, A.K., Kelemen, M.H., Stewart, K.J., Ewart, C.K., Kaleman, M.D., Valenti, S.A., & Manley, J.D. (1984). Prediction of compliance to target heart rate during walk-jog exercise in cardiac patients by a self-efficacy scale. *Medicine and Science in Sports and Exercise*, **16**, 115.

Godding, P.R., & Glasgow, R.E. (1985). Self-efficacy and outcome expectations as predictors of controlled smoking status. *Cognitive Therapy and Research*, **9**, 583-590.

Godin, G., Colantonio, A., Davis, G.M., Shephard, R.J., & Simard, C. (1986). Prediction of leisure-time exercise behavior among a group of lower-limb disabled adults. *Journal of Clinical Psychology*, **42**, 272-279.

Godin, G., Cox, M.H., & Shephard, R.J. (1983). The impact of physical fitness evaluation on behavioral intentions toward regular exercise. *Canadian Journal of Applied Sport Sciences*, **8**, 240-245.

Godin, G., Desharnais, R., Jobin, J., & Cook, J. (1987). The impact of physical fitness and health-age appraisal upon exercise intentions and behavior. *Journal of Behavioral Medicine*, **10**, 241-250.

Godin, G., & Shephard, R.J. (1985). Gender differences in perceived physical self-efficacy among older individuals. *Perceptual and Motor Skills*, **60**, 599-602.

Godin, G., & Shephard, R.J. (1986a). Psychosocial factors influencing intentions to exercise of young students from grades 7 to 9. *Research Quarterly for Exercise and Sport*, **57**, 41-52.

Godin, G., & Shephard, R.J. (1986b). Importance of type of attitude to the study of exercise-behavior. *Psychological Reports*, **58**, 991-1000.

Godin, G., Shephard, R.J., & Colantonio, A. (1986). The cognitive profile of those who intend to exercise but do not. *Public Health Reports*, **101**, 521-526.

Godin, G., Valois, P., Shephard, R.J., & Desharnais, R. (1987). Prediction of leisure-time exercise behavior: A path analysis (LISREL V) Model. *Journal of Behavioral Medicine*, **10**, 145-158.

Good, T.L., & Brophy, J.E. (1986). School effects. In M.L. Wittrock (Ed.), *Handbook of research on teaching* (3rd ed.) (pp. 328-375). New York: Macmillan.

✗ Gould, D. (1982). Sport psychology in the 1980's: Status direction, and challenges in youth sports research. *Journal of Sport Psychology*, **4**, 203-218.

Gould, D. (1984). Developing psychological skills in young athletes. In N.L. Wood (Ed.), *Coaching science update*. Ottawa: Coaching Association of Canada.

Gould, D., Feltz, D., Horn, T., & Weiss, M. (1982). Reasons for sport attrition in competitive youth swimming. *Journal of Sport Behavior*, **5**, 155-165.

Gould, D., & Horn, T. (1984). Participation motivation in young athletes. In J. Silva & R. Weinberg (Eds.), *Psychological foundations of sport* (pp. 359-370). Champaign, IL: Human Kinetics.

Gould, D., & Weiss, M. (1981). Effect of model similarity and model self-talk on self-efficacy in muscular endurance. *Journal of Sport Psychology*, **3**, 17-19.

Gruneau, R. (1983). *Class, sports, and social development*. Amherst, MA: University of Massachusetts Press.

Hall, C.S., & Lindzey, G. (1970). *Theories of Personality* (2nd Ed.). New York: Wiley.

Hall, H. (1990). *A social-cognitive approach to goal setting: The mediating effects of achievement goals and perceived ability*. Unpublished doctoral dissertation, University of Illinois.

Hall, H.K., & Byrne, T. (1988). Goal setting in sport: Clarifying anomalies. *Journal of Sport and Exercise Psychology*, **10**, 189-192.

✓ Hall, H., Weinberg, R., & Jackson, A. (1983). *The effects of goal setting upon the performance of a circuit training task*. Paper presented at the TAHPERD Conference, Corpus Christi, TX.

Hall, H., Weinberg, R., & Jackson, A. (1987). Effects of goal specificity, goal difficulty, and information feedback on endurance performance. *Journal of Sport Psychology*, **9**, 43-54.

Hamilton, J.O. (1974). Motivation and risk taking behavior: A test of Atkinson's Theory. *Journal of Personality and Social Psychology*, **29**, 856-864.

Harris, J.C. (1984). Interpreting youth baseball: Players' understandings of fun and excitement, danger and boredom. *Research Quarterly for Exercise and Sport*, **55**, 379-382.

Harris, D.V., & Harris, B. (1984). *Sports psychology: Mental skills for physical people*. Champaign, IL: Leisure Press.

Harter, S. (1975). Developmental differences in the manifestation of mastery motivation on problem-solving tasks. *Child Development*, **46**, 370-378.

Harter, S. (1978). Effectance motivation reconsidered: Toward a developmental model. *Human Development*, **21**, 34-64.

Harter, S. (1980). A model of intrinsic motivation in children: Individual differences and developmental change. In W.A. Collins (Ed.), *Minnesota symposium in child psychology: Vol. 14.* Hillsdale, NJ: Erlbaum.

Harter, S. (1981a). The development of competence motivation in the mastery of cognitive and physical skills: Is there a place for joy? In G.C. Roberts and D.M. Landers (Eds.), *Psychology of motor behavior and sport-1980* (pp. 3-29). Champaign, IL: Human Kinetics.

Harter, S. (1981b). A new self-report scale of intrinsic versus extrinsic orientation in the classroom: Motivational and informational components. *Developmental Psychology, 17,* 300-312.

Heckhansen, H. (1982). The development of achievement motivation. In W.W. Hartup (Ed.), *Review of child development research, VI,* (pp. 600-668). Chicago: University of Chicago Press.

Heider, F. (1958). *The psychology of interpersonal relations.* New York: Wiley.

Heinzelmann, F., & Bagley, R.W. (1970). Response to physical activity programs and their effects on health behavior. *Public Health Reports, 85,* 905-911.

Heitman, H.M. (1982). Motives of older adults for participating in physical activity programs. In R.C. Cantu and W.J. Gillepsie (Eds.), *Sport medicine, sport science: Bridging the gap* (pp. 199-204). Toronto: The Callamore Press.

Hogan, P.I., & Santomier, J.P. (1984). Effect of mastering swim skills on older adults' self-efficacy. *Research Quarterly for Exercise and Sport, 55,* 294-296.

Hollingsworth, B. (1975). Effects of performance goals and anxiety on learning a gross motor task. *Research Quarterly, 46,* 162-168.

Holloway, J.B., Beuter, A., & Duda, J.L. (1988). Self-efficacy and training for strength in adolescent girls. *Journal of Applied Social Psychology, 18,* 699-719.

Hoyt, M.F., & Janis, I.L. (1975). Increasing adherence to a stressful decision via the balance-sheet procedure: A field experiment on attendance at an exercise class. *Journal of Personality and Social Psychology, 31,* 833-839.

Inglis, F. (1977). *The name of the game.* London: Heineman.

Inkeles, A. (1980). Continuity and change in the American national character. *Tocqueville Review, 2*(2-3), 20-51.

Ivancevich, J.M. (1977). Different goal setting treatments and their effects on performance and job satisfaction. *Academy of Management Journal, 20,* 406-419.

Jackson, S. (1988). *Positive performance states of athletes: Toward a conceptual understanding of peak performance.* Unpublished master's thesis, University of Illinois, Urbana.

Jackson, S.A., & Roberts, G.C. (1989). *Positive performance states of athletes: Toward a conceptual understanding of peak performance.* Unpublished manuscript, University of Illinois, Urbana.

Jagacinski, C.M. & Nicholls, J.G. (1990). Reducing effort to protect perceived ability: "They'd do it but I wouldn't." *Journal of Educational Psychology*, **82**, 15-21.

James, W. (1907). *Pragmatism*. New York: Longmans, Green & Co.

Kahn, R.L. (1979). Aging and social support. In M.W. Riley (Ed.), *Aging from birth to death: Interdisciplinary perspectives* (pp. 77-91). Boulder, CO: Westview Press.

Kaplan, R.M., Atkins, C.J., & Reinsch, S. (1984). Specific efficacy expectations mediate exercise compliance in patients with COPD. *Health Psychology*, **3**, 223-242.

Kau, M.L., & Fischer, J. (1974). Self-modification of exercise behavior. *Journal of Behavior Therapy and Experimental Psychiatry*, **5**, 213-214.

Kavanagh, D., & Hausfeld, S. (1986). Physical performance and self-efficacy under happy and sad moods. *Journal of Sport Psychology*, **8**, 112-123.

Kazdin, A.E. (1981). *Behavior modification in applied settings* (2nd ed.). Homewood, IL: Dorsey Press.

Keefe, F.J., & Blumenthal, J.A. (1980). The life fitness program: A behavioral approach to making exercise a habit. *Journal of Behavior Therapy and Experimental Psychiatry*, **11**, 31-34.

Kelley, H.H. (1973). The process of causal attribution. *American Psychologist*, **28**, 107-128.

Kelley, H.H. (1983). Love and commitment. In H.H. Kelley, E. Berscheid, A. Christensen, J.H. Harvey, T.L. Huston, G. Levinger, E. McClintock, L.A. Peplau, & D.P. Peterson (Eds.), *Close relationships* (pp. 265-314). New York: W.H. Freeman.

Kelley, H.H., & Thibaut, J.W. (1978). *Interpersonal relations: A theory of interdependence*. New York: Wiley.

Kenyon, G.S. (1968). Six scales for assessing attitudes toward physical activity. *Research Quarterly*, **39**, 566-574.

Kimiecik, J.C. (1990). *Motivational determinants of exercise involvement: A social-psychological process/stage approach*. Unpublished doctoral dissertation, University of Illinois, Urbana.

Kimiecik, J.C., Allison, M., & Duda, J. (1986). Performance satisfaction, perceived competence, and game outcome: The competitive experience of Boys' Club Youth. *International Journal of Sport Psychology*, **3**, 255-268.

Kimiecik, J.C., Jackson, S.A., & Giannini, J.M. (in press). Striving for exercise goals: An examination of the motivational orientations and exercise behavior of unsupervised joggers, swimmers and cyclists. In L. Vander Velden & J. Humphrey (Eds.), *Psychology and sociology of sport: Current selected research: Vol. II*. New York: AMS Press.

King, A.C., & Frederickson, L.W. (1984). Low-cost strategies for increasing exercise behavior: Relapse preparation training and social support. *Behavior Modification*, **8**, 3-21.

King, A.C., Taylor, C.B., Haskell, W.L., & DeBusk, R.F. (1988). Strategies for increasing early adherence to and long-term maintenance of home-based exercise training in healthy middle-aged men and women. *American Journal of Cardiology*, **61**, 628-632.

Kirschenbaum, D.S. (1985). Proximity and specificity of planning: A position paper. *Cognitive Therapy and Research*, **9**, 489-506.

Kleiber, D., & Roberts, G.C. (1981). The effects of sport experience in the development on social character: An exploratory investigation. *Journal of Sport Psychology*, **3**, 114-122.

Klint, K.A., & Weiss, M.R. (1986). Dropping in and dropping out: Participation motives of current and former youth gymnasts. *Canadian Journal of Applied Sport Sciences*, **11**, 106-114.

Klint, K.A., & Weiss, M.R. (1987). Perceived competence and motives for participating in youth sports: A test of Harter's competence motivation theory. *Journal of Sport Psychology*, **9**, 55-65.

Klug, G.A., McAuley, E., & Clark, S. (1990). Factors influencing the development and maintenance of aerobic fitness: Lessons applicable to the fibrositis syndrome. *Journal of Rheumatology*, **16**, 41-50.

Knapp, D.N. (1988). Behavioral management techniques and exercise promotion. In R.K. Dishman (Ed.), *Exercise adherence: Its impact on public health*. Champaign, IL: Human Kinetics.

Koestner, R., Zuckerman, M., & Koestner, J. (1987). Praise, involvement, and intrinsic motivation. *Journal of Personality and Social Psychology*, **53**, 383-390.

Komaki, J., Barwick, K.D., & Scott, L.R. (1978). A behavioral approach to occupational safety: Pinpointing and reinforcing safe performance in a food manufacturing plant. *Journal of Applied Psychology*, **64**, 434-445.

Krolner, B., Toft, B., Nielsen, S.P., & Tandewold, E. (1983). Physical exercise as a prophylaxis against involuntary bone loss: Controlled trial. *Clinical Science*, **64**, 541-546.

Laffrey, S.C., & Isenberg, M. (1983). The relationship of internal locus of control, value placed on health, perceived importance of exercise, and participation in physical activity during leisure. *International Journal of Nursing Studies*, **20**, 187-196.

Latham, G.P., & Baldes, J.J. (1975). The "practical significance" of Locke's theory of goal setting. *Journal of Applied Psychology*, **60**, 122-124.

Latham, G.P., & Lee, T.W. (1986). Goal setting. In E.A. Locke (Ed.), *Generalizing from laboratory to field studies*. Lexington, MA: Lexington Books.

Latham, G.P., & Locke, E.A. (1975). Increasing productivity with decreasing time limits: A field replication of Parkinson's law. *Journal of Applied Psychology*, **60**, 524-526.

Latham, G.P., & Yukl, G.A. (1975). Assigned versus participative goal setting with educated with uneducated wood workers. *Journal of Applied Psychology*, **60**, 229-302.

Latham, G.P., & Yukl, G.A. (1976). The effects of assigned and participative goal setting on performance and job satisfaction. *Journal of Applied Psychology*, **61**, 166-171.

Leahy, R.L., & Hunt, T.M. (1983). A cognitive developmental approach to the development of conceptions of intelligence. In R.L. Leahy (Ed.), *The child's construction of social inequality* (pp. 135-160). New York: Academic Press.

⚮ Lee, C. (1982). Self-efficacy as a predictor of performance in competitive gymnastics. *Journal of Sport Psychology*, **7**, 283-295.

Libb, J.W., & Clements, C.B. (1969). Token reinforcement in an exercise program for hospitalized geriatric patients. *Perceptual and Motor Skills*, **28**, 957-958.

Lindsay-Reid, E., & Osborn, R.W. (1980). Readiness for exercise adoption. *Social Science Medicine*, **14**, 139-146.

Lirgg, C.D., & Feltz, D.L. (1991). Teacher versus peer models revisited: Effects on motor performance. *Research Quarterly for Exercise Sport*, **62**, 217-224.

Litt, M.D. (1988). Self-efficacy and perceived control: Cognitive mediators of pain tolerance. *Journal of Personality and Social Psychology*, **54**, 149-160.

Locke, E.A. (1966). The relationship of intentions to level of performance. *Journal of Applied Psychology*, **50**, 60-66.

Locke, E.A. (1968). Toward a theory of task motivation and incentives. *Organizational Behavior and Human Performance*, **3**, 157-189.

Locke, E.A. (1978). The ubiquity of the technique of goal setting in theories of and approaches to employee motivation. *Academy of Management Review*, **3**, 594-601.

Locke, E.A. (1980). Latham versus Komaki: A tale of two paradigms. *Journal of Applied Psychology*, **65**, 16-23.

Locke, E.A. (1982). Relation of goal level to performance with a short work period and multiple goal levels. *Journal of Applied Psychology*, **67**, 512-514.

Locke, E.A., Cartledge, N., & Knerr, C.S. (1970). Studies of the relationship between satisfaction, goal setting, and performance. *Organizational Behavior and Human Performance*, **5**, 135-138.

Locke. E.A., Frederick, E., Lee, C., & Bobko, P. (1984). Effects of self-efficacy, goals, and task strategies on task performance. *Journal of Applied Psychology*, **69**, 241-251.

Locke, E.A., & Latham, G.P. (1985). The application of goal setting to sports. *Journal of Sport Psychology*, **7**, 205-222.

Locke, E.A., Shaw, K.N., Saari, L.M., & Latham, G.P. (1981). Goal setting and task performance: 1969-1980. *Psychological Bulletin*, **90**, 125-152.

London, M., & Oldham, G.R. (1976). Effects of varying goal types and incentive systems on performance and boredom. *Academy of Management Journal*, **19**, 537-546.

Long, B.C. (1984). Aerobic conditioning and stress inoculation: A comparison of stress-management interventions. *Cognitive Therapy and Research*, **8**, 517-541.

Long, B.C. (1985). Stress-management interventions: A fifteen month follow-up of aerobic conditioning and stress inoculation training. *Cognitive Therapy and Research*, **9**, 471-478.

Long, B.C., & Haney, C.J. (1986). Enhancing physical activity in sedentary women: Information, locus of control, and attitudes. *Journal of Sport Psychology*, **8**, 8-24.

Long, B.C., & Haney, C.J. (1988). Coping strategies for working women: Aerobic exercise and relaxation interventions. *Behavior Therapy*, **19**, 75-83.

Maehr, M.L. (1974). Culture and achievement motivation. *American Psychologist*, **29**, 887-896.

Maehr, M.L. (1983). On doing well in science. Why Johnny no longer excels; why Sarah never did. In S.G. Paris, G.M. Olson, and H.W. Stevenson (Eds.), *Learning and motivation in the classroom*. Hillsdale, NJ: Lawrence Erlbaum and Associates.

Maehr, M.L. (1984). Meaning and motivation: Toward a theory of personal investment. In R. Ames & C. Ames (Eds.), *Research on motivation in education: Vol. 1. Student motivation* (p. 144). New York: Academic Press.

Maehr, M.L. (1989). Thoughts about motivation. In R. Ames & C. Ames (Eds.) *Research on motivation in education: Vol. 3. Goals and cognitions* (pp. 299-315). New York: Academic Press.

Maehr, M.L., & Ames, C. (1989). [Survey of junior high school science classes]. Unpublished raw data. University of Illinois, Institute for Research on Human Development.

Maehr, M.L., & Braskamp, L.A. (1986). *The motivation factor. A theory of personal investment*. Lexington, MA: Lexington Books.

Maehr, M.L., & Nicholls, J.G. (1980). Culture and achievement motivation: A second look. In N. Warren (Ed.), *Studies in cross-cultural psychology* (pp. 221-267). New York: Academic Press.

Mandler, G., & Sarason, S.B. (1952). A study of anxiety and learning. *Journal of Abnormal and Social Psychology*, **47**, 166-173.

Marlatt, A., & Gordon, J.R. (1985). *Relapse prevention: Maintenance strategies in the treatment of addictive behaviors*. New York: Guildford Press.

Martens, R. (1975). *Social psychology in physical activity*. New York: Harper & Row.

Martens, R. (1987). Science, knowledge, and sport psychology. *The Sport Psychologist*, **1**, 29-55.

Martin, J.E., & Dubbert, P.M. (1982a). Exercise and Health: The adherence problem. *Behavioral Medicine Update*, **4**, 16-24.

Martin, J.E., & Dubbert, P.M. (1982b). Exercise applications and promotion in behavioral medicine: Current status and future directions. *Journal of Consulting and Clinical Psychology*, **50**, 1004-1017.

Martin, J.E., & Dubbert, P.M. (1984). Behavioral management strategies for improving health and fitness. *Journal of Cardiac Rehabilitation*, **4**, 200-208.

Martin, J.E., & Dubbert, P.M. (1985). Adherence to exercise. *Exercise and Sport Sciences Review*, **13**, 137-167.

Martin, J.E., Dubbert, P.M., Katell, A.D., Thompson, J.K., Raczynski, J.R., Lake M., Smith, P.O., Webster, J.S., Sikora, T., & Cohen, R.E. (1984). Behavioral control of exercise in sedentary adults: Studies 1 through 6. *Journal of Consulting and Clinical Psychology*, **52**, 795-811.

Massie, J.F., & Shephard, R.J. (1971). Physiological and psychological effects of training—a comparison of individual and gymnasium programs, with a characterization of the exercise "dropout." *Medicine and Science in Sports*, **3**, 110-117.

Masters, J.C., Furman, W., & Barden, R.C. (1977). Effects of achievement standards, tangible rewards, and self-dispensed achievement evaluations on children's task mastery. *Child Development*, **48**, 217-224.

McArthur, L.Z., & Baron, R.M. (1983). Toward an ecological theory of social perception. *Psychological Review*, **90**, 215-238.

McAuley, E. (1985a). Modeling and self-efficacy: A Test of Bandura's model. *Journal of Sport Psychology*, **7**, 283-295.

McAuley, E. (1985b). Success and causality in sport: The influence of perception. *Journal of Sport Psychology*, **7**, 13-22.

McAuley, E. (1990a). *Efficacy perceptions and continued participation in exercise behavior*. Unpublished manuscript, University of Illinois, Urbana.

McAuley, E. (1990b). Self-referent thought in sport and physical activity. In T. Horne (Ed.), *Advances in sport psychology*. Champaign, IL: Human Kinetics.

McAuley, E. (In press). The role of efficacy cognitions in the prediction of exercise behavior in sedentary middle-aged adults. *Journal of Behavioral Science*.

McAuley, E., Courneya, K.S., & Lettunich, J. (1991). Effects of acute and long term exercise on self-efficacy responses on sedentary, middle-aged males and females. *The Gerontologist*, **31**(4), 534-542.

McAuley, E., & Duncan, T.E. (1990). The causal attribution process in sport and physical activity. In S. Graham & V. Folkes (Eds.), *Advances in Applied Social Psychology V: Applications of Attribution Theory* (pp. 37-52). Hillsdale, NJ: Erlbaum.

McAuley, E., Duncan, T.E., & McElroy, M. (1989). Self-efficacy cognitions and causal attributions for children's motor performance: An exploratory investigation. *The Journal of Genetic Psychology*. **150**, 65-73.

McAuley, E., Duncan, E.T., & Tammen, V.V. (1989). Psychometric properties of the Intrinsic Motivation Inventory in a competitive sport setting: A confirmatory factor analysis. *Research Quarterly for Exercise and Sport*, **60**, 48-58.

McAuley, E., Duncan, T.E., & Wraith, S.C. (1989, June). Intrinsic motivation and exercise behavior: A confirmatory factor analysis. Paper presented at the meeting of the North American Society for the Psychology of Sport and Physical Activity, Knoxville, TN.

McAuley, E., Duncan, T.E., Wraith, S.C., & Lettunich, M. (1991). Self-efficacy, perceptions of success, and intrinsic motivation. *Journal of Applied Social Psychology*, **21**, 139-155.

McAuley, E., & Gill, D. (1983). Reliability and validity of the physical self-efficacy scale in a competitive sport setting. *Journal of Sport Psychology*, **5**, 410-418.

McAuley, E., & Jacobson, L.B. (1991). Self-efficacy and exercise participation in sedentary adult female exercise patterns. *American Journal of Health Promotion*, **5**, 185-191.

McAuley, E., Poag, K., Gleason, A., & Wraith, S.C. (1990). Attrition from exercise programs: Attributional and affective perspectives. *Journal of Social Behavior and Personality*, **5**, 591-602.

McAuley, E., & Rowney, T. (1990). Exercise behavior and intentions: The mediating role of self-efficacy cognitions. In L. VanderVelden and J.H. Humphrey (Eds.), *Psychology and sociology of sport: Current selected research* (pp. 3-15). New York: AMS Press.

McCann, I.L., & Holmes, D.S. (1984). Influence of aerobic exercise on depression. *Journal of Personality and Social Psychology*, **46**, 1142-1147.

McClelland, D.C. (1958). Risk taking in children with high and low need for achievement. In J.W. Atkinson (Ed.), *Motives in fantasy, action, and society*. Princeton, NJ: Van Nostrand.

McClelland, D.C. (1961). *The achieving society*. New York: Free Press.

McClelland, D.C., Atkinson, J.W., Clark, R.A., & Lowell, E.W. (1953). *The achievement motive*. New York: Appleton-Century-Crofts.

McClements, J.D., & Botterill, C.B. (1979). Goal setting in shaping of future performance of athletes. In P. Kilavora & J. Daniel (Eds.), *Coach, athlete, and the sport psychologist*. Toronto, ON: University of Toronto.

McCombs, B.L. (1984). Processes and skills underlying continuing motivation to learn: Toward a definition of motivational skills training interventions. *Educational Psychologist*, **19**, 199-218.

McCombs, B.L. (1988). Motivational skills training: Combining metacognitive, cognitive and affective learning strategies. In C.E. Weinstein, E.T. Goetz, & P.A. Alexander (Eds.), *Learning and study strategies: Issues in assessment, instruction and evaluation* (pp. 141-169). New York: Academic Press.

McCready, M.L., & Long, B.C. (1985). Locus of control, attitudes toward physical activity, and exercise adherence. *Journal of Sport Psychology*, **7**, 346-359.

McCullagh, P. (1987). Model similarity effects on motor performance. *Journal of Sport Psychology*, **9**, 249-260.

McKeachie, W.J., Pintrich, P.R., & Lin. Y. (1985). Teaching learning strategies. *Educational Psychologist*, **20**, 153-160.

McPherson, B.P. (1983). *Aging as a social process: An introduction to individual and population aging*. Toronto: Butterworks.

McVicker-Hunt, J. (1965). Intrinsic motivation and its role in psychological development. In D. Levine (Ed.), *Nebraska symposium on motivation: Vol. 13*. Lincoln: University of Nebraska Press.

Meichenbaum, D. (1977). *Cognitive behavior modification: An integrated approach*. New York: Plenum Press.

Meichenbaum, D., & Turk, D.C. (1987). *Facilitating treatment adherence. A practitioner's handbook*. New York: Plenum Press.

Mento, A.J., Cartledge, N.D., & Locke, E.A. (1980). Maryland vs Michigan vs Minnesota: Another look at the relationship of expectancy and goal difficulty to task performance. *Organizational Behavior and Human Performance*, **25**, 419-440.

Mento, A.J., Steel, R.P., & Karren, R.J. (1987). A meta-analytic study of the effects of goal-setting on task performance: 1966-1984. *Organizational Behavior and Human Decision Processes*, **39**, 52-83.

Mihevic, P.M. (1981). Sensory cues for perceived exertion: A review. *Medicine and Science in Sports and Exercise*, **13**, 150-163.

Miller, A.T. (1985). A developmental study of the cognitive basis of performance impairment after failure. *Journal of Personality and Social Psychology*, **49**, 529-538.

Miller, J.T., & McAuley, E. (1987). Effects of goal setting training program on basketball free-throw, self-efficacy, and performance. *The Sport Psychologist*, **1**, 103-113.

Miner, J.B. (1984). The validity and usefulness of theories in an emerging organizational science. *Academy of Management Review*, **9**, 296-306.

Morgan, P.P., Shephard, R.J., Finucane, R., Schimmelfing, L., & Jazmaji, V. (1984). Health beliefs and exercise habits in an employee fitness programme. *Canadian Journal of Applied Sport Sciences*, **9**, 87-93.

Morgan, W.P. (1977). Involvement in vigorous physical activity with special reference to adherence. In L.I. Gedvillas & M.E. Kneer (Eds.), *National College Physical Education Association Proceedings*, Chicago.

Morgan, W.P. (1987). Reduction of state anxiety following acute physical activity. In W.P. Morgan & S.E. Goldston (Eds.), *Exercise and mental health* (pp. 105-107). Washington, DC: Hemisphere.

Motivation Factor. (1983, May 8). *New York Times*, Business Section, p. 1.

Murray, H.A. (1938). *Explorations in personality*. New York: Oxford University Press.

Naipaul, V.S. (1987, April 23). On being a writer. *New York Review of Books*, p. 7.

Newsham, S. (1989). *The effects of a task-oriented physical education program on the self-perception of third, fourth, and fifth grade students*. Unpublished doctoral dissertation, University of Southern California, Los Angeles.

Nicholls, J.G. (1976). Effort is virtuous, but it's better to have ability:

Evaluative responses to perceptions of effort and ability. *Journal of Research in Personality*, **10**, 306-315.

Nicholls, J.G. (1978). The development of the concepts of effort and ability, perception of attainment, and the understanding that difficult tasks require more ability. *Child Development*, **49**, 800-814.

Nicholls, J.G. (1981). *Striving to demonstrate and develop ability: A theory of achievement motivation.* Unpublished manuscript, Purdue University, West Lafayette, IN.

Nicholls, J.G. (1984a). Achievement motivation: Conceptions of ability, subjective experience, task choice, and performance. *Psychological Review*, **91**, 328-346.

Nicholls, J.G. (1984b). Conceptions of ability and achievement motivation. In R. Ames & C. Ames (Eds.), *Research on motivation in education: Vol. 1. Student motivation.* New York: Academic Press.

Nicholls, J.G. (1989). *The competitive ethos and democratic education.* Cambridge, MA: Harvard University Press.

Nicholls, J.G. (1990). What is ability and why are we mindful of it? A developmental perspective. In R. L. Sternberg & J. Kolligian, Jr. (Eds.), *Competence considered* (pp. 11-40). New Haven, CT: Yale University Press.

Nicholls, J.G., Cheung, P., Lauer, J., & Patashnick, M. (1989). Individual differences in academic motivation: Perceived ability, goals, beliefs, and values. *Learning and Individual Differences*, **1**, 63-84.

Nicholls, J.G., Cobb, P., Wood, T., Yackel, E., & Patashnick, M. (1990). Assessing students' theories of success in mathematics: Individual and classroom differences. *Journal for Research in Mathematics Education*, **21**, 109-122.

Nicholls, J.G., Cobb, P., Yackel, E., Wood, T., & Wheatley, G. (1990). Students theories about mathematics and their mathematical knowledge: Multiple dimensions of assessment. In G. Kulm (Ed.), *Assessing higher order thinking in mathematics* (pp. 137-154). Washington, DC: American Association for the Advancement of Science.

Nicholls, J.G., & Miller, A.T. (1984). Development and its discontents: The differentiation of the concept of ability. In J. Nicholls (Ed.), *Advances in motivation and achievement: Vol. 3. The development of achievement motivation* (pp. 185-218). Greenwich, CT: JAI Press.

Nicholls, J.G., Patashnick, M., & Nolen, S.B. (1985). Adolescents' theories of education. *Journal of Educational Psychology*, **77**, 683-692.

Nicholls, J.G., Patashnick, M., & Mettetal, G. (1986). Conceptions of ability and intelligence. *Child Development*, **57**, 636-645.

Nicholls, J.G., & Thorkildsen, T.A. (1988). Children's distinctions among matters of intellectual convention, logic, fact and personal preference. *Child Development*, **59**, 939-949.

Nicholls, J.G. & Thorkildsen, T.A. (1989). Intellectual conventions versus matters of substance: Elementary school students as curriculum theorists. *American Educational Research Journal*, **26**, 533-544.

Nisbett, R.E., & Wilson, T.D. (1977). Telling more than we can know: Verbal reports on mental processes. *Psychological Review*, **84**, 231-258.

Noland, M.P. (1981). *The efficacy of a new model to explain leisure exercise behavior.* Unpublished doctoral dissertation, University of Maryland, College Park.

Nucci, L. (1982). Conceptual development in the moral and conventional domains: Implications for values education. *Review of Educational Research*, **52**, 93-122.

O'Block, F.R., & Evans, F.H. (1984). Goal setting as a motivational technique. In J. Silva & R. Weinberg (Eds.), *Psychological foundations of sport* (pp. 188-196). Champaign, IL: Human Kinetics.

O'Connell, J.K., & Price, J.H. (1982). Health locus of control of physical fitness program participatns. *Perceptual and Motor Skills*, **29**, 551-553.

Odiorne, G.S. (1978). A backward glance. *Business Horizons*, **21**(5), 14-24.

Oldridge, N.B. (1982). Compliance and exercise in primary and secondary prevention of coronary heart disease: A review. *Preventive Medicine*, **11**, 56-70.

Oldridge, N.B., & Jones, N.L. (1983). Improving patient compliance in cardiac exercise rehabilitation: Effects of written agreement and self-monitoring. *Journal of Cardiac Rehabilitation*, **3**, 257-262.

Oldridge, N.B., Wicks, J.R., Hanley, C., Sutton, J.R., & Jones, N.L. (1978). Noncompliance in an exercise rehabilitation program for men who have suffered a myocardial infarction. *Canadian Medical Association Journal*, **18**, 361-364.

O'Leary, A. (1985). Self-efficacy and health. *Behavior and Research Therapy*, **23**, 437-451.

Olson, J.M., & Zanna, M.P. (1982). *Predicting adherence to a program of physical fitness: An empirical study.* Report to the Ontario Ministry of Tourism and Recreation, Government of Ontario, Toronto, Canada.

Orgell, S., & Duda, J.L. (1990, May). *The effects of gender and a task- versus ego-involving condition on intrinsic motivation and perceived competence in sport.* Paper presented at the annual meeting of the North American Society for the Psychology of Sport and Physical Activity, University of Houston.

Paffenbarger, R.S. (1986). Physical activity all-cause mortality, and longevity of college alumni. *New England Journal of Medicine*, **314**, 605-613.

Paffenbarger. R.S., & Hyde, R.T. (1988). Exercise adherence, coronary heart disease and longevity. In R.K. Dishman (Ed.), *Exercise adherence: Its impact on public health* (pp. 41-73). Champaign, IL: Human Kinetics.

Paffenbarger, R.S., Wing, A.L., Hyde, R.T., & Jung, D.L. (1983). Physical activity and incidence of hypertension in college alumni. *American Journal of Epidemiology*, **117**, 245-256.

Pandolf, K.B. (1983). Advances in the study and application of perceived exertion. In R.L. Terjung (Ed.), *Exercise and sport science reviews: Vol. 11* (pp. 118-158). Philadelphia, PA: Franklin Institute Press.

Paris, B. (1989, February 13). The godless girl. *New Yorker*: pp. 54-73).

Pemberton, C., Petlichkoff, L., & Ewing, M. (1986, June). *Psychometric properties of the achievement orientation questionnaire.* Paper presented at the Annual Meeting of the North American Society for the Psychology of Sport and Physical Activity, Scottsdale, AZ.

Pender, N.J., & Pender, A.R. (1986). Attitudes, subjective norms, and intentions to engage in health behaviors. *Nursing Research*, **35**, 15-18.

Pinder, C. (1984). *Work motivation*. Glenview, IL: Scott, Foresman.

Plant, R., & Ryan, R.M. (1985). Self consciousness, self-awareness, ego involvement, and intrinsic motivation: An investigation of internally controlling styles. *Journal of Personality*, **53**, 435-449.

Poag, K., & McAuley, E. (1991, June). *Goal-setting, self-efficacy, and exercise behavior.* Paper presented at the annual meeting of the North American Society for the Psychology of Sport and Physical Activity, Asilomar, CA.

Powell, B. (1990). *Children's perceptions of classroom goal structure and related motivational processes.* Unpublished master's thesis, University of Illinois, Urbana.

Powell, K.E., Spain, K.G., Christensen, G.M., & Mollenkamp, M.P. (1986). The status of the 1990 objectives for physical fitness and exercise. *Public Health Reports*, **101**, 15-21.

Rejeski, W.J. (1985). Perceived exertion: An active or passive process? *Journal of Sport Psychology*, **7**, 371-378.

Rejeski, W.J., Best, D.L., Griffith, P., & Kenney, E. (1987). Sex-role orientation and the responses of men to exercise stress. *Research Quarterly for Exercise and Sport*, **58**, 260-264.

Rejeski, W.J., & Brawley, L.R. (1983). Attribution theory in sport: Current status and new perspectives. *Journal of Sport Psychology*, **5**, 77-99.

Rejeski, W.J., & Kenney, E.A. (1988). *Fitness motivation: Preventing participant dropout*. Champaign, IL: Human Kinetics.

Riddle, P.K. (1980). Attitudes, beliefs, behavioral intentions, and behaviors of women and men toward regular jogging. *Research Quarterly for Exercise and Sport*, **51**, 663-674.

Roberts, G.C. (1974). Effects of achievement motivation and social environment on risk-taking. *Research Quarterly*, **45**, 42-55.

Roberts, G.C. (1975). Win-loss causal attributions of Little League players. *Mouvement*, **7**, 315-322.

Roberts, G.C. (1982). Achievement and motivation in sport. In R. Terjung (Ed.), *Exercise and Sport Science Reviews: Vol. 10.* Philadelphia: Franklin Institute Press.

Roberts, G.C. (1984). Achievement motivation in children's sport. In J.G. Nicholls (Ed.), *Advances in motivation and achievement: Vol. 3. The development of achievement and motivation* (pp. 251-281). Greenwich, CT: JAI Press.

Roberts, G.C. (1989). When motivation matters: The need to expand the conceptual model. In J.S. Skinner, C.B. Corbin, D.M. Landers, P.E. Martin, & C.L. Wells (Eds.), *Future directions in exercise and sport sciences* (pp. 71-83). Champaign, IL: Human Kinetics.

Roberts, G.C., & Balague, G. (1989, August). *The development of a social cognitive scale of motivation.* Paper presented at the Seventh World Congress of Sport Psychology, Singapore.

Roberts, G.C., & Duda, J. (1984). Motivation in sport: The mediating role of perceived ability. *Journal of Sport Psychology, 6*, 312-324.

Roberts, G.C., Hall, H., Jackson, S., Kimiecik, J.C., & Tonymon, P. (1990, September). *Goal orientations and perceptions of the sport experience.* Paper presented at the meeting of the Association for the Advancement of Applied Sport Psychology, San Antonio, TX.

Roberts, G.C., Kleiber, D.A., & Duda, J.L. (1981). An analysis of motivation in children's sport: The role of perceived competence in participation. *Journal of Sport Psychology, 3*, 206-216.

Rorty, R. (1983). Method and morality. In N. Haan, R. Bellah, P. Rabinow, & W. Sullivan (Eds.), *Social science as moral enquiry* (pp. 155-176). New York: Columbia University Press.

Rosenthal, M., Haskell, W.L., Solomon, R., Widstrom, A., & Reaven, G.M. (1983). Demonstration of a relationship between level of physical training and insulin stimulated glucose utilization in normal humans. *Diabetes, 32*, 408-411.

Rosswork, S.G. (1977). Goal setting: The effects on an academic task with varying magnitudes of incentive. *Journal of Educational Psychology, 69*, 710-715.

Rothkopf, E.Z. & Kaplan, R. (1972). Exploration of the effect of density and specificity of instructional objectives on learning from text. *Journal of Educational Psychology, 63*, 295-302.

Rotter, J.B. (1954). *Social learning and clinical psychology.* Englewood Cliffs, NJ: Prentice-Hall.

Rotter, J.B., Chance, J.E., & Phares, E.J. (1972). *Applications of a social learning theory of personality.* New York: Holt, Rhinehart, and Winston.

Rudisill, M.E., Meaney, K.S., McDermott, B.A., & Jibaja-Rusth, M. (1990, May). *Influence of various goal-setting orientations on children's persistence and perceived competence in three motor skills.* Paper presented at the annual meeting of the North American Society for the Psychology of Sport and Physical Activity, University of Houston.

Rudman, W. (1986). Life course, socioeconomic transitions, and sport involvement: A theory of restricted opportunity. In B.D. McPherson (Ed.), *Sport and aging* (pp. 25-35). Champaign, IL: Human Kinetics.

Rusbult, C.E. (1980a). Commitment and satisfaction to romantic associations: A test of the investment model. *Journal of Experimental Social Psychology, 16*, 172-186.

Rusbult, C.E. (1980b). Satisfaction and commitment in friendships. *Representative Research in Social Psychology, 11*, 96-105.

Rusbult, C.E. (1983). A longitudinal test of the investment model: The development (and deterioration) of satisfaction and commitment in heterosexual involvements. *Journal of Personality and Social Psychology*, **45**, 101-117.

Rusbult, C.E., & Farrell, D. (1983). A longitudinal test of the investment model: The impact on job satisfaction, job commitment, and turnover of variations in rewards, costs, alternatives, and investments. *Journal of Applied Psychology*, **68**, 429-438.

Ryan, R.M. (1982). Control and information in the intrapersonal sphere: An extension of cognitive evaluation theory. *Journal of Personality and Social Psychology*, **43**, 450-461.

Ryan, R.M., & Deci, E.L. (1989). Bridging the research traditions of task/ego involvement and intrinsic/extrinsic motivation: Comment of Butler (1987). *Journal of Educational Psychology*, **81**, 265-268.

Ryan, R.M., & Grolnick, W.S. (1986). Origins and pawns in the classroom: Self-report and projective assessments of individual differences in children's perceptions. *Journal of Personality and Social Psychology*, **50**, 550-558.

Ryan, R.M., Mims, V., & Koestner, R. (1983). The relationship of reward contingency and interpersonal context to intrinsic motivation: A review and test using cognitive evaluation theory. *Journal of Personality and Social Psychology*, **45**, 736-750.

Ryan, T.A. (1970). *Intentional behavior: An approach to human motivation*. New York: Ronald Press.

Rychlak, J.F. (1968). *A philosophy of science of personality theory*. Boston: Houghton Mifflin.

Ryckman, R.M., Robbins, M.A., Thronton, B., & Cantrell, P. (1982). Development and validation of a physical self-efficacy scale. *Journal of Personality and Social Psychology*, **42**, 891-900.

Sallis, J.F., Haskell, W.L., Fortmann, S.P., Vranizan, M.S., Taylor, C.B., & Solomon, D.S. (1986). Predictors of adoption and maintenance of physical activity in a community sample. *Preventive Medicine*, **15**, 331-341.

Sallis, J.F., Priski, R.B., Grossman, R.M., Patterson, T.L., & Nader, P.R. (1988). The development of self-efficacy scales for health related diet and exercise behaviors. *Health Education Research*, **3**, 283-292.

Sapp, M., & Haubenstricker, J. (1978). *Motivation for joining and reasons for not continuing in youth sports programs in Michigan*. Paper presented at American Alliance for Health, Physical Education, Recreation & Dance Conference, Kansas City.

Sarason, S.B., Davidson, K., Lighthall, F., Waite, F., & Ruebrush, B. (1960). *Anxiety in elementary school children*. New York: Wiley.

Sarason, I.G., & Sarason, B.R. (Eds.) (1985). *Social support: Theory, research and applications*. The Hague, Netherlands: Matinus Nijhof.

Scanlan, T.K. (1978a). Antecedents of competitiveness. In R. Magill, M. Ash, & F. Smoll (Eds.), *Children in sport: A contemporary anthology* (pp. 48-69). Champaign, IL: Human Kinetics.

Scanlan, T.K. (1978b). Social evaluation: A key developmental element in the competitive process. In R. Magill, M. Ash, & F. Smoll (Eds.), *Children in sport: A contemporary anthology* (pp. 138-152). Champaign, IL: Human Kinetics.

Scanlan, T.K., Carpenter, P.J., Simons, J.P., & Keeler, B. (1990). *Stage of involvement and commitment to a youth sport program.* Paper presented at the annual conference of the Association for the Advancement of Applied Sport Psychology, San Antonio, TX.

Scanlan, T.K., Carpenter, P.J., Simons, J.P., Keeler, B., & Schmidt, G.W. (1990). *A model of sport commitment.* Paper presented at the annual conference of the North American Society for Psychology of Sport and Physical Activity, Houston, TX.

Scanlan, T.K., & Lewthwaite, R. (1986). Social psychological aspects of the competitive sport experience for male youth sport participants: IV. Predictors of enjoyment. *Journal of Sport Psychology*, **8**, 25-35.

Scanlan, T.K., Simons, J.P., Schmidt, G.W., Carpenter, P.J., & Keeler, B. (1991). *The Sport Commitment Model: An introduction and empirical test.* Manuscript submitted for publication.

Scanlan, T.K., Stein, G.L., & Ravizza, K. (1989). An in-depth study of former elite figure skaters: 2. Sources of enjoyment. *Journal of Sport and Exercise Psychology*, **11**, 65-83.

Schoenfeld, A.H. (1988). When good teaching leads to bad results: The disasters of "well-taught" mathematics courses. *Educational Psychologist*, **23**, 145-166.

Schunk, D.H., & Gunn, T.P. (1986). Self-efficacy and skill development: Influence of task strategies and attributions. *Journal of Educational Research*, **79**, 238-244.

Schunk, D.H., & Rice, J.M. (1986). Extended attributional feedback: Sequence effects during remedial reading instruction. *Journal of Early Adolescence*, **6**, 55-66.

Seals, D.R., Hagberg, J.M., Hurley, Z.B.F., Ehsani, A.A., & Holloszy, J.O. (1984). Effects of endurance training on glucose tolerance and plasma lipid levels in older men and women. *Journal of the American Medical Association*, **252**, 645-649.

Shephard, R.J. (1985). Motivation: The key to fitness compliance. *The Physician and Sportsmedicine*, **13**, 88-101.

Shephard, R.J., Morgan, P., & Finucane, R.E. (1980). Factors influencing participation in an employee fitness program. *JOM*, **22**, 389-398.

Sherer, M., Maddux, J.E., Mercandante, B., Prentice-Dunn, S., Jacobs, B., & Rogers, R.W. (1982). The self-efficacy scale: Construction and validation. *Psychological Reports*, **51**, 663-671.

Silva, J. (1983). The perceived legitimacy of rule violating behavior in sport. *Journal of Sport Psychology*, **5**, 438-448.

Silva, T., & Nicholls, J.G. (1990). *Students as writing theorists.* Unpublished manuscript.

Simons, J.P., Scanlan, T.K., Carpenter, P.J., & Schmidt, G.W. (1990). *A test of the sport commitment model.* Paper presented at the annual conference of the North American Society for Psychology of Sport and Physical Activity, Houston, TX.

Siscovick, D.S., Laporte, R.E., & Newman, J.E. (1985). The disease-specific benefits and risks of physical activity and exercise. *Public Health Reports,* **100**, 180-188.

Slenker, S.E., Price, J.H., & O'Connell, J.K. (1985). Health locus of control of joggers and nonexercisers. *Perceptual and Motor Skills,* **61**, 323-328.

Slenker, S.E., Price, J.H., Roberts, S.M., & Jurs, S.G. (1984). Joggers versus nonexercisers: An analysis of knowledge, attitudes and beliefs about jogging. *Research Quarterly for Exercise and Sport,* **55**, 371-378.

Smetana, J. (1981). Preschool children's perceptions of moral and social rules. *Child Development,* **52**, 1333-1336.

Smith, R. (1988). The logic and design of case study research. *The Sport Psychologist,* **2**, 1-12.

Smith, R.E., Smoll, F.L., & Curtis, B. (1979). Coach effectiveness training: A cognitive-behavioral approach to enhancing relationship skills in youth sport coaches. *Journal of Sport Psychology,* **1**(1), 59-75.

Smith, R.E., Zane, N.W.S., Smoll, F.L., & Coppell, D.B. (1983). Behavioral assessment in youth sports: Coaching behaviors and children's attitudes. *Medicine and Science in Sports and Exercise,* **15**, 208-214.

Smoll, F.L., & Smith, R.E. (1984). Leadership research in young athletes. In J. Silva, III & R.S. Weinberg (Eds.), *Psychological foundations of sport.* Champaign, IL: Human Kinetics.

Sonstroem, R.J. (1976). The validity of self-perceptions regarding physical and athletic ability. *Medicine and Science in Sports,* **8**, 126-132.

Sonstroem, R.J. (1978). Physical estimation and attraction scales: Rationale and research. *Medicine and Science in Sports and Exercise,* **10**, 97-102.

Sonstroem, R.J. (1982). Attitudes and beliefs in the prediction of exercise participation. In R.C. Cantu and W.J. Gillepsie (Eds.), *Sport Medicine, Sport Science: Bridging the Gap* (pp. 3-16). Toronto: The Callamore Press.

Sonstroem, R.J., & Kampper, K.P. (1980). Prediction of athletic participation in middle school males. *Research Quarterly for Exercise and Sport,* **51**, 685-694.

Sonstroem, R.J., & Morgan, W.P. (1989). Exercise and self-esteem: Rationale and model. *Medicine and Science in Sports and Exercise,* **21**, 329-337.

Sonstroem, R.J., & Walker, M.I. (1973). Relationship of attitudes and locus of control to exercise and physical fitness. *Perceptual and Motor Skills,* **36**, 1031-1034.

Spence, J.T. & Helmreich, R.L. (1983). Achievement-related motives and behaviors. In J.T. Spence (Ed.), *Achievement and achievement motives* (pp. 7-74). San Francisco: Freeman.

Spink, K.S., & Roberts, G. (1980). Ambiguity of outcome and causal attributions. *Journal of Sport Psychology,* **2**(3), 237-244.

Steers, R.M., & Porter, L.W. (1974). The role of task-goal attributes in employee performance. *Psychological Bulletin,* **81**, 434-452.

Sternberg, R., Conway, B., Ketron, J., & Bernstein, M. (1981). Peoples' conceptions of intelligence. *Journal of Personality and Social Psychology,* **41**, 37-55.

Stipek, D., & MacIver, D. (1989). Developmental change in children's assessment of intellectual competence. *Child Development,* **60**, 521-538.

Stitcher, T. (1989). *The effects of goal setting on peak performance in a competitive athletic setting.* Unpublished doctoral dissertation, North Texas State University, Denton.

Stitcher, T., Weinberg, R., & Jackson, A. (1983). *Goal setting and its effects on endurance performance.* Paper presented at the TAHPERD conference, Corpus Christi, TX.

Taggart, A.C., Taggart, J., & Siedentop, D. (1986). Effects of a home-based activity program: A study with low fitness elementary school children. *Behavior Modification,* **10**, 487-507.

Tappe, M.K., & Duda, J.L. (1988). Personal investment predictors of life satisfaction among physically active middle-aged and older adults. *Journal of Psychology,* **122**, 557-568.

Tappe, M.K., Duda, J.L., & Ehrnwald, P. (1990). Personal investment predictors of exercise behavior among adolescents. *Canadian Journal of Sport Sciences,* **15**(3), 185-192.

Taylor, C.B., Bandura, A., Ewart, C.K., Miller, N.H., & DeBusk, R.T. (1985). Exercise testing to enhance wives' confidence in their husbands' cardiac capabilities soon after clinically uncomplicated acute myocardial infarction. *American Journal of Cardiology,* **55**, 6335-6338.

Taylor, C.B., Sallis, J.F., & Needle, R. (1985). The relation of physical activity and exercise to mental health. *Public Health Reports,* **100**, 195-202.

Taylor, F.W. (1967). *The principles of scientific management.* New York: Norton. (Originally published 1911)

Taylor, S.E. (1986). *Health Psychology.* New York: Random House.

Thayer, R.E. (1987). Energy, tiredness, and tension effects of a sugar snack versus moderate exercise. *Journal of Personality and Social Psychology,* **52**, 472-474.

Thompson, C.E., & Wankel, L.M. (1980). The effects of perceived activity choice upon frequency of exercise behavior. *Journal of Applied Social Psychology,* **10**, 436-443.

Thorkildsen, T. (1988). Theories of education among academically precocious adolescents. *Contemporary Educational Psychology,* **13**, 323-330.

Thorkildsen, T.A. (1989a). Justice in the classroom: The student's view. *Child Development,* **60**, 323-334.

Thorkildsen, T.A., (1989b). Pluralism in children's reasoning about social justice. *Child Development*, **60**, 965-972.

Tolman, E.C. (1932). *Purposive behavior in animals and men*. New York: Century.

Tolman, E.C. (1934). Theories of learning. In F.A. Moss (Ed.), *Comparative psychology*. Englewood Cliffs, NJ: Prentice-Hall.

Tolmin, S. (1983). The construal of reality: Criticism in modern and post modern science. In W.J.T. Mitchell (Ed.), *The politics of interpretation* (pp. 99-117). Chicago: University of Chicago Press.

Triandis, H.C. (1977). *Interpersonal behavior*. Belmont, CA: Brooks/Cole.

Tubbs, M.E. (1986). Goal setting: A meta-analytic examination of the empirical evidence. *Journal of Applied Psychology*, **71**, 474-483.

Turiel, E. (1983). *The development of social knowledge: Morality and convention*. Cambridge, England: Cambridge University Press.

U.S. Department of Health and Human Services. (1979). *Surgeon General's Report: Promoting health-preventing disease, 1990 objectives for the nation*. Washington, DC: Public Health Services, National Institutes of Health.

U.S. Department of Health and Human Services (1980). *Promoting health and preventing disease*. Washington, DC: Public Health Services, National Institutes of Health.

Ulrich, B.D. (1987). Perceptions of physical competence, motor competence, and participation in organized sport: Their interrelationships in young children. *Research Quarterly for Exercise and Sport*, **58**, 57-67.

Vallerand, R.J., Deci, E.L., & Ryan, R.M. (1988). Intrinsic motivation in sport. In K. Pandolf (Ed.), *Exercise and Sport Sciences Reviews* (pp. 389-425). New York: MacMillan.

Vallerand, R.J., Gauvin, L., & Halliwell, W.R. (1986). Negative effects of competition on children's intrinsic motivation. *Journal of Social Psychology*, **126**, 649-657.

Valois, P., Desharnais, R., & Godin, G. (1988). A comparison of the Fishbein and Ajzen and the Triandis Attitudinal Models for the prediction of exercise intention and behavior. *Journal of Behavioral Medicine*, **11**, 459-472.

Vealey, R.S. (1984). *The conceptualization and measurement of sport confidence*. Unpublished doctoral dissertation, University of Illinois, Urbana.

Vealey, R.S. (1986). Conceptualization of sport-confidence and competitive orientation: Preliminary investigation and instrument development. *Journal of Sport Psychology*, **8**, 221-246.

Vealey, R.S., & Campbell, J.L. (1988). Achievement goals of adolescent figure skaters: Impact on self-confidence, anxiety and performance. *Journal of Adolescence Research*, **3**, 227-243.

Vernon, P.E. (1969). *Intelligence and cultural environment*. London: Methuen.

Wallston, K.A., Wallston, B.S., & DeVallis, R. (1978). *Health Education Monographs*, **6**, 160-170.

Wankel, L.M. (1984). Decision-making and social support strategies for increasing exercise involvement. *Journal of Cardiac Rehabilitation*, **4**, 124-135.

Wankel, L.M. (1985). Personal and situational factors affecting exercise involvement: The importance of enjoyment. *Research Quarterly for Exercise and Sport*, **56**, 275-282.

Wankel, L.M., & Kreisel, P.S.J. (1983). *A comparison of the effectiveness of structured social support and group decision balance-sheet approaches to motivating exercise adherence.* Unpublished research report prepared for Fitness and Amateur Sport, Canada, Project #218, Ottawa, ON.

Wankel, L.M., & Kreisel, P.S.J. (1985a). Factors underlying enjoyment of youth sports: Sport and age group comparisons. *Journal of Sport Psychology*, **7**, 51-64.

Wankel, L.M., & Kreisel, P.S.J. (1985b). Methodological considerations in youth sport motivation research: A comparison of open-ended and paired comparison approaches. *Journal of Sport Psychology*, **7**, 65-74.

Wankel, L.M., & Sefton, J.M. (1989). A season-long investigation of fun in youth sports. *Journal of Sport and Exercise Psychology*, **11** 355-366.

Wankel, L.M., & Thompson, C. (1977). Motivating people to be physically active: Self-persuasion vs. balanced decision making. *Applied Social Psychology*, **7**, 332-340.

Wankel, L.M., & Yardley, J.K. (1982). An investigation of the effectiveness of a structured social support program for increasing exercise adherence of high and low self-motivated adults. In D. Ng (Ed.), *Proceedings of the Leisure Research Section.* Saskatoon, Canadian Parks/Recreation Association Conference.

Wankel, L.M., Yardley, J.K., & Graham, J. (1985). The effects of motivational interventions upon the exercise adherence of high and low self-motivated adults. *Canadian Journal of Applied Sports Sciences*, **10**, 147-156.

Ward, A., & Morgan, W.P. (1984). Adherence patterns of healthy men and women enrolled in an adult exercise program. *Journal of Cardiac Rehabilitation*, **4**, 143-152.

Webb, H. (1969). Professionalization of attitudes toward play among adolescents. In G. Kenyon (Ed.), *Aspects of contemporary sport sociology* (pp. 161-178). Chicago: The Athletic Institute.

Weber, J., & Wertheim, E.H. (1989). Relationships of self-monitoring, special attention, body fat percentage, and self-motivation to attendance at a community gymnasium. *Journal of Sport and Exercise Psychology*, **11**, 105-114.

Weinberg, R. (1985). Relationship between self-efficacy and cognitive strategies in enhancing endurance performance. *International Journal of Sport Psychology*, **17**, 280-293.

Weinberg, R., Bruya, L.D., & Jackson, A. (1985). The effects of goal proximity and goal specificity on endurance performance. *Journal of Sport Psychology*, **7**, 296-305.

Weinberg, R., Bruya, L.D., & Jackson, A. (1990). Goals and competition: A reaction to Hall and Byrne. *Journal of Sport and Exercise Psychology*, **12**, 92-96.

Weinberg, R., Bruya, L., Jackson, A., & Garland, H. (1987). Goal difficulty and endurance performance: A challenge to the goal attainability assumption. *Journal of Sport Behavior*, **10**, 82-92.

Weinberg, R., Bruya, L.D., Longino, J., & Jackson, A. (1988). Effect of goal proximity and specificity on endurance performance of primary-grade children. *Journal of Sport and Exercise Psychology*, **10**, 81-91.

Weinberg, R., Gould, D., & Jackson, A. (1979). Expectations and performance: An empirical test of Bandura's self-efficacy theory. *Journal of Sport Psychology*, **1**, 320-331.

Weinberg, R., Gould, D., Yukelson, D., & Jackson, A. (1981). The effect of preexisting and manipulated self-efficacy on a competitive muscular endurance task. *Journal of Sport Psychology*, **3**, 345-354.

Weinberg, R., & Ragan, J. (1979). Effects of competition, success/failure, and sex on intrinsic motivation. *Research Quarterly*, **50**, 503-510.

Weinberg, R., Sinardi, M., & Jackson, A. (1982). Effect of bar height and modeling on anxiety, self-confidence and gymnastic performance. *International Gymnast*, **2**, 11-13.

Weiner, B. (1972). *Theories of motivation: From mechanics to cognition.* Chicago: Markham.

Weiner, B. (1979). A theory of motivation for some classroom experiences. *Journal of Educational Psychology*, **71**, 3-25.

Weiner, B. (1986). *An attributional theory of motivation and emotion.* New York: Springer-Verlag.

Weiner, B., Frieze, I., Kukla, A., Reed, L., Rest, S., & Rosenbaum, R.M. (1971). Perceiving the causes of success and failure. In E.E. Jones, D.E. Kanose, H.H. Kelley, R.E. Nisbett, S. Valins, & B. Weiner (Eds.), *Attribution: perceiving the causes of behavior* (pp. 95-120). Morristown, NJ: General Learning Press.

Weiss, M.R., & Bredemeier, B.J. (1983). Developmental sport psychology: A theoretical perspective for studying children in sport. *Journal of Sport Psychology*, **5**, 216-230.

Weiss, M.R., & Petlichkoff, L.M. (1989). Children's motivation for participation in and withdrawal from sport: Identifying the missing links. *Pediatric Exercise Science*, **1**, 195-211.

Weiss, M.R., Wiese, D.M., & Klint, K.A. (1989). Head over heels with success: The relationship between self-efficacy and performance in competitive youth gymnastics. *Journal of Sport and Exercise Psychology*, **11**, 444-451.

Weisz, J. (1984). Contingency judgments and achievement behavior: Deciding what is controllable and when to try. In J.G. Nicholls (Ed.), *Advances in motivation and achievement: Vol. 3. The development of achievement motivation* (pp. 107-136). Greenwich, CT: JAI Press.

Weitzer, J.E. (1989). *Childhood socialization into physical activity: Parental roles in perceptions of competence and goal orientation.* Unpublished master's thesis, University of Wisconsin, Milwaukee.

White, R.W. (1959). Motivation reconsidered: The concept of competence. *Psychological Reveiw, 66,* 297-333.

White, S.A., Duda, J.L., & Sullivan, C. (1991). *The relationship of gender, level of sport involvement, and participation motivation to goal orientation.* Unpublished manuscript.

Whitehead, J. (1986). A cross-national comparison of attributions underlying achievement orientations in adolescent sport. In J. Watkins, T. Reilly, & L. Burwitz (Eds.), *Sport Sciences* (pp. 297-302). London, New York: E. & F.N. Spon.

Whitehead, J. (1989, November). *Achievement motivation and persistence in adolescent sport.* Paper presented at the symposium on Motivation in Sport and Exercise, University of Illinois, Urbana.

Whitehead, J. (in press). Why children might choose to do sport—or stop. In M.J. Lee (Ed.), *Coaching young people.* Leeds, England: National Coaching Foundation.,

Whitehead, J., & Dalby, R.A. (1987). *The development of effort and ability attributions in sport.* Paper presented at a conference of the Institute for the Study of Children in Sport, Bedford College of Higher Education, Bedford, England.

Wilkes, R.L., & Summers, J.J. (1984). Cognitions, mediating variables, and strength performance. *Journal of Sport Psychology, 6,* 351-359.

Wood, R.E., & Bandura, A. (1989). Impact of conceptions of ability on self-regulatory mechanisms and complex decision-making. *Journal of Personality and Social Psychology, 56,* 407-415.

Wood, R.E., Mento, A.J., & Locke, E.A. (1987). Task complexity as a moderator of goal effects: A meta-analysis. *Journal of Applied Psychology, 72,* 416-425.

Wurtele, S.K., & Maddux, J.E. (1987). Relative contributions of protection motivation theory components in predicting exercise intentions and behavior. *Health Psychology. 6,* 453-466.

Wysocki, T., Hall, G., Iwata, B., & Riordan, M. (1979). Behavioral management of exercise: Contracting for aerobic points. *Journal of Applied Behavior Analysis, 12,* 55-64.

Yan Lan, L., & Gill, D.L. (1984). The relationships among self-efficacy, stress responses, and a cognitive feedback manipulation. *Journal of Sport Psychology, 6,* 227-238.

Yukl, G.A., & Latham, G.P. (1978). Interrelationships among employee participation, individual differences, goal difficulty, goal acceptance, goal instrumentality, and performance. *Personnel Psychology*, **31**, 305-323.

Index

Page numbers in *italics* indicate figures or tables.
Page numbers followed by "n" refer to notes.

subject's commitment to research on,
189-191
subjects' pre-existing motivation in
research on, 189-190
task characteristics in research on,
188-189
and training programs in sports/exercise,
186-187, 192-193
Weinberg's suggestions for future
research on, 192-197
Goal specificity, 178-185, 186, 195
Godding, P. R., 111
Godin, G., 112, 115, 131, 133, 145-146,
149, 157
Good, T. L., 174
Gordon, J. R., 126
Gould, D., 27, 78, 94, 97, 180, 183,
185, 203
Graham, J., 151, 153
Griffin, W., 150
Griffith, P., 87
Grolnick, W. S., 164
Gross, J. B., 203
Grossman, R. M., 121
Group discussion, 151-152
Grouping dimension of learning environ-
ment, 172, 173
Gruger, C., 113
Gruneau, R., 39, 53
Gunn, T. P., 104

H

Habit strength in exercise behavior, 146,
156
Hagberg, J. M., 130
Hall, C. S., 132
Hall, G., 150
Hall, H.
on goal perspectives, 67, 68
on goal-setting, 25
on goal specificity, 182, 183
on perception of ability, 21, 70
on performance, 76, 77, 78, 80
Hall, H. K.
on goal proximity, 184-185
on goal-setting, 25, 187, 189, 191-192
on goal specificity, 182
on self-efficacy and goals, 125
Halliwell, W. R., 73-74
Hamilton, J. O., 75
Hanesian, H., 58
Haney, C. J., 114-115, 133, 143
Hanley, C., 131
Harlow, 9
Harris, B., 185
Harris, D. V., 185
Harris, J. C., 204, 206, 207
Harter, S., 11, 13, 14, 20, 24-25, 29n,
69, 199, 206, 207

Haskell, W. L., 112, 130, 149
Hatfield, B. D., 97, 110
Haubenstricker, J., 203
Hausfeld, S., 99
HBM. See Health belief model
Health belief model (HBM), 139-142,
140, 155
Health Locus of Control Scale (HLCS),
142-143
Heart attack, 111, 117, 123, 131, 150
Heckhausen, H., 55n
Hedonism, 6
Heider, F., 9, 34, 134
Heinzelmann, F., 125, 151, 152, 155, 156
Heitman, H. M., 157
Helmreich, R. L., 46
Heuristic function of theory, 133-134
Hierarchy of needs, 141, 155
High blood pressure, 130
HLCS. See Health Locus of Control Scale
Hogan, P. I., 97
Hollingsworth, B., 180
Holloszy, J. O., 130
Holloway, J. B., 103, 110, 116-117
Holmes, D. S., 130
Horn, T., 78, 203
Hoyt, M. F., 151, 152
Huddleston, S., 203
Hunt, T. M., 37
Hurley, Z. B. F., 130
Huston, L., 83
Hyde, R. T., 130
Hypertension, 130

I

Ickes, W., 135
Ilgen, D. R., 179
Imagery, 98-99
IMI. See Intrinsic Motivation Inventory
Incentives in personal investment theory,
86
Incentive values of success and failure, 5
Inclusion levels in evaluation of theory,
135-136
Individual differences
effect on goal perspectives, 59, 60-64,
90, 163-164
as a variable in research on exercise be-
havior, 156
Inglis, F., 40, 52
Inkeles, A., 4
Intelligence
children's concepts of, 33, 37-38, 42,
54n-55n
fairness and concepts of, 42
in lay achievement theories, 45, 46, 56n
Intensity, 6, 75, 110, 139, 193. See also
Effort
Intentions
exercise, 133, 145-148, 149

Contributors

Glyn C. Roberts, PhD
Editor

Glyn C. Roberts is a professor of kinesiology at the University of Illinois in the sport psychology program. He earned his undergraduate degree at Loughborough University in England, his master's degree from the University of Massachusetts, and his PhD from the University of Illinois. Roberts is a past president of the North American Society of Sport Psychology and Physical Activity, is currently on the executive committee of the International Association of Applied Psychology, and is the general secretary of the International Society of Sport Psychology. Roberts is a fellow  in the American Academy of Physical Education and the Association for the Advancement of Applied Sport Psychology. Roberts has published extensively on the issue of motivation in sport, especially as it impacts children. Roberts also is a sport psychology consultant to the United States Gymnastic Federation. Roberts enjoys tennis, jogging, and golf.

Carole Ames, PhD

Carole Ames is professor and chair of the Department of
Educational Psychology at the University of Illinois. She
received her bachelor's and master's degrees from Indiana
University and her PhD from Purdue University. Her
research focuses on the role of environmental factors in shaping the motivation patterns of children. Most recently, she
has been developing and studying an intervention that re-
structures the motivational climate of schools and classrooms.
She has published widely on the motivation of children and
with co-author, Russell Ames, has edited a series of volumes
on motivation research in education.

Joan L. Duda, PhD

Joan L. Duda teaches graduate and undergraduate courses
in the social psychological aspects of sport and exercise at
Purdue University. She is an active member of the North
American Society for the Psychology of Sport and Physical
Activity, the Association for the Advancement of Applied
Sport Psychology, and the Research Consortium of the
American Alliance of Health, Physical Education, Recreation
and Dance and is currently the chair for the North American
Society of Sport Psychology and Physical Activity Sport
Psychology Academy. Duda earned her doctorate in sport

psychology from the University of Illinois. She has written numerous publications on the motivational factors influencing behavior and enjoyment in movement contexts. As an undergraduate at Rutgers, Duda was an intercollegiate
participant in basketball, softball, and tennis. She still enjoys these activities, as
well as golf, music, and travel.

Deborah L. Feltz, PhD

Deborah L. Feltz is professor of physical education and chairperson of the Department of Physical Education and Exercise Science at Michigan State University. Feltz received her bachelor's degree in physical education from the State University of New York at Buffalo and master's and doctoral degrees in physical education from Pennsylvania State University. Feltz's research interests have centered on the interrelationships of self-confidence, anxiety, and sport performance. Her work has resulted in more than 70 professional publications and numerous honors and awards. Feltz is a member of the North American Society for the Psychology of Sport and Physical Activity, a Fellow in the Research Consortium of AAHPERD, a fellow of the American Psychological Association, and a member of the Sport Psychology Advisory Committee to the United States Olympic Committee.

Edward McAuley, PhD

Edward McAuley is associate professor in the Department of Kinesiology at the University of Illinois. He received his doctoral degree from the University of Iowa. His research interests are primarily in motivational aspects of exercise and health psychology, with particular emphasis on how social psychological variables influence behavioral, cognitive, and affective aspects of physical activity. McAuley has published widely in the areas of self-efficacy and attribution theories as they relate to human movement. He enjoys running, music, and his family.

John G. Nicholls, PhD

John G. Nicholls is professor of educational psychology at the University of Illinois at Chicago. The New Zealand native previously taught at Purdue University, the University of Illinois, and the Victoria University of Wellington, New Zealand. His PhD is from Victoria University. Since coming to the Midwest Nicholls has retired from mountaineering but manages to get some sense of adventure from exploring topics such as those outlined in his chapter in this volume.

W. Jack Rejeski, PhD

W. Jack Rejeski is professor of health and sport science at Wake Forest University in Winston-Salem, NC. He teaches exercise and health psychology and is a clinical counselor with the cardiac rehabilitation program. Rejeski earned his PhD from the University of Connecticut in 1978 with a major field of study in personality/social psychology. Rejeski is the coauthor of *Fitness Motivation* and has researched affective and perceptual changes accompanying exercise, acute exercise as a buffer to stress reactivity, and the social psychobiology of anabolic steroid abuse. He is a member of the American Psychological Association and the North American Society for the Psychological Study of Sport and Physical Activity.

Tara K. Scanlan, PhD

Tara K. Scanlan received her PhD from the University of Illinois and is a professor in the Department of Psychology at UCLA. Her research focuses on the social psychology of sport, including youth sport participants and elite athletes. She has published primarily in the areas of motivation and stress. Scanlan is a former president of the North American Society for the Psychology of Sport and Physical Activity and is a fellow in the American Academy of Physical Education and the Association for the Advancement of Applied Sport Psychology.

Jeffery P. Simons, PhD

Jeffery P. Simons is on the Department of Kinesiology faculty at the University of Colorado at Boulder. He formerly was associate director of the KidSport Project, a joint research effort of the UCLA Sport Psychology Laboratory and the Amateur Athletic Foundation of Los Angeles. Besides youth sport, Simons is interested in psychological skills training techniques and has served as a performance consultant to many competitive athletes, coaches, and teams. He has conducted applied sport psychology seminars for several national and international sport governing bodies and is a sport psych consultant to The Athletics Congress.

Robert Weinberg, PhD

Robert Weinberg is a Regents Professor in the Department of Kinesiology at the University of North Texas. He received master's degrees in both psychology and kinesiology as well as a doctoral-degree specializing in sport psychology from UCLA. His research interests focus on the effects of psychological factors on motor performance, including motivation, mental preparation strategies, and anxiety. He is widely published in the field of sport psychology and serves on numerous editorial boards. He also works extensively in applied sport psychology, focusing on the development of  psychological skills for improving performance and enhancing personal growth. His recreational pursuits include tennis, basketball, and cycling.